THE M & E HANDBOOK SERIES

British Government and Politics

F. Randall
B.Sc (Soc), DPA (Lond)

MACDONALD AND EVANS

Macdonald and Evans Ltd.
Estover, Plymouth PL6 7PZ

First published 1979

© Macdonald & Evans Ltd. 1979

7121 0247 7

Printed in Great Britain by
Hazell Watson & Viney Ltd,
Aylesbury, Bucks

Preface

This HANDBOOK is intended for the use of students preparing for examinations in Politics and Government, and British Constitution. The standard is based on the "A" Level papers set by the University of London and the Associated Examining Board. It should also be useful for other examinations such as the Ordinary National Certificate in Public Administration, those of the Institute of Municipal Treasurers and Accountants and Papers I and II in Public Administration in the Local Government Training Board Certificate in Municipal Administration.

The book is mainly concerned with central government although, in response to changes in various syllabuses, it contains a chapter on local government.

Different examining boards look for differing approaches. Courses at "O" Level tend to be more traditional, in that the emphasis is placed on factual information; "A" Level courses, particularly that set by the University of London with effect from June 1978, place more emphasis on the broad, analytical approach. The Local Government Training Board, on the other hand, expects candidates to have a reasonably detailed knowledge of reports, White Papers and legislation.

These different approaches mean that the HANDBOOK, if it is to be generally useful, must cover a wide range of topics embracing the essence of the subject. It is not, and is not intended to be, a substitute for wide reading of standard works and of contemporary reports.

Government and politics change, as do the syllabuses of examinations. The student should be very clear in his mind as to the approach to the subject which is required by the examining body. He will then be able to use this book with discrimination, using those parts which meet his needs, testing his knowledge by means of the Progress Tests and supplementing it by recommended reading.

November 1978   F.R.

Contents

Preface   v
List of Tables   xi

PART ONE: POLITICAL IDEAS

I   *Government and Democracy*   1
The sociology of government; Towards democracy; Constitutional monarchy; Parliamentary democracy; The machinery of government; Separation of the powers

II *Government and Society*   16
Political culture; Public opinion; Pressure groups

III *Government and Freedom*   26
Elective dictatorship and residual freedoms; Natural rights; Power and authority; A Bill of Rights; Open government

IV *Types of Government*   39
Constitutional government; Parliamentary government; Party government; Reform of the legislature

V *Concepts*   55
Participation; Ideology; Traditionalism, technocracy and meritocracy; Representative and responsible government

VI *Issues and Parties*   66
Political issues; Political parties; Politics and social class

PART TWO: INSTITUTIONS

VII *The Legal System*   77
Law, morality and custom; The rule of law; Sources of English law; The courts; Police; Legal reform

VIII *Local Government*   92
　　　Background; The Redcliffe-Maud Report; The
　　　reform of local government; The functions of
　　　local government; Local authority and the com-
　　　munity; Local authority finance

IX *Decentralisation and Devolution*   109
　　　Background; Devolution; Some alternatives;
　　　The Kilbrandon Report; The government's ap-
　　　proach; Electoral reform

X *Supra-National Government*   124
　　　Natural law; The European Community; Impli-
　　　cations of Community membership; The referen-
　　　dum; Parliamentary sovereignty; Direct elections
　　　to the European Assembly

PART THREE: POLITICAL ISSUES

XI *Education*   137
　　　The purpose of education; Schools and teachers;
　　　Other educational issues; Current situation and
　　　future trends

XII *Industry and Employment*   149
　　　Nationalisation; Trade unions; Employment dis-
　　　advantage; Unemployment

XIII *Housing and the Environment*   162
　　　The housing problem; Home ownership; Rented
　　　property; Homelessness; The environment

XIV *Immigration and Racialism*   173
　　　The problem; Some possible solutions; Race
　　　relations legislation; The future

XV *Poverty*   184
　　　Problems; Proposals to deal with poverty; Legis-
　　　lation

XVI *Health*   198
　　　The development of the health service; Problems;
　　　Present situation and future directions

PART FOUR: PUBLIC ADMINISTRATION

XVII   *The Civil Service*   211
        Development; Bureaucracy; The Fulton Report;
        Post-Fulton developments; Criticisms of the Civil
        Service

XVIII   *Policy Making*   227
        Political parties; The Prime Minister; The Cab-
        inet; Policy-making considerations; Civil Servants

XIX   *Legislative and Administrative Control*   239
        Administrative agencies; Delegated legislation;
        Administrative tribunals; Public corporations;
        Central control

        APPENDICES   251
        I Bibliography; II Examination technique; III Test
        papers

        Index   265

List of Tables

I	Aristotle's view of government	2
II	How a Bill becomes law	12
III	Results of failure to separate the powers	14
IV	Functions of principal local authorities in England and Wales	101
V	Educational landmarks, 1944–77	147
VI	Percentage of population in various types of tenure	163
VII	Number of Civil Servants 1969–77	219
VIII	Civil Service expenditure and manpower	219
IX	Categories of non-industrial staff in the Civil Service	223

PART ONE

POLITICAL IDEAS

CHAPTER I

Government and Democracy

THE SOCIOLOGY OF GOVERNMENT

1. The sociology of government. All societies have a form of government. The simplest can be seen in the most primitive societies. One person, often the eldest male, performs all the functions of a leader. Such a man, aided probably by the tribal elders, is responsible for an oligarchy, i.e. rule by a few people. His place in society is secure but it is only likely to remain so if he follows the normal customs, practices and traditions of his group. In political terms this is known as the political culture (*see* II). As societies evolve the kinship patterns give way to groupings based on conquest. The stronger groups oppress the weaker and eventually the weaker leaders agree to serve the stronger in return for protection. Thus in Britain, a thousand years ago, the kings of Mercia and Wessex became vassals and the beginnings of the United Kingdom began to emerge. The feudal system, as it is called, lasted for many years and became, eventually, the modern Britain with which this book is concerned. The history of that progression is fascinating but it is beyond the scope of this study. Before dispensing with the historical perspective, however, it is worth reminding ourselves that Aristotle, one of the greatest of all political philosophers, writing in the fourth century B.C. recognised six forms of government.

2. Aristotle's view. Aristotle, who lived from 384 B.C. to 322 B.C., distinguished three types of government and sub-divided these into "good" and "bad" forms (*see* Table I). Whether a form of government was good or bad depended, in his view, on whose interests it served.

Ideally, Aristotle considered monarchy the best form of govern-

TABLE I.   ARISTOTLE'S VIEW OF GOVERNMENT

Type of government	Good form	Bad form
By one man	Monarchy	Tyranny
1 y the few	Aristocracy	Oligarchy
By many	Polity	Democracy

ment, since the sovereign had a legitimate right to rule. The "enlightened despot" was therefore the ideal ruler. But if he was not enlightened, if he was weak, cruel or capricious, then tyranny would result. Aristotle recognised that the skills needed to govern were rare and he thought that those who seemed most fitted to rule would be the philosophers. Such men would be trained from infancy and would form an aristocracy dedicated to the service of the populace. But such dedication might be misused. It might become selfish and the ruling group could use its power for its own ends, government would then become debased.

In talking about "polity" and "democracy" it should be noted that the meaning of the words have altered, and that what Aristotle called "polity" would today be called "democracy". It should also be borne in mind that he was discussing the government of ancient Greek city-states and that forms of government suitable for such states may not be suitable for complex modern matters.

TOWARDS DEMOCRACY

3. Democracy. The dictionary defines democracy as: "A state having government by all people, direct or representative; form of society ignoring hereditary class distinctions and tolerating minority views". Such a definition begs almost as many questions as it answers. It allows the word to be used by almost any form of government which is prepared to pay lip-service to the ideal. Phrases like "the will of the people" or "government in the interests of the majority" do not help very much. Who are "the people"? In a socialist society the word frequently refers to workers and intellectuals. Would capitalists count as people in such a society? (One might note in passing that Aristotle, a man in advance of his time in other respects, did not regard slaves as people in this context.) And what about the interests of the majority? Who decides what these interests are; and, if there is such a thing as a silent majority, how will its interests become known?

4. Pre-conditions for democracy. If democracy is considered to be a good thing, and most governments seeking popular approval would so describe themselves, then one must ask what conditions are necessary for it to work? The major ones are as follows:

(*a*) *The right of dissent* must be safeguarded. Parliament contains both H.M. Government and H.M. Opposition. Voltaire, writing at a time of great political stress, said, "I disagree with what you say, but will defend to the death your right to say it".

(*b*) *Pluralism.* There can be no true democracy where only one party is allowed.

(*c*) *Undogmatic attitudes.* Laying down the law and allowing no argument may make for effective government, though this is unlikely. It cannot make for democratic government.

(*d*) *Free flow of information.* Democracy implies choice, but one cannot choose properly except on the basis of adequate information. Parliamentary debates are reported verbatim in *Hansard*. Parliament has its own radio broadcasts and public discussion is encouraged by means of White Papers and other publications. Whether this is adequate remains an open question, but certainly without such a flow of information it would be misleading for a government to call itself democratic.

(*e*) *Interest.* Plato called attention to the dangers of apathy two thousand years ago. At that time he said that it killed democracy. The statement is still true today.

5. Government and state. The terms government and state are sometimes used as though they were synonymous, but there is an important difference.

(*a*) *The state* is the larger framework within which governments work.

(*b*) *Government* is the collective name for the group which rules the country. Whilst in theory the government can be one man, i.e. a dictatorship, in practice it must always be a group, since even the most autocratic tyrant must have a court or body of followers. Other types of government include:

(*i*) *Plutocracy.* The rule of the wealthy. It is partly to avoid this danger that the expenses of parliamentary candidates are restricted (*see* IV, **11**).

(*ii*) *Theocracy*. The rule of the priestly class, e.g. Tibet in the days of the Dalai Lama, i.e. prior to 1968.

(*c*) *Monarchy*. Here a sovereign is the head, both of government and the state (*see* 6). States with elected or non-hereditary heads are known as republics.

CONSTITUTIONAL MONARCHY

6. Constitutional monarchy. Britain is a constitutional monarchy, that is, a monarchy in which the sovereign has mainly advisory and ceremonial responsibilities. The other major form of monarchy is the absolute monarchy, in which the monarch is also the ruler. The constitutional position is summed up in the famous phrase "The Queen reigns but does not rule".

(*a*) The advantages of monarchy may be summed up as follows.

(*i*) The Queen personifies the state.

(*ii*) The hereditary principle ensures that there is always a recognised legal sovereign. The sovereign is the person on whom the crown is conferred and "the crown" is therefore always in being ("the king is dead; long live the king").

(*iii*) The monarch is traditionally above politics and is, therefore, able to express a view not generally regarded as politically motivated.

(*iv*) In the case of a long reign, e.g. Queen Victoria's, the monarch provides continuity and may develop a perspective unattainable to the politician.

(*b*) The disadvantages may be summarised as follows.

(*i*) Hereditary rulers are not necessarily best fitted to rule; indeed the European monarchs of the eighteenth and nineteenth centuries, by restricting royal marriages to a small circle, ran the risk of in-breeding.

(*ii*) The cost of maintaining the royal family is considerable. The Civil List, an annual grant from Parliament, cost over £2 million in 1977. In addition, over three-quarters of all expenditure arising from the royal family's official duties is paid by government departments. Both the Queen and the Prince of Wales have considerable private fortunes and some critics, notably Mr William Hamilton, M.P. for Fife Central, feel that the country does not get value for its money. His book, *My Queen and I* (Quartet Books, 1975), is an interesting exposition of this view.

7. The function of the sovereign. Walter Bagehot, in his classic work, *The British Constitution* (1867), described the monarch as having a "dignified" function. By this he meant that the job of giving the seal of approval to the functions of government, and thus legitimising them, can only be performed, in Britain at least, by the monarch. Although the decision to award a knighthood, or some other honour, may be taken by the Prime Minister on the advice of his colleagues (*see* XVIII, **7**), it is the Queen alone who has the right to confer the honour. She too will represent the state on important ceremonial occasions; and she it is who symbolises unity, not only between members of the Commonwealth (of which she is head) but also of the nation as a whole. In this connection it is worth remembering that she caused a minor stir among some nationalists when, in the course of a Jubilee speech, she said that she was head of the *United* Kingdom and hoped to remain so.

8. The royal prerogative. The prerogative, or right, of the Queen to exercise certain powers is an ancient one, and the powers which she currently exercises are but a pale shadow of those held by some of her predecessors. Since all official acts are carried out in her name (by Her Majesty's ministers, Her Majesty's judges etc.) it follows that the prerogative can only be exercised subject to certain conditions. In choosing ministers, and particularly the Prime Minister, she must act impartially and in accordance with convention (*see* IV, **6**). Thus in choosing the Prime Minister she will normally ask the leader of the majority party in the House of Commons. It could happen however that no one party had a clear majority, in which case she would consult all the interested parties with a view to selecting the person most able to head a coalition. Where possible she should accept the advice of a responsible minister, frequently the former Prime Minister.

In practice, the prerogative is exercised by a responsible minster on her behalf, but such acts are still presented as representing the will of the sovereign. In expressing this will the Queen has a number of instruments, i.e. documents having the status of a royal command. They include:

(*a*) *Orders in Council*. Such orders, e.g. the issue of writs for the calling of a new Parliament are made "by and with the consent of the Privy Council".

(*b*) *Proclamations*. Declarations of war and peace, and the decisions of the Privy Council to summon or prorogue (dissolve)

Parliament are all made "by command of Her Majesty" and her signature is attested by the Lord Chancellor who affixes the Great Seal of the Realm to such documents.

(c) *Sign Manual Warrant*. This is a document by which the Queen signifies her pleasure for specific purposes such as the granting of charters, the commissioning of officers in H.M. Forces or the commissioning of counsellors of state to act on her behalf during absence or illness.

9. Some decisions are purely formal. The Royal Pardon is granted to those people found guilty by the courts and subsequently proved to be innocent. But although it is the Queen's prerogative it is in fact the Home Secretary who actually exercises it. Similarly, although no Bill can become law without the Royal Assent (which is given in Norman French), this has not been withheld since 1707. Even if the monarch disapproves of a measure, as did King George V on the question of Irish Home Rule, the convention still demands that Assent is given.

(a) The speech from the throne which outlines, at the beginning of each parliamentary session, the legislative programme of the government is, in fact, composed by the government.

(b) The sovereign is "the fount of all honour" and when a government, or more correctly the Prime Minister, feels that an honour should be bestowed for political or other services it is the monarch who bestows it.

(c) Some personal powers remain. Some honours, such as the Order of Merit, remain at the personal disposal of the monarch. Although the Queen's role may appear to be purely formal she exercises considerable personal influence. Bagehot recognised three rights: the right to be consulted, the right to encourage and the right to warn. The Queen is entitled to be informed of Cabinet decisions and is regularly supplied with all important state papers. By this means the monarch can, if possessed of diligence and common sense, be an important influence divorced from party politics.

PARLIAMENTARY DEMOCRACY

10. Parliamentary democracy. The essence of parliamentary government is debate, the end product of which is legislation. The world "Parliament" is derived from the French *parler*, to talk; and the early English Parliaments conducted their debates in Norman French. In Britain we normally refer to "Parliament" but the correct term is "The Queen in Parliament". The sovereign is an integral part of the parliamentary system, together with the House of Lords and the House of Commons. There may be argument as to the relative importance of these three components but most people would concede that in the twentieth century the House of Commons has become the most important. It is also the part of Parliament which is elected. Whether this makes it either democratic or representative is for the reader to decide.

11. The House of Lords. The House of Lords is not an elected body and the argument for calling it either democratic or representative is, therefore, more difficult to sustain. Until the early years of this century it had considerable power. It could veto any Bill submitted to it by the House of Commons and in so doing could be regarded as thwarting the will of the people. In 1909 Lloyd George attempted to pass a Finance Bill sometimes referred to as "The People's Budget". Lords rejected the Bill and Lloyd George therefore called for a general election on the issues of the powers of the House of Lords. He proposed that the powers of the Lords should be reduced and threatened that if they refused to pass a Bill restricting their powers he would ask the King (Edward VII) to create sufficient peers to ensure the passing of the Bill. In the event King Edward VII died and it was left to his successor (King George V) to agree to such a course of action, should it be necessary. The House of Lords had, however, seen the writing on the wall and agreed to the proposed legislation.

The Parliament Act 1911 considerably reduced the power of the Lords; and their powers were further reduced by another Act of the same name in 1949. The Lords now only have powers to:

(*a*) initiate non-controversial legislation;
(*b*) revise or amend non-monetary Bills;
(*c*) delay a Bill for one year only; this power is used sparingly, and the Lords cannot delay a Money Bill for more than a month;
(*d*) introduce legislation affecting the peerage;
(*e*) sit as the highest court in the land. (*See* also IV, 9.)

12. A minor role? From this it would appear that the House of Lords has only a minor role to play. Such, however, is not the case. Non-controversial Bills may be better dealt with in the deliberative atmosphere of the Lords. There may be occasions on which the normal order is reversed; the Bill is given its first reading in the Lords and then passed to the House of Commons. Regardless of the order in which a Bill passes through Parliament it cannot become law until it has received the Royal Assent (*see* Table II).

13. Criticism. Criticism of the House of Lords often centres on its unrepresentative and unelected character. Most criticisms can be matched with counter arguments, and the strength of both criticisms and counter arguments is a matter of opinion rather than fact.

(*a*) *It is hereditary.* So is the monarchy and, in any case, the creation of life peerages dilutes the principle.

(*b*) *It is conservative.* This could be counted as an advantage if it provided a bulwark against hasty or ill-conceived legislation.

(*c*) *It is unrepresentative.* So, it could be argued, is the House of Commons (*see* V, 13).

(*d*) *It is ineffective.* Its ineffectiveness is due to curbs deliberately placed on its activities.

(*e*) *It has too much power* (*see* (*d*)). You cannot have it both ways.

(*f*) *Attendance is poor.* True, but both Lords and Commons share this fault at times. It would be fairer to say that by attending in force, when its interests are threatened, members may bring undue weight to bear.

(*g*) *It is undemocratic.* It might claim that since its members do not have to submit to election it can, on occasion, express the will of the people better than the House of Commons.

THE MACHINERY OF GOVERNMENT

14. The machinery of government. It has been said that the Queen reigns but does not rule (*see* I, 6). The ruling function of government is performed by the machinery of government which, in turn, relies a great deal on convention (*see* IV, 6). Machinery of government is a complex of institutions and procedures through which the business of government is conducted. Its main components are:

(*a*) government, i.e. the party in power;

(*b*) the party system;

(*c*) the Cabinet and the principle of "collective responsibility". This principle asserts that every government decision is the responsibility of all members of the government. Cabinet decisions are always presented as unanimous, although it may be well-known within the party that not all members are in agreement. In such a situation the individual members have a choice. They may either accept the decision or resign from the Cabinet on principle;

(d) Her Majesty's Opposition.

15. Aims and principles. On 15th October 1970, a White Paper was published under the title *The Reorganisation of Central Government*, the aim of which was to suggest ways in which the machinery of government could be rationalised. It was felt that governments tried to do too much and that the machinery, particularly those parts which dealt with the making and implementing of decisions, was not sufficiently responsive to new pressures and problems. The White Paper therefore put forward a number of aims and principles by which the machinery of government could be made more effective.

(a) The aims were:

(i) to improve the quality of policy formation and decision-taking;

(ii) to make the structure of government correspond with coherent fields of policy and administration;

(iii) to ensure that the machinery of government was responsive to the needs of society and to introduce more flexibility into the methods of implementing decisions.

(b) The principles to be followed in achieving these aims were the following.

(i) *An analytical approach.* An approach which asked questions such as "Does the proposed legislation accord with the policies of the government?" and "How important are these policies?"

(ii) *A functional approach.* Government departments were to be organised by reference to the task to be done, or the objective to be achieved, rather than by reference to the needs of the client group. In this way it was felt that better use would be made of specialists employed by the government.

(iii) *A geographical approach.* It was felt that there was merit in relating the process of government to specific geographical areas and their particular needs (*see* IX).

(iv) *To group related ministries together.* Thus, for example, the separate ministries of Trade and Industry were to be recognised as having common ground, more rationally covered by one ministry (although they have since been reseparated).

16. Modifications. The maintenance and overhaul of the machinery of government is a responsibility which is shared by the government of the day, the civil service and, above all, the Prime Minister. He has been elected to govern on the basis of a programme which will be carried out by the executive (*see* XVIII, 5). An incoming Prime Minister must take the machinery of government as he finds it. His attempts to modify it may take up, as both Mr. Heath's and Mr. Wilson's did, a great deal of time and effort and may well become the subject of party controversy. But he cannot leave it unaltered. To do so would be to make it less responsive to new pressures and new problems.

Any trend towards fewer and larger departments of state has both advantages and disadvantages. On the credit side it can be said that such ministries are more economical to run, and that they present better opportunities for the proper deployment of skilled manpower. It can also be said that more aspects of the work of the government can be represented in the Cabinet by fewer people.

Critics of "super ministries" point out that the amalgamation of a number of government departments under one label is more apparent than real. The Department of Health and Social Security was formed by an amalgamation of the Ministries of Health and Social Security in 1968, and the Ministry of Social Security itself was an amalgamation of the Ministry of Pensions and National Insurance and the National Assistance Board in 1966. Although there is now only one Secretary of State, sometimes called an overlord, answerable for all the functions of the department, there are three ministers, each responsible for different aspects of the work of the department. The health and local authority social services part of the department still works largely independently of the social security aspects.

SEPARATION OF THE POWERS

17. Executive power. Parliament passes laws and does so, as we have seen, in the name of the sovereign. The laws are administered by government departments, or ministries, headed by a member of the government (a Minister or a Secretary of State) who is answerable to Parliament for all the official acts carried out by his department. The Crown, i.e. the government acting in the name of the Queen, can be held responsible both to Parliament and to the courts for its actions. It can prosecute on behalf of the nation and it can in turn be prosecuted, particularly if its actions are considered to be beyond the powers conferred on it by Parliament. Such an action, usually known by its Latin name *ultra vires*, is an important safeguard of the liberties of the citizen.

18. Legislative powers. Parliament, or more correctly "the Queen in Parliament", is the supreme law-making authority in Britain. It is, in theory at any rate, the body which controls the executive. No Bill can become law until it has passed through various stages (*see* Table II). Most of the major legislation starts in the House of Commons and, if passed by them, is sent to the House of Lords. Lords, at one time the major partner, now has very limited powers (*see* IV, **9**). This limitation of their powers is deliberate and there is a case to be made for abolishing the second chamber completely (*see* **13**).

Bills coming before Parliament may be classified as follows.

(*a*) *Public Bills.* These are matters of concern to the nation as a whole. They include:

(*i*) money Bills (*see* IV, **9**(*b*));

(*ii*) Bills on other matters of general application, frequently reflecting the programme which the government pledged itself to implement when it was elected;

(*iii*) private member's Bills. These are Bills which are sponsored by individual M.P.s. A ballot is held at the beginning of each parliamentary session and the winners are allowed to introduce legislation which is not part of the government's programme. Such legislation is not likely to pass through all the stages necessary to become law unless the government is prepared to support it. The Abortion Act 1968 (*see* XVI, **10**), however, is an example of a successful private member's Bill.

(*b*) *Private Bills.* These are Bills which have a local or personal relevance only. Such Bills include some measures passed by local authorities and legislation concerning landed property.

(*c*) *Hybrid Bills* are partly public and partly private. They may be defined as public Bills which affect specific private interests.

19. Judicial power. The judges, often referred to as the judiciary, interpret the law and are responsible for its enforcement. Theirs

TABLE II. HOW A BILL BECOMES LAW

First reading	Formal stage. The title of the Bill is read out and copies are made available for further study.
Second reading	Bill is debated in principle.
Committee stage	Standing Committee undertakes detailed consideration (sometimes done by a "Committee of the whole House").
Report stage	Debate on amendments.
Third reading	Formal or verbal amendments only.
Royal Assent	Formal stage without which no Bill can become law.

NOTE: The procedure is the same in both Lords and Commons.

is the job of pronouncing on the law, both written and unwritten. To do this they must be completely independent. On occasion their legal interpretation may be opposed to popular sentiment and demands are made for their dismissal.

This happened in *R.* v. *Holdsworth* (1977) when three appeal judges reduced a sentence in a case of indecent assault. It was said that the defendant, a regular soldier, would have a promising career destroyed if the original sentence was allowed to stand. It transpired that even the reduced sentence was insufficient to prevent him being discharged from the army. An organisation calling itself "Women Against Rape" demanded that the appeal judges should be sacked. The demand was not met: if it had been it would have created a dangerous precedent in that any judge delivering what he knew to be an unpopular verdict would run the risk of being sacked.

The demand was not taken very seriously by the authorities, but even if it had been it is extremely unlikely that the judges would have been dismissed. They pronounced on the law as they saw it and the only way they could have been dismissed for so doing would be in response to an address by both Houses of Parliament calling for this action to be taken. The Act of Settlement 1701, under which this procedure was devised, was intended to cover only the most serious misconduct on the part of the judiciary and would certainly not be invoked to save them from temporary unpopularity.

20. Separation of the powers. The three powers described above, executive, legislative and judicial, are in themselves formidable; exercised together they could be disastrous. Seventeenth century philosophers such as John Locke were concerned at the threat of tyranny but it was a Frenchman, the Baron de Montesquieu, who, in his book *The Spirit of the Laws* (1748), put forward the theory of the separation of powers. Montesquieu compared the situation in the England of George III with that of France under Louise XV and advocated that the powers should be exercised separately. He did not insist that there should be complete separation, which would in any case be impossible, but he did advocate that, in general, this should be the case.

21. Separation of the powers in the U.S.A. The framers of the American constitution, building on the ideas of Montesquieu, incorporated a series of checks and balances into their system of government in order that the separation of the powers should be an integral part of government. The American constitution is, of course, a written one and the Declaration of Independence affirms its belief that "governments derive their just powers from the consent of the governed".

(*a*) The judiciary (the Supreme Court) decides whether or not any law passed in the U.S.A. is constitutional, and to this extent it acts independently of the legislature of which it is a part.

(*b*) The legislature (Congress) is deliberately separated from the executive, personified by the President and his cabinet, none of whom can be members of Congress. The legislature is elected for a fixed period and members can be re-elected.

(*c*) The executive has great powers. Although the President cannot himself introduce Bills into Congress he has powers of veto over congressional legislation and his administration appoints heads of departments of state with the approval of the upper house of Congress (the Senate). Two further points should be noted. The President is not necessarily a member of the majority party in Congress and he cannot be re-elected more than once.

22. Separation of the powers in Britain. The theory of the working of the separation of the powers in Britain assumes that as far as possible they should be exercised separately but that, in fact, there cannot be complete separation. Britain has no written constitution although it has, of course, a large and growing body

of written law. The separation of the powers is therefore something which has emerged in the course of time rather than as a
result of a clearly planned decision. As a result there are a number
of anomalies.

(a) Both the sovereign and the Lord Chancellor are part of the
legislature, the judiciary and the executive.

(b) The House of Lords is part of the legislature but as the
home of the Law Lords (see IV, 8(e)) it is the highest court of
appeal in the land, and thus part of the judiciary.

(c) The growth of delegated legislation (see XIX) has meant
that some legislative and judicial functions are undertaken by the
executive.

(d) There are however some checks and balances. For example,
no Member of Parliament can hold an office of profit under the
Crown (House of Commons (Disqualification) Act 1957) and no
Member can voluntarily relinquish his seat (Erskine May, *Parliamentary Practice*, Butterworth, 1976). The typically British solution to this particular problem is for there to be two sinecures in
the gift of the Treasury for which the member who wishes to resign can apply. The sinecures are the Stewardship of the Chiltern
Hundreds and the post of Bailiff of the Manor of Northstead,
both of which have a small, almost nominal, salary. Once appointed to one of these posts the M.P. is held to be occupying an
office of profit under the Crown and hence to be ineligible to be
a Member of Parliament.

23. Results of failure to separate powers. If the powers are not
separated there are a number of ills which Montesquieu claimed
would follow. They are shown in Table III.

Whilst the theory itself may be sound it has its critics. Montes-

TABLE III.   RESULTS OF FAILURE TO SEPARATE THE POWERS

Combination	Result
Legislature plus executive	Oppressive laws
Legislature plus judiciary	Arbitrary laws, i.e. judges would legislate rather than arbitrate.
Executive plus judiciary	Arbitrary power, i.e. such power would not have legal authority
All three combined	Tyranny

quieu recognised that complete separation of the powers was impossible and an eminent modern writer, Professor Finer, has pointed out that the powers can only be separate if one assumes that the content is different. In fact it is the agencies administering them which differ. If two or more agencies have the same object, as they do in the case of delegated legislation, why should they not combine?

PROGRESS TEST 1

1. What do you understand by "democracy"?   (3–5)

2. Set out the case for and against the monarchy.   (6–9)

3. How was the power of the House of Lords reduced in 1911? (11)

4. The House of Lords is not elected. Does this mean that it is necessarily undemocratic?   (3, 4, 13)

5. What is the "machinery of government" and how did the White Paper, *The Reorganisation of Central Government*, suggest that it should be rationalised?   (14–16)

6. What is meant by the "separation of the powers"?   (17–23)

CHAPTER II

Government and Society

POLITICAL CULTURE

1. Political culture. Hobbes's phrase, "even tyrants must sleep", is a reminder that governments must command a measure of popular support to be effective, and this support is provided by the political culture. It may be defined as the social background to political ideas and actions. It is the traditions which help to form the political climate of a particular society. Within the society there may be conflict about the ways in which it should be governed, but there will be a consensus as to the framework of rules and procedures which decide how such conflicts should be resolved.

The British system of government, a constitutional monarchy presiding over a parliamentary democracy, has evolved from British history and tradition. The normal and recognised way of achieving political power is by parliamentary election and, broadly speaking, the method is acceptable to its society as a whole. Democratic elections can be seen as an acceptable way of commanding a large measure of agreement. The military *coup*, or the widespread use of bribery or intimidation, are generally not acceptable in Britain.

2. Political culture is more than just tradition. It involves a whole system of beliefs, religious, moral and political. Kings of England were for centuries said to rule by divine right and even today the Queen's official title includes the phrase, "Elizabeth, by the Grace of God". Such beliefs are given material expression in artifacts which have a symbolic significance. The Union Jack is an amalgamation of the flags of England, Ireland and Scotland. In America, the Stars and Stripes represents the fusion of separate states into a united whole.

The importance of artifacts, and the values they symbolise, are best seen in the great ceremonial occasions, such as a coronation, where every part of a long service has a symbolic significance and where each item of the regalia has its traditional associations.

3. Élites. An élite is a small group within a society, frequently recognised as being superior in some sense, who are influential within the society. Such a group is clearly important in any discussion of the government and politics of the society and many writers, particularly sociologists, believe that such people normally form the government. Thus V. Pareto, in his book *Mind and Society* (Dover Publications, 1935), claims that in any given society there are two élites at any particular time. One is in power, the governing élite, and the other is waiting in the wings. This second, or non-governing, élite forms the alternative government.

This theory, known as the circulation of élites, can be seen clearly in Britain where H.M. Government wields power and H.M. Opposition stands ready complete with shadow cabinet and a leader who will, if the party comes to power, become the Prime Minister. C. Wright Mills, in *The Power Élite* (Oxford University Press, 1956), stresses the group nature of such élites, i.e. they may be composed of individuals of outstanding ability but it is their combined abilities, rather than the brilliance of any one individual, which gives the group its strength.

A more recent writer, Anthony Sampson, in *The New Anatomy of Britain* (Hodder and Stoughton, 1971), has shown that the "old boy network" and "the establishment" are closely related and that even in the Britain of the 1970s it is still possible to be born into a ruling class.

W. G. Runciman, in *Social Science and Political Theory* (Cambridge University Press, 1969), recognises élites but says that there are a number of these in society at any given time, and that they serve different purposes. Thus, an intellectual élite, the think-tank, may influence governments to a considerable degree but it is not composed of the same people who form the governing élite.

Communism, it should be noted, rejects the theory of élites since Marx believed that it was whole social classes which formed the ruling component of a society. A good case could be made, however, for calling the rulers of Russia an élite since, even if it is conceded that Russia is not yet a Communist state (H. Marcuse, *Soviet Marxism*, Pelican, 1971) and that they represent the fellow members of their social class, they are still a very small proportion of the population. Perhaps the whole concept can be summed up by another sociologist, R. Michels, who claimed that in any organised body in society the ruling function was performed by a small group. This led him to propound the iron law of oligarchy, "Who says organisation says oligarchy".

PUBLIC OPINION

4. Public opinion. Everybody knows what public opinion is but it is a vague concept, difficult to define, constantly changing and almost impossible to measure accurately (*see* 7). It is, however, an important indicator of social trends and, in particular, of the popularity or unpopularity of governments. They have of course some indication of their popularity in the letters which are sent to M.P.s and to government departments but such letters may not be very representative; indeed the sort of person who actually puts pen to paper instead of merely intending to do so is himself unrepresentative of the majority of us.

5. The mass media. The term mass media includes television, radio, newspapers and magazines all of which are important disseminators of news and views and agents in the formation of public opinion, "It must be true, I read it in the papers". It follows that a government which wishes overtly to control public opinion will exercise control over the media. Totalitarian regimes will therefore own or control the press, radio and television and censorship will be seen not as an intrusion on the liberty of the subject but as a right and necessary part of the business of government. The British government does not own any newspapers and the Wireless and Telegraphy Acts 1949 and 1967, whilst retaining ultimate control in the hands of the government who are answerable to Parliament, entrusts the day-to-day running to independent authorities, i.e. the British Broadcasting Corporation and the Independent Broadcasting Authority (*see* XIX, 9(*f*)).

6. Control over the media. There are occasions, however, when it is said to be in the national interest that there shall be some control over the media, and in such conditions restrictions are imposed on freedom of speech. Thus, during the Second World War the Defence of the Realm Act 1939 gave the government exceptional powers. These powers were, however, given grudgingly and were withdrawn when the war ended.

Legal restrictions are not the only sanctions open to the government. D notices are confidential official requests to newspapers and publishers not to divulge certain information on the grounds that it might be harmful to national security. Failure to comply with such notices is not, in itself, illegal; but a journalist publishing such information runs the risk of prosecution under the Official Secrets Act 1911.

This Act deals only with official matters and does not impose general censorship (*see* III, 3(*b*)) although critics claim that "official matters" are too widely defined. More important than the possible legal sanction is the fact that a journalist using restricted information supplied on a confidential basis could find that such information would not be available to him next time he needed it.

7. Measuring public opinion. Since public opinion is so nebulous it defies accurate measurement. This does not mean, however, that it cannot be measured. Newspapers and magazines have, for many years, conducted polls among their readers to ascertain public opinion about various matters; but it was left to an American, Dr. Gallup, to put polling on a scientific basis. The essential point about modern polls is that they try to deal with a representative sample of the population.

This is more complicated than it sounds, since a sample may be fully representative of a small section of the population and completely unrepresentative of the rest. A poll of all workers in a large factory, for example, would represent the workers' views. If the subject of the poll was attitudes to trade unions it is unlikely that it would represent the views of management or the non-working population. It is even possible that it would be unrepresentative of the views of workers in another industry. Then too there is evidence to suggest that people who take part in polls may themselves be unrepresentative, since clearly they cannot speak for those who do not normally respond when asked to take part in a survey.

The Gallup Poll was founded in 1941 and was nearly wrecked at the outset by just this sort of problem. A prediction of the outcome of an American presidential election was wildly wrong and, on investigating afterwards why this should be so, the pollsters discovered that the estimates had been based on the replies to a series of telephone enquiries. Anybody not on the phone was not therefore asked and such people represented a considerable proportion of the electorate with different views from those of the phone owners.

8. The value of public opinion. It may be said that public opinion is valuable because the government, any government, needs to know the wishes of the governed. Pressure groups (*see* 10) provide a focus for public opinion but opinion itself remains vague and subject to change. If laws are made in defiance of public opinion they may be widely disregarded and thus become bad law. The National Industrial Relations Court, set up under the Industrial Relations Act 1971 (*see* XII, 7), proved to be so unpopular with the trade union movement that it was eventually scrapped as unworkable. On the other hand, responsible government (*see* V, 15) must, in some cases, be in advance of public opinion.

Thus, although vociferous pressure groups campaigned for revision of the laws on homosexuality and capital punishment (*see* 10), the revision of such laws was not supported by public opinion. It may, in any case, be singularly ill-informed and it can be manipulated as is shown in the books by Vance Packard in the 1950s, notably, *The Hidden Persuaders*. But if public opinion is ill-informed or irrational, it is still the opinion of the governed and, as such, is worthy of consideration. It is worth remembering incidentally that the British jury system (*see* VII, 13) is based on the assumption that twelve ordinary men and women will normally be able to reach a sensible, non-expert verdict in even the most complex of cases. Whilst there is clearly a case for listening to the experts, and governments have access to whatever expert help and advice they need, experts still only represent one kind of opinion and it is a minority one. It may well be that ill-informed, irrational public opinion which has been derived from the everyday experiences of ordinary people is, in the end, more important.

9. A consensus. Public opinion which is rooted in political culture (*see* 7) forms a consensus, i.e. a basic agreement about what governments have a "right" to do. Such an agreement may well not include the particular point at issue. It could express itself in some such phrase as, "I think that they are wrong to take that particular course, but if that is what they intend to do then they are entitled to do it (however I reserve my right to oppose them by whatever lawful means are in my power)".

PRESSURE GROUPS

10. Pressure groups. One way in which public opinion may make its voice heard effectively is by means of a pressure group, which may be defined as a body of people banded together to influence the course of public policy. Such groups may be organised for a specific purpose, e.g. the Anti-Vivisection Society, or they may be in existence for some more general purpose and act as pressure groups for a specific purpose arising from their general beliefs. Thus the Roman Catholic Church is basically a religious organisation but provides a pressure group to influence proposed changes in the law on abortion. The way in which this can be done is described by B. Pymm in *Pressure Groups and the Permissive Society* (David and Charles, 1974), an account of the lobbying of different groups on three separate moral issues in the 1970s.

(*a*) The issues were the reform of the law on abortion, capital punishment and homosexuality.

(*b*) The method was to lobby M.P.s, to encourage the passing of private member's Bills (*see* I, **18**) on these topics and to provide parliamentary spokesmen with relevant information.

(*c*) Other national events were a major factor. In the early days of the campaign the Profumo case diverted public opinion and, later, the miners' strike (1974) and the economic situation in 1976–7 meant that Bills were lost because the government was too busy with other things to allow adequate time for their discussion.

11. How groups work. Pressure groups can work in a number of ways and through a number of agencies.

(*a*) *Active politics.* A pressure group may decide that the only way it can make its voice heard effectively is to get one of its supporters into Parliament. The group will therefore turn itself into a political organisation, or join an existing one, and campaign on a particular "platform".

(*b*) *A public relations campaign.* The education of the public on a particular issue may well change the climate of public opinion. The issue of Britain's entry into the European Economic Community was widely canvassed in the late 1960s and early 1970s (*see* X, **3**). In 1974 the Labour Party came into power committed to a re-negotiation of Britain's terms of entry. It was the referendum on 5th June 1975, however, which finally endorsed the decision; and the referendum was preceded by a sustained campaign from both pro-marketeers and anti-marketeers which cut across party divisions and sought to educate public opinion as to the implications of this decision.

(*c*) *Electioneering*. Candidates in general elections and by-elections are invariably the target of pressure groups.

(*d*) *Industrial action*. It has been said that the Heath government of 1970 was brought down by the intransigence of the miners. That same trade union strength supported the Labour government which succeeded Mr. Heath. It should be noted that "industrial action" covers a wide range of activities other than strikes. It can involve other forms of non-co-operation or it can include co-operation, as in the case of the social contract (*see* III, 4).

(*e*) *Lobbying*. Most legislatures have places where constituents and others can meet their elected representatives and plead their cause or discuss their problems. Such places, rooms, corridors or offices, are known as "lobbies" and the process itself is known as "lobbying".

(*f*) *Protest*. Pressure groups can act positively, in that they actively champion a cause or they can act in a negative way, in that their main emphasis is on opposition. Opposition can take many forms. They include marches, sit-ins and campaigns in which supporters are encouraged to write to their M.P.

12. Pressure points. Pressure is exerted at different points and for different purposes.

(*a*) *Politicians*. They are the elected representatives and groups can bring pressure to bear by promising or withholding their votes.

(*b*) *Civil Servants*. They are the people who carry out the legislation and they advise ministers on matters of policy. It is also part of the responsibility of the higher civil service to consider the views of interested parties when changes in legislation are proposed. For example, the Home Office working parties on prison conditions include representatives of the Howard League for Penal Reform. For this reason groups can frequently exert their most effective pressure through the Civil Service.

(*c*) *The Public*. The public at large form public opinion and to do so effectively they may well need educating. One of the functions of a pressure group is to ensure that its case is well known and sympathetically received by the public.

13. Political pressure groups. All political parties have pressure groups, ranging in size and importance from small groups of enthusiasts bonded together temporarily to focus attention on a specific issue to large, old-established bodies employing numbers of professional staff. Their links with the parent party range from official recognition and support to embarrassed disclaimers.

(a) Groups associated with the *Conservative Party* include:

(i) the Bow Group, founded in 1951, and representing the intellectual approach;

(ii) the 1922 Committee, an influential group of back-benchers;

(iii) the Monday Club, formed originally in 1961 to oppose Harold Macmillan's "wind of change" speech and still an important barometer of Conservative opinions;

(iv) the Selsdon Group (1973), mainly young Conservatives concerned to reduce the amount of government intervention in everyday life;

(v) the Centre for Policy Studies, founded by Sir Keith Joseph in 1974, and concerned with research, particularly into social problems.

(b) Groups associated with the *Labour Party* include:

(i) the Fabian Society, founded in 1884 and representing the academic approach to politics. The society produces a great deal of literature, particularly Fabian pamphlets on social and political matters. There are some 800 titles in the series;

(ii) the Tribune Group, founded in 1937, largely as a response to thinking about the Spanish civil war. It has about eighty associated M.P.s and publishes a regular newspaper.

(iii) the Campaign for Labour Democracy, founded in 1972 as a pressure group within the Labour Party. It aims to establish a procedure whereby all members of the party seeking re-election to Parliament should be nominated on each occasion by the local committee. Advocates of the proposal claim that this would make M.P.s more responsive to the local electorate and thus be more democratic. Opponents claim that the Campaign is run by "left-wing activists" and that, far from enhancing democracy, the proposal would allow a major decision to be made by a small unrepresentative group.

(c) *Other groups.* All the major parties have youth groups and there are a large number of left-wing groups who claim that their policies are more truly socialist than those of the Labour Party. They include the Revolutionary Socialist League and the Social Democratic Alliance. The Gladstone Club, founded in 1973, claims to represent all shades of political opinion.

There are also a number of groups outside the immediate political field whose views are nevertheless well represented in Parliament. The links between the Labour Party and the trade union movement are well known (*see* XII, 4). In the general election of October 1974 there were 154 Labour members who were members of trade unions. The total number of trade unionists of the other parties was twenty-four, (*Cassell's Parliamentary Directory* 1975). The interests of the National Chamber of Trade, the National Farmers' Union and the British Medical Association are well represented by Conservative M.P.s.

14. Influence. It will be clear that public opinion and the activities of pressure groups exercise considerable influence. It should be noted that influence may be exerted both on the governors and on the governed. Ways of exerting influence include the following.

(*a*) *The giving of information.* We have seen that a government in control of the media is in a stronger position than one which is not. Any information-giving agency therefore has power at its disposal.

(*b*) *Threat of sanctions.* Only a government can impose legal sanctions. Fines, imprisonment and executions are all punishments which are unlawful unless carried out by due process of law. To talk of the I.R.A. "executing" traitors is, therefore, either a misuse of language or an anticipation of a different form of government. Such action is murder. There are, however, a number of sanctions which are imposed by agencies other than governments. Parents, teachers and religious organisations, for example, have both authority and power (*see* III) and are able to reinforce it by sanctions ranging from disapproval to, in the case of religious organisations, excommunication.

(*c*) *Personal relationships.* Parents, friends and others can frequently exert influence because the person whom they wish to influence is likely to be sympathetic to their point of view.

(*d*) *Prototypes of initiation.* This is a sociological term which is used to describe the sort of influence exerted by fashion. No one is forced to follow fashion; the reasons why people do so are complicated. They include, however, the feeling that it is in some way right to do so.

PROGRESS TEST 2

1. What is meant by "political culture"? **(1, 2)**

2. What evidence is there for the existence of élites in Britain? **(3)**

3. Define "public opinion" and state why it is considered important. **(4–9)**

4. What are "pressure groups" and how do they work? **(10–12)**

5. List some of the more important political pressure groups. **(13)**

6. In what ways may influence be exerted on the government? **(14)**

CHAPTER III

Government and Freedom

ELECTIVE DICTATORSHIP AND RESIDUAL FREEDOMS

1. Elective dictatorship. In the Richard Dimbleby Lecture, 1976, Lord Hailsham, Lord Chancellor in the previous administration, described the power of Parliament as being absolute and unlimited, and pointed out that in this Britain was unique. He was not suggesting that this power was abused, although clearly it has been in the past, but merely that if Parliament chose to abuse its powers the ordinary citizen would have no redress short of revolution.

One of the traditional checks on the power of the House of Commons was the existence of a second chamber; but the House of Lords is now very restricted in its functions (*see* IV, **9**) and there is a case to be made for either its abolition or its replacement by a second chamber elected on a different basis to the House of Commons. The American Congress has its House of Representatives and its Senate elected in different ways.

2. Legislation. Since the turn of the century, legislation has increased enormously.

(*a*) In 1911 the Liberal government, often thought of as a great reforming body, produced about 430 pages of legislation. In 1975 the Labour government, suffering from a very small majority in Parliament, and thus unable, one would have thought, to legislate as it desired was, nevertheless, able to produce no less than 13,000 pages of legislation.

(*b*) At the turn of the century the budget was of the order of £100 million; by the late 1970s it was in excess of £50,000 million not including local authority spending.

The mass of legislation, and the fact that more and more aspects of daily life are covered by legislation, means that the sovereignty of Parliament and the rule of law (*see* VII, **5**) are increasingly in conflict. In this situation Parliament can always win and the considerations which might prevent this happening are moral and political, not legal.

3. Residual freedoms. If modern government is as ubiquitous as Lord Hailsham believes, by what definition is Britain still called a free country? It is true that the citizen is free to do whatever he likes so long as the law does not proscribe it and it is also true that, except in a very theoretical way, he has freedom of thought. Subliminal advertising, for example, in which pictures are flashed on a television screen too quickly to be seen but which make an impression on the sub-concious mind, is technically possible. But it is illegal. A citizen thus has freedom under the law and this gives him four basic rights.

(*a*) *Freedom of person.* It was laid down as long ago as 1215 in Magna Carta that, "No free man shall be taken or imprisoned or dispossessed or outlawed . . . unless by lawful judgment of his peers or the law of the land" and this principle still survives. Anybody whose personal freedom is endangered can have recourse to a number of actions, all of which will be supported by the law. They include the following.

(*i*) Self-defence. It is a defence in law to show that the reason you attacked somebody was to defend yourself.

(*ii*) Prosecution for assault. Conversely if you yourself are attacked your opponent can be summonsed for assault and if found guilty will be punished.

(*iii*) Actions for wrongful arrest and/or false imprisonment. The police have certain powers (*see* VII, **17**) but can only exercise these powers in accordance with very specific rules. Any arrest or imprisonment which can be shown to have contravened these rules is actionable.

(*iv*) Habeas corpus. If a person is arrested he must be charged with a specific offence. If he is not so charged the person acting for him can apply to Queen's Bench for a writ of habeas corpus. This writ commands the judge to show legal cause for his detention (Habeas Corpus Acts 1675 and 1816).

(*b*) *Freedom of speech.* This is not a right to say whatever one thinks whenever one wishes. It is the right to say whatever one wishes so long as it does not infringe a specific law. Freedom of speech applies to the publication of words in any form and the main barriers to publication are as follows.

(*i*) Slander. Spoken language which is defamatory, i.e.

words which injure another person's reputation (Defamation Act 1952).

(*ii*) Libel. The publication of slanderous statements by other means, i.e. books, plays, broadcasts, is equally against the law. It is a defence in a libel case if the defendant can show that the defamation was unintentional and that he is prepared to make suitable amends (Defamation Act 1952).

(*iii*) Official Secrets. Information obtained for official purposes must not be disclosed to an unauthorised person (Official Secrets Act 1911). The Act was originally intended to deal with espionage and similar matters but it has been used to prevent the disclosure of almost any sort of official matter, e.g. the circumstances of a claimant for supplementary benefit. Critics, both within official circles and outside them, have long felt that this Act is being used for purposes for which it was not intended and that, in the interests of open government (*see* 11), there is a good case to be made for it to be reconsidered. In July 1978, the government published a White Paper containing proposals for reform of the legislation (*Reform of Section 2 of the Official Secrets Act 1911*, Cmnd. 7285).

(*iv*) Incitement to disaffection. It has been the practice of some pacifist groups in recent years to try to encourage soldiers serving in Northern Ireland to desert. Whether one considers this laudable or deplorable is a matter of opinion. What is not a matter of opinion is that such an act is contrary to the Incitement to Disaffection Act 1936.

(*v*) Conduct likely to cause a breach of the peace. In general terms, anything which is said or done which is likely to stir up hatred or ill-feeling can be an offence against the Public Order Act 1936. In practice, of course, the law is administered humanely and to secure a conviction it would be necessary to show that the words complained of were likely to cause a grave disturbance. The Act was amended by the Race Relations Act 1976 to include the situation where provocative words were likely, "having regard to all the circumstances", to stir up hatred against any racial group in Great Britain.

(*vi*) Censorship. There is no general power of censorship as such although special powers may be necessary to protect the national interest in times of war. Plays were at one time censored by the Lord Chamberlain but this practice ceased with the Theatres Act 1968. Films are still subject to censorship, mainly on grounds of obscenity, and the power of censorship is vested in local authorities (Cinematograph Acts 1909–1952). In practice such authorities usually rely on the certificate issued by the British Board of Film Censors, a non-statutory body answerable to the film industry, although its president is appointed in consultation with the Home Secretary and the local authorities.

(c) *Freedom of association and assembly.* People may assemble in large numbers and may march and protest in various ways so long as their purpose is a legal one. But a law-abiding, peaceful protest may get out of hand and may then become a danger to public order. The mass picketing of the Grunwick film processing laboratories at Cricklewood in the summer of 1977 was an example of this sort of situation. As a result of this incident there were demands for the laws on picketing to be reconsidered. The concept of "peaceful picketing", with pickets having the right to stop lorries at the picket line and to explain the case of the strikers in a reasonable atmosphere may seem attractive when discussed in the calm precincts of Westminster, but can look different at the scene of a bitter and long drawn-out strike.

(d) *Freedom of religion.* There is no legalised religious intolerance in Britain. Churches or religious groups are not proscribed for their religious views, or even their political opinions, although they may be prosecuted if, as a result of these views, they perform or condone acts which would otherwise be illegal. There is however an established church, the Church of England, and the Test Act 1673 laid down that only members of the established church could hold certain official positions. The Act was repealed in 1828 and a further Act, the Catholic Emancipation Act 1829, removed barriers which had, until then, prevented Catholics from taking their full part in public life. The only area now remaining where there is a religious barrier is the succession to the throne. The Act of Settlement 1701 still insists that the monarch, as Defender of the Faith, shall be a member of the established church.

NATURAL RIGHTS

4. Natural rights. The American Declaration of Independence asserts that man has an inalienable right, i.e. one that cannot be taken away, to "life, liberty and the pursuit of happiness". If these rights are inalienable then it follows that they are in some sense "natural". Both Hobbes and Locke accepted the idea of such rights but pointed out that civilised man does not live in a state of nature. He lives in a complex society and he is ruled by a sovereign power. Hobbes's view was that, by definition, the sovereign's power was absolute and that he had the right to command the allegiance of his subjects. But the sovereign's rights are not inalienable. He forefeits them if he fails to protect his subjects.

These mutual rights, those of the sovereign and the subjects, form a social contract, by means of which both ruler and ruled recognise duties and responsibilities to each other. The concept was central to the thinking of another writer on political matters, Jean-Jacques Rousseau (1712–78) whose book, *Du contrat social: ou, principes du droit politique* (1762), expounded the theory of the "general will" by which the interests of the people were served. The duty of the government was to find this will and apply it. The duty of the people was to express it.

The concept of natural rights was born of the political situation in the seventeenth century (Hobbes lived from 1588 to 1679 and Locke from 1632 to 1704). One might reasonably ask whether a seventeenth-century concept still applies in the twentieth century. The Labour government of 1974 obviously thought so. They resurrected the phrase "social contract" and re-defined it. The modern social contract, which critics would argue died in 1977 with the third stage of the government's incomes policy, was basically an agreement between the government and the Trades Union Congress in which the T.U.C. would endeavour to persuade its members to moderate their wage demands and, in return for this service, the government would provide a social wage, i.e. non-monetary benefits, or forms of tax relief which, it was said, would have been of greater value to the workers than a nominal increase in wages which would have been useless because of the effects of inflation.

5. The social wage. This itself was not a new idea. The Poor Law was an Elizabethan concept and, although until the mid-nineteenth century such help was only available to the poorest, there was a growing recognition that society had a duty to its less fortunate members. The earliest Factory Act, for example, in 1802, was a belated recognition that workers would work better if there were curbs on the extent to which they could be exploited. But it was the Reform Act 1867 and legislation between then and the end of the nineteenth century which really laid the foundation of today's welfare state.

Its origins are various. The industrial revolution and subsequent industrial expansion had suggested the economic advantages of a concern for welfare. Some individuals, philosophers like Jeremy Bentham, philanthropists like Lord Shaftesbury and political activists like Sidney and Beatrice Webb all made their own contributions for their own motives. The Reform Act 1832 extended the franchise and workers with votes became people to be considered. The Victorians set up numerous societies to deal with the social problems of their age. One of these was the Charity Organisation Society (now known as the Family Welfare Association) whose original concern was with the "deserving poor".

But it was not really until the Beveridge Report of 1942, *Social Insurance and Allied Services*, that the concept of the "deserving poor" was changed. That Report, designed as an attack on Want, was also a recognition that poverty, ignorance, disease etc., were not just personal misfortunes; they were the responsibility of government. A government which accepted its responsibility could justly claim to be fulfilling its part of a social contract and the social wage thus provided would be seen as a right, and not as a form of charity. The social wage would be seen by government as "enlightened self-interest", a phrase which was used by another great Victorian philanthropist, Octavia Hill who, by stressing this motive, persuaded wealthy patrons to subsidise the building of artisans' dwellings.

POWER AND AUTHORITY

6. Power and authority. Power may be defined as the ability to impose one's will on others; authority as the right to do so. The ability to do so may rest on sheer physical force or on one person having more intellectual capacity than another or on domination, i.e. some people have the ability to impose their will on others by force of personality. Power may also come through manipulation or influence.

The right to impose one's will on others may be defined as legitimated power and such authority must be acknowledged, widely accepted and institutionalised. The sociologist Max Weber recognises three types of authority, all of which can be seen in different aspects of the British system of government.

(*a*) *Legal-rational* authority is the sort of authority which rests on a belief in the legitimacy of the rulers, and on the right of those issuing orders to do so. A man who is arrested may ask by what authority he is charged and he will be told which particular law he is believed to have contravened. Generally speaking, whether innocent or guilty of the particular crime, he will take for granted the legitimacy of the system under which he is charged (the actions of I.R.A. members in refusing to recognise the authority of the court which is trying them are atypical).

(b) *Traditional* authority rests on established belief. Britain is a monarchy and has been for some time. Critics of the monarchy may feel that it is out-moded and should be replaced, but few would deny the right of the monarch to rule even if they feel that the right should no longer be bestowed.

(c) *Charismatic* authority, unlike the other two types, is a personal authority; the strength of character possessed by great leaders which causes men to follow them. It has been ascribed to leaders as different as Christ, Napoleon, Joan of Arc, Ghandi and Hitler. Such authority does not survive the death of the leader although the party or movement of which he was head may carry on by virtue of one of the other types of authority.

7. Liberty and equality. Freedom under the law is an important concept (*see* 3). But what does freedom mean? It does not mean complete absence of restraint, for that would lead to anarchy. Such "freedom" would benefit the strong at the expense of the weak. Nor does it mean submission to an authority of which one approves. Rousseau's "general will", if it could be shown to exist, would be a state of freedom in which the sovereign would not need to restrain his subjects since, by definition, he was doing that which they would want done. Sir Isaiah Berlin, in a pamphlet entitled *Two Concepts of Liberty* (Clarendon Press, 1958), distinguishes between "freedom to" and "freedom from". It makes no sense to say that a person is free *to* develop his personality if he does not have freedom *from* hunger. He cannot consider his development whilst he is starving.

These ideas are not new. Oliver Cromwell's Commonwealth was an attempt to set up a government which was free from the tyranny of monarchy. It was only partially successful, in that it was superseded by a monarchy again, but at least some lessons had been learnt. The French Revolution, with its slogan "liberty, equality and fraternity", was a more successful attempt to destroy the power of the monarchy and the "declaration of the rights of man and of citizens" by the French National Assembly in 1789 listed equality, liberty and brotherhood as basic human rights, together with the right to property and security. One need hardly add that there were not many aristocratic Frenchmen around to endorse this view; nor would they, had they been there, necessarily have agreed that the right to resist oppression was inalienable.

It may be necessary to restrain some freedoms in order that others may flourish. It would be generally agreed that without laws against theft, murder and other crimes there could be no true freedom in society. In a free society, however, such restraint can only be exercised by what Hobbes called "coercive sovereign power". The question of the amount of freedom which a free society can permit itself is neatly summed up in the subject-matter of an essay competition established in memory of the late Ross McWhirter. The subject for 1977 was: "How can a democratic country protect its citizens against subversion without sacrificing individual freedom?"

It might appear at first glance that liberty and equality are indivisible: that a society which is not free cannot be equal, nor an unequal society free. Equality however does not mean treating all members of a society equally. Some have greater needs than others and their treatment needs to be unequal if they are to have equal opportunity. In Aristotle's view, "Injustice arises as much from treating unequals equally as from treating equals unequally". The Equal Pay Act 1970 and the Sex Discrimination Act 1975 (*see* XII, **13**) both recognise particular inequalities whilst striving to create a more general equality.

A BILL OF RIGHTS

8. Bill of Rights. King James II ascended the throne in February 1685; a few months later Parliament was prorogued. It did not meet again until 1689 when, James having fled, the crown was offered to William of Orange and his wife Mary. Since there was no king on the throne at the time the document offering them the throne could not be an Act of Parliament (*see* Table II). It was in fact a Bill and, as the Bill of Rights 1689, it was a major constitutional landmark. It did not introduce any radical constitutional changes, apart from changing the line of succession to the throne, but it did set out to vindicate and assert the rights of both Parliament and the people, rights which James was said to have infringed. In particular it reiterated five basic points:

(*a*) that Parliament, not the king, was responsible for levying taxes;

(*b*) that the right of petitioning the sovereign, and thus by-passing Parliament, was illegal;

(*c*) that the king was not allowed to maintain a standing army;

(*d*) that Parliament had the right to act freely and independently of the sovereign; and

(*e*) that Parliament was responsible for the redress of grievances (*see* IV, **16**) and, therefore, should be free to meet as and when necessary.

Perhaps the time has come for a new Bill of Rights. The idea has already been accepted in principle, in that Britain was a party to the Universal Declaration of Human Rights made by the General Assembly of the United Nations in 1948 and ratified by the European Convention on Human Rights in 1951. But the Convention is merely a declaration of intent and has no legal standing. Even if it were enshrined in law by an Act of Parliament it would not be immune from amendment, suspension or repeal by the same legal process.

A Bill of Rights, in other words, can only be effective if it has an in-built guarantee that it will not be subject to alteration except in the most unusual circumstances and according to stringent procedures. If a Bill of Rights were to become law then it would have to incorporate special features; for example that it could not be changed by the normal parliamentary majority (which might be only two or three votes). A majority of, say, two-thirds would ensure that the matter was decided irrespective of party views.

It has been held that "Parliament cannot bind its successors", and this is part of what is meant by the sovereignty of Parliament (*see* X, **14**), but such a Bill would clearly bind successive governments. Convention, however, is an important part of British government (*see* IV, **6**) and there is no reason to suppose that the rights enshrined in such a Bill would not be covered by convention. Such a matter would not, after all, be a party political issue.

9. The new rights. Freedom of person, speech, association, assembly and religion are already accepted in Britain (*see* **3**), but these are residual freedoms. There is no general statute which says that these freedoms are guaranteed. Indeed there are limitations on each of them. Freedom of association, for example, permits and encourages membership of a trade union. It was not always

so. The Combination Acts of 1799 and 1801 had made membership of trade unions illegal and early trade unionists, including
the "Tolpuddle Martyrs" were transported for this very crime.
The repeal of these Acts in 1924 led to positive discrimination in
favour of trade unions. The increasing influence of the T.U.C.
on government (see XII, 4) and legislation such as the Trade
Unions and Labour Relations (Amendment) Act 1976, designed
to protect the interests of trade unionists, may yet endanger the
rights of a citizen not to belong to a union (see XII, 9).

General rights then are accepted but, since they are not absolute and not covered by legislation, they can be infringed. In a
situation where a general right appeared to be infringed by a
specific law it would be for the courts to decide between them.
Such a situation would not present a new principle. In libel cases
at present the court must decide between the aspects of defamation of character and freedom of speech. The difference would
be that whilst freedom of speech is at present recognised it does
not have appropriate legal backing. A Bill of Rights setting out a
citizen's right to such freedom could preserve the right rather
more clearly.

10. Privacy and rights. There is no general right to privacy in
Britain and a recent report on the subject, the *Report of the Committee on Privacy* (the Younger Committee, Cmnd. 5012), urged
that careful consideration should be given to the dangers in-
herent in the advance of technology. A White Paper, *Computers
and Privacy* (Cmnd. 6353), recommended legislation to cover such
situations and, in particular, echoed the recommendations of the
Younger Committee.

(*a*) Information collected for a specific purpose should not be
used for other purposes.

(*b*) Access to computerised information should be confined
to authorised persons.

(*c*) The amount of information collected should be the minimum required for the purpose.

(*d*) The identity of informants, in surveys etc., and information about them should be stored separately.

(*e*) Computerised information should be available to the person to whom it refers, so that he can comment on it and correct
it if necessary.

(*f*) There should be security procedures built in to the data collection process and such security levels should be stipulated when research is being planned.

(g) Systems of data collection should be monitored.

(h) All information collected about individuals for research purposes should be destroyed when the purpose for which it was collected has been served.

(i) All data should be as accurate as possible.

(j) Value-judgments in social surveys, etc., should be coded with care.

A number of other rights, like the right to a fair trial in public and the right to education, are already covered by existing laws. But such laws can be set aside in certain circumstances, e.g. the right to a public trial can be denied if the case is one involving matters which, in the opinion of the judge, it would not be in the public interest to disclose. A general right would ensure that such considerations would be weighed equitably, with the state's rights not necessarily taking precedence over those of the individual.

There are a number of other rights or groups of people who appear to be overlooked in the present state of the law. The so-called "tug-of-love" cases, in which hapless children seemed to be pawns in a matrimonial dog-fight, produced a number of demands for an official procedure which would ensure that the rights of children were fully considered. Perhaps the most important right, however, which could be incorporated in a new Bill of Rights would be the automatic right to legal remedy where it could be shown that the "basic" rights of an individual had been infringed.

OPEN GOVERNMENT

11. Open government. Niccoló Machiavelli (1469–1527) gave his name to the adjective "Machiavellian", frequently regarded as synonymous with "devious". In his book *The Prince*, for example, he advised the prince to maintain a respectable appearance, but to feel free to use this as a cloak to hide whatever activities he might be engaged in which might have been unpopular but which were, nevertheless, necessary in the interests of the state.

The cloak of secrecy is frequently used in this way and there are occasions when it may be justified. In the world of crime, for example, it would be folly to insist that the police always dealt openly with the public since, by doing so, they would present the criminal with an unfair advantage which would be used to the detriment of the law-abiding citizen. It is, however, only a short step from conceding this point to creating secret police and the totalitarian regimes which would accompany them. A distinction must always be made between necessary secrecy and unnecessary secrecy.

The Fulton Report on the Civil Service (1968) (*see* **XVII, 6**) recognised this problem and commented, "We think that the administrative process is surrounded by too much secrecy. The public interest would be better served if there were a greater amount of openness". Fulton's solution was that there should be more consultation.

The White Paper on *The Reorganisation of Central Government*, 1970 (Cmnd. 4506) recognised a similar problem and thought that the creation of fewer, and larger, government departments would solve it. Various suggestions for procedural reform in the House of Commons also had the problem of open government in mind and the *Royal Commission on the Constitution* 1969–73 (The Kilbrandon Report, 1973, Cmnd. 5460) was also conscious, not only of secrecy, but of the fact that such secrecy was frequently represented as being in the public interest. It was recognised that more open government would encourage public debate and that this would inevitably cause delays. The Commission also felt that the publication of Green Papers, intended to stimulate discussion, had not been entirely successful since such papers tended to seem more authoritative than they claimed.

12. Parliament on the air. The suggestion was made from time to time that the proceedings in Parliament should be broadcast. This was already done in a limited way, in that programmes like *Today in Parliament* were broadcast regularly and the Opening of Parliament and the Queen's Speech were televised. Such glimpses were, however, exceptional and the proposal, agreed by the Labour government in July 1977, that there should be full broadcasting of all parliamentary proceedings is not without its dangers. Broadcasting of such proceedings was tried experimentally in 1975 and, since 11th April 1978 the Prime Minister's question time has been broadcast on Radio Four every Tuesday and Thursday. The April 1978 Budget proceedings were perhaps a more realistic demonstration of the advantages and disadvantages of regular, complete parliamentary coverage. On the credit side it is clearly a step towards open government and it may be that an aspiring M.P. could cultivate a critical, informed and positive approach which would not only impress his constituents but would also contribute to the efficiency of the proceedings of the House. On the debit side however it is possible that a series of parliamentary debates would not make particularly interesting listening and so defeat the object of the exercise. There would also of course be an ever-present temptation for M.P.s to "play to the gallery". The cost of complete broadcast coverage of parliamentary debates was estimated as £310,000 in 1976 and the technical difficulties in "wiring up" the whole House are considerable. Even when the wiring is completed and the full scheme is fully operational the broadcasts will not cover *all* parliamentary business since there will be two rooms, for use of Select Committees and similar bodies, which will not be wired for sound (*Hansard*, 26th July 1977).

PROGRESS TEST 3

1. What freedoms are there in an elective dictatorship? (1–3)
2. What is meant by "natural rights"? (4)
3. Define "power" and "authority" and distinguish between liberty and equality. (6, 7)
4. Make a case for a Bill of Rights in Britain. (8–10)
5. What is meant by open government? (11, 12)

CHAPTER IV

Types of Government

CONSTITUTIONAL GOVERNMENT

1. Constitutional government. Any state, i.e. any community organised as a political entity, needs a government, since in all but the very smallest communities there will be need for a focus of authority to frame the rules by which the society is to be governed and to ensure that such rules (laws) are carried out. Government has been described as a necessary evil; necessary for the reasons given above and evil because any action by the state infringes the liberty of the individual. Acton's dictum is also true that, "power corrupts, absolute power tends to corrupt absolutely".

A constitution may be defined as the rules which stipulate how a state may be governed. Such rules do not have to be written, indeed the British constitution is partly written and partly unwritten. However, all constitutions will have certain features in common. They will specify:

(a) the laws, how they are to be made and the methods of enforcement;

(b) the form of government, i.e. a monarchy, a dictatorship, a republic etc.; and

(c) the powers of government, i.e. to what extent and in what direction can the government operate and, possibly, what happens if the government attempts to exceed its powers

2. Unconstitutional and anti-constitutional. It should be noted that the terms "unconstitutional" and "anti-constitutional" are not synonymous. An act is unconstitutional if it infringes what is generally accepted to be a constitutional principle. Both the referendum and the mandate were at one time widely considered to be unconstitutional in Britain. The question of the terms of Britain's entry into the Common Market was felt however to be of such importance and, more significantly perhaps, was so clearly not a party-political issue that the hitherto unconstitu-

39

tional referendum was thought to be a useful way of resolving the issue, and the referendum therefore received recognition. The mandate, the idea that a party having won an election has been given blanket powers to push through its party programme, is not recognised by constitutional lawyers (*see* XVIII, **18**). Some critics, particularly if they represent the opposition to a minority government, insist that for a government to claim such a right is unconstitutional, although it would be difficult to prove that it was illegal.

Anti-constitutional acts, on the other hand, are likely to be widely regarded as bordering on the illegal and are quite clearly aimed at undermining the constitution. Such acts, if successful, would not simply alter the constitution, they would supplant it. Thus a military *coup* as a means of achieving a change of government would not be simply unconstitutional, it would clearly be anti-constitutional.

3. Unitary and federal constitutions. A unitary constitution is one in which the central government is sovereign. It alone makes the laws and it alone is responsible for carrying them out. It can of course delegate its authority and in Britain this is done frequently (*see* XIX, **3**). Parliament is, however, the supreme legislative authority in the United Kingdom and its supremacy extends over Britain (England, Scotland and Wales) and Northern Ireland, but not the Channel Islands nor the Isle of Man, both of which are Crown dependencies. In 1920 a Northern Ireland Parliament (Stormont) was set up but was prorogued indefinitely in 1972 because of the disturbed situation there. Since then Northern Ireland has been ruled direct from Westminster and talks about a revised constitutional arrangement have broken down on a number of occasions because of the intransigent attitude of the political factions.

A federal constitution, on the other hand, is one in which a number of states are united for some purposes of government. States which are united in this way still retain some sovereignty but the constitution, i.e. the agreement to federate, is supreme. Such an agreement, invariably written, will specify the degree of autonomy to be enjoyed by member states.

In the American constitution, for example, the tenth amendment lists the respective powers of state government and federal government. Those federations in which the majority of power is wielded by states, rather than the central government, are known as confederations. Switzerland is a good example since the cantons, the twenty-two republics which make up the country of Switzerland, are more independent than the individual states which together comprise the United States of America.

In federations the powers of government are divided rather than delegated and the law-making function is shared. In such a situation an independent body will adjudicate in cases where conflict arises as to the allocation of power. In the U.S.A. the Supreme Court performs this function and in West Germany the federal government (the *Bund*) has specified powers. Those powers which are not so specified are the responsibility of the *Länder* (the regions).

4. Rigid and flexible constitutions. A constitution can be either rigid or flexible. A country with a flexible constitution can change its constitution by the normal processes of the law. No special procedure was required for example when Britain virtually broke the power of the House of Lords by means of the Parliament Act 1911. Rigid constitutions are invariably written and such a constitution can only be changed by a special, usually rather elaborate, procedure, for example, one of the following.

(*a*) Amendment to the constitution may only be possible if a specified proportion of the legislature agrees to it. In the U.S.A. a quorum of two-thirds of the members of both Houses of Congress is necessary.

(*b*) In Switzerland the constitution may only be changed as a result of a referendum.

(*c*) The ordinary legislature may be empowered to change the constitution by means of a special process. Thus in South Africa a majority of both parts of the legislature is required; and this majority must be obtained by both Houses in joint session.

(*d*) There may be a special body who alone can interpret the constitution. The Supreme Court exercises this function on occasion in the U.S.A.

5. The Commission on the Constitution. The Royal Commission on the Constitution 1969–73 (which produced the Kilbrandon Report) was an attempt to discover what people thought was wrong with the government and what should be done about it. The Commission carried out a survey designed to test attitudes to matters like participation, nationalism and devolution.

At the end of four years the Commission concluded that, although there was no evidence of "seething discontent throughout

the land", there was considerable evidence of a general dissatisfaction and, as a result, they proposed a form of devolution.
Their solution to the problem (discussed in IX) was based
broadly on the belief that people felt that government was too remote, and that they would like to have more say in the running
of the country.

6. Convention. Legal rules are an important part of the British
constitution, but an equally important part is played by conventions. These unwritten rules may be defined as those practices
which the government would feel bound to follow even though
they do not have the force of law. Being "non-legal" has the advantage that such conventions can be discarded if outmoded, or
created if legislation does not seem appropriate.

They can also be the subject of legislation. Thus the convention that "the King can do no wrong" is still true in that the
sovereign cannot be called to account for individual misdemean-
ors. Until 1947 however the convention covered not only the
sovereign in person but also the servants of the sovereign. The
Crown Proceedings Act 1947 removed this anomaly and made it
possible to sue a Crown servant for tort (an action in which
damages could be paid).

PARLIAMENTARY GOVERNMENT

7. The House of Lords. The House of Lords, or the Upper House
as it is also known, was an entirely hereditary chamber until the
Life Peerages Act 1958 enabled peerages to be bestowed for the
life-time of the peer only, i.e. they could not be inherited. The
hereditary principle was further eroded by the Peerages Act 1963
which allowed peers to disclaim their title.

The Act was the culmination of a campaign by the second
Viscount Stansgate, twice elected M.P. for Bristol South in 1960
but denied his right to sit because he was a peer. The Act enabled
him to renounce his peerage and he took his seat in the name of
Anthony Wedgwood-Benn. Lord Home, on becoming Prime
Minister in 1963, also disclaimed his peerage and was known as
Sir Alec Douglas Home until a peerage, the traditional reward
for a Prime Minister when he retires, restored his title. This time,
however, it was only a life peerage, and no hereditary peerages
have, in fact, been granted since 1945. The Peerages Act 1963
also allowed those ladies who were peeresses in their own right

to sit in the House of Lords for the first time. In spite of changes, both in the composition and the powers of the Upper House, it still retains its traditional character and further efforts to change it have met with limited success (*see* **24**).

8. Composition. There are about 1,000 peers eligible to sit in the House of Lords. In practice only about a quarter of this number do so. The Archbishops of Canterbury and York, together with twenty-four senior bishops, are known as the Lords Spiritual. Other peers including the Law Lords (*see* **9**(*e*)) are Lords Temporal and include all Scottish peers. Since 1957 peers have been entitled to an allowance of up to £6.50 per day, plus certain expenses for every day that they attend. Peers who do not intend to exercise their right to sit in the House of Lords may apply for leave of absence and about 200 have done so since this provision was introduced in 1958.

9. Powers. The main powers left to the Lords as a result of the Parliament Acts 1911 and 1949 are as follows.

(*a*) *Initiation of legislation.* Most legislation originates in the House of Commons but some non-controversial Bills start in the Upper House. The Companies Act 1948, for example, involved a great deal of work at the Committee stage and therefore received its first reading in the House of Lords.

(*b*) *Revision or amendment of any Bill, except a Money Bill.* A Money Bill is one which deals with financial matters and which the Speaker has certified as coming within that category. The power to revise and amend is important in the case of non-controversial Bills and there are occasions when the Lords, not being subject to the electorate, can make a useful contribution which the party politicians would feel unable to make.

(*c*) *Rejection of a Bill.* This power is restricted to one year, after which the rejected Bill becomes law. The Lords have no power to reject a Money Bill and the power to reject is used sparingly. It is sometimes justified on the grounds that it provides time for mature reflection (a week in politics is a long time). Critics claim that thwarting the will of the Commons is undemocratic (*see* I, **3**) but the power is in practice that of delay rather than rejection.

(*d*) *Legislation affecting peerages.* This is invariably introduced by the Lords although the initiative for such legislation may well come from the Commons. The House of Lords is, after all, the body most affected by such legislation and it must, in any case, pass through both Houses to become law.

(*e*) *Judicial power*. In addition to its legislative power the House of Lords acts as the supreme Court of Appeal. This function is exercised by the Law Lords, i.e. the Lord Chancellor and the Lords of Appeal in Ordinary. This is of course at variance with the theory of the separation of the powers (*see* I, **20–23**) but the legislative and judicial functions are in practice exercised separately.

10. The House of Commons. The House of Commons consists of 635 members, 516 for England, 36 for Wales, 71 for Scotland and 12 for Northern Ireland. Each member represents a constituency, the boundaries of which are kept under review by four Boundary Commissions, one each for England, Wales, Scotland and Northern Ireland, who recommend a redistribution of seats if this appears to be justified by changes in the structure of the population. The number of electors represented by a single M.P. varies from 53,336 in south-east England to 86,076 in Northern Ireland (*Hansard*, 26th October 1977). Members are paid a basic salary of £6,474 and office holders, including the Leader of the Opposition, are paid salaries in addition. Certain allowances, averaging about £1,000 per year, are also payable for expenses. The seating arrangements of the House of Commons are shown in Fig. 1.

11. Method of election. To become a Member of Parliament a candidate must be a British subject over twenty-one years of age and he must obtain the largest number of votes cast in his constituency. This system, sometimes called "first past the post", has been criticised as being unfair to minority parties (*see* **19**(*c*)). Whilst it is not a requirement that a candidate must be a member of a political party almost all successful candidates are. If for no other reason the cost of an election would preclude most independents.

A candidate is allowed to spend up to £1,075 on his election expenses, plus 6 pence for each eight electors in a borough constituency or 6 pence for six electors in a county constituency (*Britain 1977*, H.M.S.O.). He may send a copy of his election address post-free to all electors in his constituency but he must deposit £150 with the returning officer to become a candidate. This deposit is forfeit if he polls less than one-eighth of the votes cast. The rule is designed to prevent frivolous nominations but

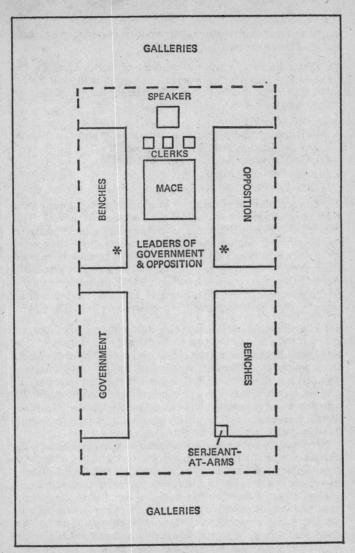

FIG. 1 *Seating in the House of Commons.*

may sometimes deter a serious candidate from a party which cannot afford such losses.

12. Disqualification. Certain categories of persons cannot become M.P.s. This does not prevent their candidature but it does mean that in the event of an election victory they would not be able to take their seat. Categories include:

  (*a*) peers (*see* 7);

  (*b*) clergymen and priests (but not non-conformist ministers, e.g. Rev. Ian Paisley, M.P. for Antrim North);

  (*c*) Civil Servants, judges and ambassadors;

  (*d*) members of H.M. forces;

  (*e*) undischarged bankrupts.

13. The organisation of business. At the beginning of each week the Leader of the House outlines the business of the week. This business will usually be decided as a result of consultation between the government and opposition, since co-operation is necessary if the work is to be accomplished. If agreement cannot be reached the opposition will register a protest, but they cannot prevent it. About half of the time will be taken up with the implementation of the government's legislative programme and the rest will be miscellaneous business, including question time (*see* XIX, 5(*b*)).

14. The officers of the House. The chief officer is the Speaker. Paradoxically, he does not speak in debates. His duty is to preside over the business of the House and he is elected by M.P.s from among their number. By convention, his election is unopposed but this convention has been broken on occasion. In general, however, this does not happen since he is chosen for his experience and is expected to be completely impartial. He represents the House on ceremonial occasions and is the guardian of its ancient privileges.

His deputy is known as the Chairman of Ways and Means. He also is elected by his fellow members, together with two others who act as Deputy Speakers. Like the Speaker the Deputies do not take part either in debates or in voting when acting in this capacity.

The Leader of the House is a leading member of the government and it is he, together with the Chief Whip (also known as the Patronage Secretary), who arranges the debates. If the Labour Party forms the government the appointment of the Chief Whip is made by the Prime Minister, but if the party is in opposition he is elected by Labour M.P.s. In the Conservative Party the appointment is made by the party leader who, in the normal course of events, will be either the Prime Minister or the Leader of the Opposition.

The Chief Whip is also responsible for seeing that members are present when required to vote and he is assisted in this duty by junior whips. The method of requiring members to be present is to underline important matters on the order paper. An item underlined three times is known as a "three-line whip" and a member who defies this subtle hint may have the whip withdrawn. This process involves the withdrawal of all party support from the member and could, in serious cases, result in his expulsion from the party.

The Clerk of the House of Commons is an administrator, not an M.P. He is a Civil Servant and his function is to deal with the vast amount of behind-the-scenes activity, preparation of order papers, liaison with government departments, etc.

The Serjeant-at-Arms, also technically a Civil Servant, is usually a distinguished retired soldier. He attends upon the Speaker on ceremonial occasions and is responsible, with his staff, for discipline and the security of the building.

15. Formal procedure. Procedure tends to be formal and is laid down in standing orders. If a question arises as to the interpretation of these orders the Speaker will be called upon to give a ruling. Such rulings rely heavily on precedent, and the writings of authorities such as Erskine May. They are invariably accepted. He also decides who shall speak and when, a process known as "catching the Speaker's eye", and he has a number of other duties related to the business of the House. He appoints a panel of M.P.s from which chairmen of Standing Committees are chosen and, when a Bill is to be referred to a committee, it is the Speaker who decides which committee it shall be sent to. If an M.P. wishes to raise a matter which he claims to be of "urgent public importance" the Speaker must decide whether the claim is justified and, if so, make time available for discussion.

16. The redress of grievances. Law-making is a major function of Parliament; redress of grievances is another. There are a number of ways in which citizens who feel that they have been wronged can seek redress through Parliament.

(a) *Question Time.* On four days of each week an hour of Parliamentary time is allocated to members who may question a minister on any matter for which he is responsible. Two days' notice is normally given but an urgent question, demanding an immediate answer, may be asked if the Speaker has given his prior consent. Answers are prepared by Civil Servants and may be given in either written or oral form. The broad difference between the two is that written questions ask for information and oral questions demand action. When the minister has replied to an oral question the questioner and other members have the right to ask supplementary questions and a member still unsatisfied has the right to raise the matter either in the adjournment debate, i.e. at the end of the normal day's business, or under standing orders.

(*b*) *The Parliamentary Commissioner* (usually known as the Ombudsman) receives complaints from the public about maladministration. His work is described in XIX, **14–16**, but the point to stress is that he can only act at the request of a member of the House of Commons, and he reports his findings to the House.

(*c*) *Parliamentary sovereignty.* Since Parliament is the supreme legislative body it has the power to redress any grievance which may be expressed. The power may not be used, but it is there. Both Houses share it. The Commons, as an elected assembly, is answerable to the electorate and the Lords, as the highest appellate authority, can interpret the law (*see* X, **14**).

PARTY GOVERNMENT

17. Party government. There are at least eight parties represented in the British Parliament but for the past 200 years government has been shared between two major parties, firstly Whigs and Tories, later Liberals and Conservatives and, since 1922, Conservatives and Labour. The rise of the Labour Party in the 1920s and the decline of the Liberal Party at about the same time created a situation in which there could have been three major parties, but the balance was never sufficiently equal for three parties to be serious contenders for government at the same time.

There are occasions of course when the parties sink their differences and form a coalition. This happened between 1939 and 1945 and all three parties were represented in a National Coalition Government. But the pressures which created this situation disappeared with the cessation of hostilities and the first general election after the war resulted in a clear majority for Labour and a return to two major parties. The Lib-Lab pact, by which Mr.

Callaghan's Labour government retained power in the second half of 1977 by accepting Liberal support, could hardly be called a coalition since the government thus formed was basically Labour.

Party government may be defined as the situation in which a number of political groups have a potential administration. The party which wins the election forms the government with its leader becoming the Prime Minister and its leading members becoming the Cabinet (*see* XVIII, **19**). The other major party becomes the Opposition, its leader the Leader of the Opposition and its leading members the Shadow Cabinet.

18. Advantages of party government. It has been said of British government that it is illogical but it works. When the Palace of Westminster was rebuilt after the fire of 1834, the seating and lobby arrangements of the debating chamber were designed to reflect the long tradition of the British system of party government which, in practice, is a two-party system, with the following advantages.

(*a*) It provides strong government. Between the two World Wars French governments changed frequently because there were a number of competing parties, none of whom were able to form a stable government.

(*b*) It reflects natural divisions in politics between those who wish to retain traditional institutions (conservatives) and those who wish for change (radicals).

(*c*) Voters are given a simple choice and can either endorse or reject the policies of the outgoing administration. It should be noted that most elections are decided, not by the party faithfuls, but by the floating voter whose allegiance will tend to be given to the party which appears most likely to be able to form a competent administration.

(*d*) It strengthens the major parties. If party government is a fact of political life it makes sense that there should be alternative governments from which the voters can choose. Parties can allow a range of opinions to be considered within their structure and both major parties have "wings" which represent the more extreme interpretation of their policies.

19. Disadvantages of party government. The major disadvantage of party government is that it leaves little scope for independence. Even if an Independent M.P. were elected, and this is unlikely since voters tend to vote for parties rather than individuals, he would not have the support which parties provide. The only legislation he could hope to introduce would be a private member's Bill and competition for the right to introduce these is fierce. Other disadvantages of party government include the following.

(a) Party discipline prevents members supporting minority views, which tend to be overlooked in the interests of solidarity.

(b) The personal element is lost. An M.P. is supposed to represent all his constituents, not just those who voted for him.

(c) Minority parties are unfairly treated. It takes far more votes to elect a Liberal M.P. than an M.P. of the two major parties. The *Hansard Committee on Electoral Reform* was unanimous in its view that one justification for reform was the unfairness of the present system to minority parties.

(d) A small group may have too much influence. In 1976 Reginald Prentice, M.P. for Newham East, was told by his local party committee that they would not re-adopt him as a candidate at the next election. Although he was at that time a Labour M.P. (he subsequently joined the Conservative Party) he claimed that this decision was a "left-wing conspiracy" and that the small group of activists who had caused his downfall were not representative of Labour Party supporters, and even less representative of Labour Party voters. In September 1977 Maureen Colquhoun, M.P. for Northampton, suffered a similar fate and made similar charges against her local committee. The Campaign for Labour Democracy seeks to make Labour M.P.s more directly answerable to local committees and is frequently said to be unrepresentative.

20. Totalitarian regimes. One alternative to party government is the totalitarian regime in which there is effectively only one party. Examples of such states include Communist China, the fascist government in pre-war Italy and the Soviet Union. In such systems the state has much greater power and the dominant ideology suffuses all parts of the life of the society. Social organisations and institutions are regarded as a legitimate concern of government. Writing, painting and the arts are encouraged to the extent that they serve the purposes of the state. Dissidents, e.g. the writer Solzhenitsyn in the Soviet Union, are seen as traitors.

21. Payment for political parties. The *Report of the Committee on Financial Aid to Political Parties* 1976 (Cmnd. 6601) recommended that payment should be made from public funds for political parties. The argument was that if parties depended entirely on their supporters for funds they were too dependent upon them. Other countries, Austria, Sweden and the U.S.A. among them, make such payments and it is argued that political parties which do not have to raise funds are therefore free to concentrate their energies on more important matters.

On the other hand, a subsidy from public funds was estimated to cost about £2.25 million per year and the proposal was made at a time of economic stringency. One might add that the electorate had had no say in these proposals and might very well object.

The proposals, which have not yet been implemented, envisaged a system of state grants based on electoral support, together with some re-imbursement of local election expenses. If adopted it was suggested that the scheme should be extended to cover direct elections to the European Parliament (*see* X, **18**) and to devolved assemblies. To qualify for a grant, a party must:

(*a*) have saved its candidates' deposits in at least six constituencies; *or*

(*b*) have had at least two M.P.s in the previous Parliament; *or*

(*c*) had one candidate and polled at least 150,000 votes.

REFORM OF THE LEGISLATURE

22. Reform of the legislature. Parliament is constantly changing and the society which it serves is also changing. But the institution which has served previous generations may well need an overhaul. In *Britain 1977* (H.M.S.O. 1977) the section devoted to "parliamentary procedure" states that, "A major review of parliamentary procedure is planned" (p. 33). A number of suggestions have been made from time to time. Some of them seem self-evident, some are debatable.

23. Reform of the House of Commons. Most of the discussion of reform of the House of Commons centres on the most efficient way of getting through the increasing amount of work which it undertakes.

(*a*) More parliamentary work could be delegated to committees.

(*b*) M.P.s should have better facilities. The U.S. Congress has an impressive library, an abundance of secretarial help and paid researchers to help the legislators. Britain lags far behind.

(*c*) Voting procedures could be rationalised. The present system, by which members come to the debating chamber to cast their votes in the lobbies when the division bell rings, is archaic and time-consuming. Push-button voting, possibly electronically recorded, would be quicker and more reliable.

(*d*) Formality could be reduced. Any regular reader of *Hansard* will attest to the fact that a great deal of parliamentary time is wasted on seeming irrelevances.

(*e*) A time limit on speeches. Filibustering, i.e. the delaying of the passage of legislation by prolonged talking, for example, is perhaps more common in America than in Britain; but there are occasions when a Bill fails to get through Parliament because its opponents "talk it out". This happened to the private member's Bill on abortion in 1977.

(*f*) More time for questions. Given the importance of Question Time, and the possibilities of making more time available, it would seem that an extended Question Time would be desirable.

(*g*) More sittings. A Select Committee on procedure recommended this proposal some years ago. The experiment was tried, with two sittings in the morning, but was abandoned in 1967.

(*h*) M.P.s to be full-time. This suggestion is made from time to time, on the grounds that being an M.P. is a full-time job. Opponents of the proposal claim that the "outside interests" of M.P.s are valuable, in that they give M.P.s a broader perspective. The proposal, if adopted, would reduce the "amateur" status of M.P.s. Whether this is a good or bad thing is a matter of opinion.

(*i*) The referendum should be used more. The use of the referendum in the debate on the Common Market (*see* X, **10**) was an innovation. Its advocates claim that it makes for more representative government but opponents insist that very few political questions can be answered by a straight "yes" or "no" and that, in any case, it would make the constitution more rigid.

(*j*) The use of the "initiative". In Switzerland a minimum number of citizens who are concerned with constitutional change can compel the government to debate the issue, in the same way that most organisations can demand an extraordinary general meeting if sufficient numbers of their members want one.

(*k*) Electoral reform (*see* IX, **16**).

24. Reform in the House of Lords. Most discussion of reform of the House of Lords centres on its hereditary and hence unrepresentative nature. Such discussion has been heated and, at times,

bitter but, beyond the reduction of the power of the Lords following the Parliament Acts of 1911 and 1949, very little has been
done.

The Bryce Committee met in 1917 and produced a comprehensive report, the *Report of the Conference on the Reform of the
Second Chamber*, 1918 (Cmnd. 9038) which suggested that membership of the Lords should be by election. Three-quarters of the
members would be elected by the Commons on a geographic
basis and the remainder, who would be peers and bishops, would
be elected by a joint committee of Lords and Commons. Membership would be for twelve years. This report, and others which
followed it, provoked discussion but not much action because,
whilst there was widespread agreement that the time had come
for reform, there was equally widespread disagreement as to the
form that it should take.

A White Paper, *House of Lords Reform*, 1968 (Cmnd. 3799)
called for reform and said that the reformed House must have a
degree of independence sufficient to enable it to make an effective
contribution to the process of government. The following recommendations were made.

(*a*) It should be a two-tier structure, with voting and non-
voting peers. All would have the right to speak but only some
could vote.

(*b*) Voting peers should be paid a salary.

(*c*) Hereditary peers should not automatically have the right to
a seat in the House of Lords.

(*d*) The power of Lords to delay legislation should be restricted
to six months.

A Bill to give effect to the intentions of the White Paper was
introduced shortly afterwards but was withdrawn because of
backbench opposition. Other suggestions which have been made
for reform include:

(*a*) direct election; in the absence of detailed proposals such a
suggestion would seem to indicate a second House of Commons
with restricted membership and possibly overlapping powers;

(*b*) indirect election, e.g. by local authorities;

(*c*) nomination by the government, but both this and (*b*) might
over-emphasise the political nature of such an assembly.

The Labour government of 1974 was pledged to reform the
House of Lords but has not so far found time to incorporate this

measure within its legislative programme. The pledge to do so was renewed at the Labour Party conference in 1977.

PROGRESS TEST 4

1. What is meant by (*a*) constitutional, (*b*) unconstitutional and (*c*) anti-constitutional? **(1, 2)**

2. What is the difference between unitary and federal constitutions? **(3)**

3. What is the function of the Supreme Court in the U.S.A.? **(4)**

4. Why are conventions important? **(6)**

5. What are the functions of the House of Lords and how have they changed since 1911? **(7–9)**

6. What are the qualifications necessary to become an M.P.? **(11)**

7. List the officers of the House of Commons. **(14)**

8. What is meant by "redress of grievances"? **(16)**

9. What are the advantages and disadvantages of party government? **(18, 19)**

10. If the proposal to pay political parties is accepted, what will they need to do to qualify for a grant? **(21)**

11. In what ways is it suggested that the House of Commons and the House of Lords might be reformed? **(22–24)**

CHAPTER V

Concepts

PARTICIPATION

1. Participation. In October 1968 Richard Crossman M.P. gave a lecture entitled "The Politics of Television" in the course of which he deplored what he called "plebiscitary democracy". In the context of the speech it was clear that this referred to the growing practice of organising demonstrations and marches as a means of influencing the government over policies with which the demonstrators disagreed. The lecture emphasised the need for participation but the concept, although popular with both politicians and the public, is ill-defined and frequently mis-represented. To participate means to have a share in, but to what extent do electors have a share in government? To what extent do they want to share, either in the process of government or in the working out of the legislation which results from it?

2. Participation in government. There are, one could claim, 635 people who share in government. They are the members of the House of Commons. The actual circle of direct participants could be enlarged to include the House of Lords and, in some senses, the Civil Service. All these people are directly involved in either making the law or administering it. Spreading the net wider one could claim that the electorate, about forty million people, had an indirect share in decision making. Some 72.8 per cent of these voted at the general election of October 1974.

Membership of political parties might be a more accurate guide to active political interest and taking these figures, which incidentally are high by comparison with other European countries, one finds that of the two major parties the Conservatives have about 2.8 million members and Labour 6.3 million (J. Blondel, *Voters, Parties and Leaders*, Penguin, 1976). The Labour Party figure however includes trade union membership. Probably about 10 per cent of party members are active. This would mean that only about three per cent of the electorate were politically active. This does not include full-time paid officials of either of the major parties but there are probably less than 1,000 full-time officials including those of minor political parties.

3. Participation in practice. The Skeffington Report, *People and Planning*, 1969, The Kilbrandon Report, *Royal Commission on the Constitution*, 1973 (Cmnd. 5460) and the Plowden Report, *Children and their Primary Schools*, 1967 (H.M.S.O.) were about different topics but they, together with a number of other official and semi-official reports in the last decade, stressed the need for public participation in the working out of government policies. Participation was thought to be of value because it reduced political apathy and was felt to be a more positive contribution to the life of the nation than the marches and demonstrations to which Richard Crossman had objected. Politicians who expressed these views at political meetings could be sure of acclaim, but there was a tendency to overlook the fact that such meetings would, in the main, be attended by political activists who were not necessarily representative.

4. Objections to participation. The call for more participation is based to some extent on the argument that people are dissatisfied. Levels of political awareness and activity might equally be interpreted as showing that people are, in general, quite satisfied with the way things are going, and not particularly concerned to change them. There is some evidence to suggest that "participation" is not a generalised activity; that it is largely the province of the middle-aged to elderly, the middle class and the better-educated sections of the community. This aspect is well documented in a Fabian Occasional Paper (No. 5), entitled *Public Service for the Community* which looked at the Regional Hospital Boards and Hospital Management Committees prior to the reorganisation of the National Health Service in 1973. The same section of the community was also found to provide a disproportionate number of local councillors (Lord Redcliffe-Maud and B. Wood, *English Local Government Reformed*, Oxford University Press, 1974).

5. Examples of participation. Examples of the way in which an element of participation is increasingly found in legislation can be found in almost any Act of Parliament dealing with social problems in the 1960s and 1970s. The following examples relate to the issues discussed in Part III.

(*a*) *Education* (*see* XI). The Russell Report, *Adult Education:*

A Plan for Development (H.M.S.O., 1973) recognises the important part played by voluntary organisations in the development of adult education. It recommends that such organisations, e.g. the Workers' Educational Association, should be encouraged and, where necessary, financed.

(*b*) *Employment* (*see* XII). The Health and Safety at Work etc. Act 1974 instituted a system of safety representatives and safety committees in order to enable employees to participate with management in the improvement of standards of health and safety.

(*c*) *Housing and the environment* (*see* XIII). The Skeffington Report (*see* XIII, **17**) had recognised the importance of participation. On a national level this took the form of the appointment of community development officers, charged with the responsibility of encouraging local participation. At a local level a number of councils took the opportunity to involve local residents in improvement schemes. An account of one of these can be found in *The Swinbrook Case: Report of the Housing Committee to a Meeting of the Greater London Council on 6th March* 1973 (G.L.C., 1973).

(*d*) *Immigration and Racialism* (*see* XIV). The White Paper, *Immigration from the Commonwealth*, 1965 (Cmnd. 2739) recommended the setting up of a committee to deal with the problems of immigrants. Part of the function of this committee was to set up a series of local voluntary liaison committees serviced by a full-time liaison officer whose salary would be paid partly by the government and partly by the local authority.

(*e*) *Industrial Relations* (*see* XII). The White Paper, *In Place of Strife* (1968) was an attempt by a Labour government to avoid legislation in a notoriously difficult area. It proposed in effect that trade unions and management should settle their differences without the need for government pressure in the form of legal sanctions. Since, however, the T.U.C. (among others) was unhappy about the element of participation involved it was left to the Conservative government to bring in the Industrial Relations Act 1971. This Act was also unpopular with the unions since it gave less scope for participation than the Labour proposals. It was repealed when Labour returned to power in 1974.

(*f*) *Poverty* (*see* XV). Supplementary Benefit appeal tribunals, to which a claimant can refer if he is dissatisfied with the amount of supplementary benefit he receives, are the responsibility of the Secretary of State for Social Services who is required, when appointing members, to appoint one to represent work-people.

(*g*) *Health Services* (*see* XVI). The National Health Service Reorganisation Act 1973 set up a series of about 200 Community Health Councils whose main function was to represent the consumers' viewpoint.

IDEOLOGY

6. Ideology. Political beliefs may form the basis of a specific party programme. They may, on the other hand, simply represent a cluster of ideas related to a central theme. It is this central system of beliefs which, when related to actions, becomes an ideology. For example, the animals in George Orwell's *Animal Farm* decided, at an early stage, that they were completely opposed to all that man stood for. This central belief was expressed ideologically as "four legs good, two legs bad". On another level, the complexities of the Marxist dogma can be reduced to an ideology of "the class struggle".

In the early days of the Labour Party there was a clear-cut division between the Labour and the Conservative ideologies. Labour sought to change society, the Conservatives to defend it. Some commentators, e.g. S. Beer in his book, *Modern British Politics* (Faber, 1965), believe that the coming of the welfare state after the Second World War brought the two parties closer, and that the consensus removed a great deal of the ideological differences. It is probably true however that the Labour Party is more ideologically inclined than the Conservatives.

An ideology can be defined as a secular religion. It is frequently held with what might be called religious fervour and indeed there is some evidence, e.g. T. Adorno *et al, The Authoritarian Personality* (Wiley, 1958), to suggest that those people who are "religiously inclined" are more likely to adopt an ideology than are agnostics. During the Russian revolution, for example, Trotsky recruited the bulk of his South Russian Workers' Union from members of religious sects.

The belief in a millennium is typically a religious phenomenon, but political ideologists may frequently have a similar long-term goal, whether it be "come the revolution" or Hitler's prediction that the Third Reich would last for a thousand years. Such a belief is often closely associated with social conditions and may be held by the poorer, more deprived classes. For example, when Karl Marx referred to religion as "the opiate of the people" he meant that it enabled people to believe that, however bad things may be in this life, there is a good time coming.

7. How do ideologies start? The word *ideology* was first used by the French philosopher Destutt de Tracy in the early nineteenth century. He coined the word to describe a "science of ideas" but it is now more frequently used to denote belief systems which can move people to take action. Such systems are usually either religious or political. The contemporary philosopher John Plamanetz sees all ideology as something which arises out of a system of beliefs. People tend first to accept the tenets of a particular group and then, "for reasons having to do with emotional safety" they tend to adopt the ideas behind such views and show respect for them. The convert to Christianity, for example, may well join a church and, as a result of its teaching resolve to adopt a certain way of life based on Biblical teaching. Similarly a socialist might be drawn to the Communist Party and, as a result of his understanding of its doctrines may then see the world in terms of the Marxist class struggle. The point about an ideology is that it has more to do with *how* people think than *what* they think.

8. Is ideology finished? D. Bell, in his book *The End of Ideology* (Collier-Macmillan, 1962), thought that ideology was on its way out. The old ideologies had served their purpose and were gone and there were no new ones taking their place. But that was in the early 1960s when women's liberation, for example, had barely begun to make itself heard. The question is still open.

9. Ideology in practice. A government with a strong ideological basis is frequently a totalitarian government. This is particularly so when the ideology justifies the concentration of power into a few hands, those of the ruling party. Opposition may be seen not as a healthy corrective which will prevent abuse but as treason. Three examples will suffice.

(*a*) *Communism*, whether on the Russian or Chinese model for example, sees social change as a major objective; in the interests of achieving this objective the state exercises strong powers over large areas of the life of its citizens. It claims to use these powers for the benefit of its citizens and Stalin was therefore able to say, when he introduced a new constitution for Russia in 1936, that it was "the most democratic in the world".

(*b*) *Nazism* (National Socialism) saw racial purity as being an important element in man's struggle for survival. The master race (Aryans) were best fitted to rule, aided by subject races. Jews, who were seen as destroyers of the Aryan culture, were to be eliminated. *Mein Kampf*, the book in which Hitler set out his theories, owes a lot to the German philosopher Friedrich Nietzsche, who died in 1900.

(c) *Fascism* has its roots in nineteenth century idealism. It sees the best form of government as that in which a strong leader accepts responsibility for all aspects of the life of the society. It is therefore nearer to a totalitarian form of government than to democracy. It is a romantic and nationalistic concept which tends to be supported by the middle and upper classes. Its best known modern form is the Italy of Mussolini which was born in the aftermath of the 1914–18 war. The Fascist Party flourished between the wars and during the Second World War. It survived the death of Mussolini in 1945 and is currently (1978) struggling for survival with its arch-enemy the Communist Party which, it will be clear from (a) above, represents almost exactly the opposite end of the political spectrum.

(i) Sir Oswald Mosley's British Union of Fascists was prominent in East London in the 1930s. Its meetings and marches, like those of the National Front, were frequently occasions of public disorder and led to the passing of the Public Order Act 1936 (*see* III, 3(*b*) (*v*)), under which a planned march by the National Front in Tameside, Manchester was banned in 1977.

TRADITIONALISM, TECHNOCRACY AND MERITOCRACY

10. Traditionalism. Edmund Burke, in his *Reflections on the French Revolution* (1791) made the point that something which had stood the test of time should not lightly be cast aside. This is basically the position of the traditionalist. There may be a case for change in society, indeed it is inevitable, but such change, in the area of government at least, must be brought about in a traditional manner.

Weber's "traditional authority" (*see* III, 6(*b*)) recognises the legitimacy of traditional power. Paradoxically, the revolutionaries of 1688 who unseated King James II and invited William and Mary to rule in his place did so on traditionalist grounds (*see* III, 8). They claimed that, since James had subverted the traditional concept of kingship, their action in overthrowing him was a means of preserving the tradition.

There are three arguments in favour of traditionalism.

(*a*) All political activity, even the most revolutionary, derives from tradition.

(*b*) Specific solutions to the problems of a society can only be related to the traditions of that society. An ideology, which deals in generalities, needs to be related to tradition if it is to be implemented.

(*c*) The "pursuit of imitations" is a phrase used by Professor Oakshott in the book, *Philosophy, Politics and Society* (ed. P. Laslett and W. G. Runciman, Blackwells, 1956). By this he meant that there are trends in society and that traditional politics seeks to recognise these trends and go along with them.

11. Technocracy. Technocracy is defined in the *Concise Oxford Dictionary* as "organisation and management of a country's industrial resources by technical experts for the good of the whole community". The phrase "industrial resources" suggests that the role of the technocrat is limited to these fields but a number of commentators see technocrats as having a more central part to play. Thus J. Burnham, in *The Managerial Revolution* (J. Day, 1941) says that technical management is replacing both capitalism and communism.

Democracy depends upon common sense and participation: technocracy depends on the spread of scientific knowledge. Are these two compatible? C. P. Snow, in his book, *Science and Government* (O.U.P., 1961) underlined the dilemma and talked about two cultures, one scientific and the other political. The problem is for government to control science and not vice versa. Science has its own language, its own ethics and its own terms of reference, and these may well be incomprehensible to the layman for the following reasons.

(*a*) The role of the expert in decision-making may well be crucial.

(*i*) Winston Churchill, on the advice of experts, took the decision to drop the atomic bomb.

(*ii*) President Eisenhower, in his farewell address in 1961, warned of the influence of technology.

(*b*) Technology is associated with supra-national industry and such large conglomerates represent great political power, e.g. North Sea oil.

(*c*) Governments now have it within their power to control

populations. How is this power to be used; and who decides: the politicians or the technologists? If technologists decide, they may be said to have power without responsibility and that, as Baldwin said, is the prerogative of the harlot throughout the ages.

12. Meritocracy. A meritocracy may be defined as a society in which status is achieved by the exercise of ability. This is contrasted with a traditional society in which status is ascribed by birth. The changing structure of Labour government, and particularly the composition of Labour cabinets, is often seen as an illustration of the rise of the meritocracy. The early socialists were workers representing their fellow-workers. A majority had left school at an early age and few possessed the diplomas and degrees which typify the meritocrat. By 1960 only about a third of the Parliamentary Labour Party and about 17 per cent of the Cabinet could claim to be "working class". In the present (1978) Cabinet, according to available information, sixteen of the twenty-four members are graduates.

Whilst it is easy to overestimate the dangers of meritocracy (government by those with paper qualifications rather than political experience) it should be remembered that they are, in a sense, more representative of their society. The fear, expressed by B. Hindess and N. Johnson in their book, *The Decline of Working Class Politics* (MacGibbon and Kee, 1971), that the government could become entirely middle-class, and thus unrepresentative of a large proportion of the population, would appear to be groundless.

REPRESENTATIVE AND RESPONSIBLE GOVERNMENT

13. Representative government. To say that a government is representative is to imply that representativeness is a good thing. The word "democracy" carries such connotations that it is perhaps worth asking "what is a representative"? A Member of Parliament can claim to represent his constituents in at least four ways:

    (*a*) by doing what the majority of his constituents want;
    (*b*) by doing what he believes the nation wants;
    (*c*) by doing what he believes to be the best for his constituents;

(*d*) by doing what he believes to be best for the nation.

Clement Attlee, in a speech in the House of Commons in 1933, said that it was impossible to reflect all the opinions held in Britain; and that if it were possible it would be undesirable. The recognition that not all views can be represented means that those who claim to be representatives must, in some way, justify their claim. Most representatives could be classified in one of four ways.

(*a*) *Descriptive*. This type of representative is a sample of a larger group; the pensioner who puts forward the old people's view or the student leader who claims to speak for the youngsters or the nationalist M.P.

(*b*) *Symbolic*. Part of the role of the sovereign is to symbolise the will of the nation. Whilst this symbolism may be something of a formality there is, nevertheless, a sense in which the Queen can claim to express a view which is detached from party politics.

(*c*) *Ascriptive*. The ascriptive representative may be accredited by a section of the community. Although he represents them he is not strictly a representative. The white M.P. who represents a black constituency in South Africa is an obvious example. The public school product who claims to represent "the workers" may well be another.

(*d*) *Interest*. This type of representative exemplifies a particular point of view. The "dyed-in-the-wool Tory" or the "out and out socialist" represent far more than just the party programmes of the Conservative and Labour parties.

14. Accountability. The essential feature of representative government is that it shall be accountable to those whom it claims to represent. Prior to the Reform Act 1832 only about 3 per cent of the adult population was entitled to vote. That Act increased the proportion to about 5 per cent and various other legislation in the next hundred years gradually increased the franchise. It was not until 1948, however, that the Representation of the People Act effectively ensured that the principle of "one man one vote" was observed. The Representation of the People Act 1969 reduced the age at which a person could vote from 21 to 18 so that, for practical purposes, Britain now has universal adult suffrage.

Parliament is, of course, answerable to the electorate in other ways. Its proceedings are reported in *Hansard* and Question Time gives an opportunity for members to question ministers. The

Prime Minister does not make a regular speech on the state of the nation, as does the U.S. President, but he can be, and is, held accountable for the actions of his administration.

15. Responsible government. Parliamentary government is said to be both representative and responsible. It is representative because those who are governed share the responsibility for decision-making. Their views are taken into account. Royal Commissions, for example, usually invite and consider evidence from anybody who is interested enough to present it. However imperfectly, representative government seeks to govern with the consent of those who are governed. It is responsible because it takes account of public opinion.

This does not necessarily mean that it follows public opinion, merely that it is one feature in the decision-making. There may well be occasions indeed when the government deliberately disregards public opinion because it recognises a moral duty to advocate unpopular policies. Thus the government's advocacy of wage restraint in 1978 was represented as an exercise in governmental responsibility.

Finally it should be noted that the convention of ministerial responsibility holds ministers accountable to Parliament for the transgressions of their departments. Sometimes, as in the Critchel Down case, the minister does not offer his resignation. In that particular case some land was acquired for war-time purposes and, after the war, the Minister of Agriculture, Sir Thomas Dugdale, refused to let the original owner have an opportunity to buy it back. The owner, who had a number of friends in the Cabinet, refused to accept this action and created such a fuss that a public enquiry was held. The enquiry found that the owner had been unfairly treated and the minister apologised. He did not feel it necessary to offer his resignation but public opinion eventually forced him to do so. Full details are given in the *Report of the Public Enquiry into the Disposal of Land at Critchel Down* (Cmnd. 9176).

Occasionally the entire government may be held to be at fault. Opposition members traditionally shout "Resign" whenever the government comes under fire but if the Opposition demand a vote of confidence on a major issue, and the government is defeated, convention demands that the government's credibility shall be tested at the polls. This process is referred to as "going to the country" and was the position in which Mr. Heath's administration found itself in 1974 when the miners' strike threatened the economic stability of the country.

16. Unwelcome decisions. It is an interesting psychological fact that responsible government which is prepared to put aside public opinion is not necessarily thought worse of for doing so. The book, *Must Labour Lose* by M. Abrams and R. Rose (Penguin, 1960) uses the results of a survey conducted by the magazine *Socialist Commentary* to show that, given a choice, people would prefer to be governed by leaders who were "strong enough to make unwelcome decisions". Edmund Burke, a great parliamentarian, put the point memorably to the electors of Bristol when, having been returned for that constituency in 1774, he reminded them that, "Your representative owes you not his industry only, but his judgment; and he betrays instead of serving you, if he sacrifices it to your opinion" (*Works*, vol. II, E. Burke).

PROGRESS TEST 5

1. In what sense can the average citizen be said to participate in government? (1, 2)

2. Legislation incorporating participation is becoming more common. List some examples of such legislation and indicate the disadvantages. (3–5)

3. What is meant by "ideology"? (6–8)

4. Give examples of political ideologies. (9)

5. Write brief notes on traditionalism, technocracy and meritocracy. (10–12)

6. Distinguish between representative and responsible government. (13–15)

CHAPTER VI

Issues and Parties

POLITICAL ISSUES

1. Political issues. A political issue may be defined as an issue which is thought to be capable of solution by political means. There may, however, be disagreement as to whether an issue is capable of such a solution. Politicians may believe that a certain course of action would be of benefit to the government of the country, and thus that it is a political issue. The general public, on the other hand, may have a different view. Political culture (*see* II, 1) is an important determinant of the way in which such issues are defined. Some issues may be agreed in principle by most people; the disagreement is about how they should be resolved. There has never been a time in Britain when the economy was not recognised as an important political issue. Neither has there been agreement as to how it should be managed, or indeed whether it should be managed.

Political issues are complex and arguments about how they should be resolved are sometimes about the ends to be achieved by legislation and sometimes about the means. Should legislation to ease the problems of immigration be aimed at repatriating immigrants or integrating them? Clearly one cannot begin to talk about detailed legislation until this particular question is answered. Whatever solutions are proposed few would deny that there is a problem. The extent to which it is a problem to any particular person will depend on his individual circumstances, his history, his beliefs, his interests and where he lives.

The National Front march in Lewisham in August 1977 was ostensibly about the problem raised by an increasingly large immigrant population in that area. In fact it highlighted at least three other political issues of equal, if not greater, significance.

(*a*) *Racialism.* A large proportion of the so-called immigrants were second generation British subjects who happened to be coloured. The issue was not therefore one of immigration but whether there were any grounds for differences in treatment based solely on colour.

(*b*) *Freedom of expression.* Should a party whose methods of expressing their views would be bound to cause disruption be allowed to propagate them freely? Should the police be put in the position of having to keep the peace in a situation where opponents of the march had publicly expressed their intention to prevent it, by violence if necessary?

(*c*) *The rule of law.* It would have been possible, within the framework of existing laws, to have banned the march (*see* V, 9(*c*)) as, indeed, was a later march in Hyde, Tameside. But the question remains, is such a move within the spirit of the "rule of law" or does it simply obey the letter of the law but create a situation in which respect for the law is brought into disrepute (because laws designed to extend freedom were being used to restrict it)? This particular problem seems to have been resolved by the Metropolitan Police Commissioner's ban on political marches in the Greater London area for a period of time in 1978 which included the date of the National Front's proposed march through Ilford.

2. Some issues. All the problems and issues outlined in Part III of this book are political issues and have been for many years. There are a number of other issues which have been dominant on the political horizon throughout the past ten years and some of these are outlined below. A fuller treatment of these and related issues is contained in *Issues in British Politics Since 1945* by L. J. Macfarlane (Longman, 1975).

(*a*) *Standard of living and cost of living.* A National Opinion Poll in 1970 showed that 67 per cent of the respondents felt that these were the most important political issues. They continued to be seen as such throughout the 1970s. Both the major parties laid great stress, in their election manifestos, on the importance of improving living standards by cutting the cost of living. The Conservative proposal in 1966 to reduce taxation and thus encourage initiative was matched by a Labour proposal to introduce a new pension scheme and thus enable all sections of the community to share in the increasing standards of living enjoyed by the wealthier sections of the community. By October 1974 the Conservative proposals included a statutory prices and incomes policy and the Labour solution was a wealth tax. Both parties had agreed that pensions should be rationalised and the Social Security Pensions Act 1975 was passed by the Labour government (*see* XV, 22).

(b) *Defence*. This issue was perhaps of more interest to the politicians than the public. Aspects ranged from the matter of Britain's nuclear deterrent, through the question of the sale of arms to South Africa, to the cost of maintaining troops in Northern Ireland. On all these issues members of the major parties held conflicting views and pressure groups (*see* II, 8) made their views known about the various policies which were suggested. On the cost of defence there was a fairly clear division of opinion between the parties, with Labour seeking to cut costs and Conservatives insisting that it was unsafe to do so.

(c) *The state of the economy*. This is of course closely related to standards of living and, with severe inflation in the mid-1970s it became a major issue. Politicians of both parties offered their panaceas for this particular trouble. The Conservative commitment to free enterprise and the Labour view that there should be a planned economy both aimed at the same target, namely that of economic growth which would bring with it a greater share of economic well-being for all. In the event, as so often in politics, the solution was a compromise with a Labour Chancellor of the Exchequer putting forward budget proposals which some Conservatives were proud to claim as theirs.

(d) *Nationalisation*. A commitment to nationalisation is written into clause four of the Labour Party constitution and some form of public ownership has always been advocated by Labour governments. The exact enterprises, and the terms under which they were to be administered has, however, varied over the years. The iron and steel and road haulage industries present the classic case in which the major parties fought out their battle over nationalisation over a series of elections. When Labour won the post-war election they nationalised (1949). A Conservative victory at the next election brought de-nationalisation (1953) and a subsequent Labour victory in 1964 resulted in re-nationalisation. Such a state of affairs could not continue indefinitely and a new pattern now seems to be emerging. Labour governments no longer insist on automatic nationalisation, instead they sometimes subsidise those industries which they consider to be of importance and, as the price of the subsidy, insist on having a say in the running of the enterprise. It remains to be seen whether the National Enterprise Board, set up by the Labour government which was elected in 1974, will be altered by an incoming Conservative government (*see* XII).

(e) *Devolution*. Devolution has been an important minority

issue for many years (*see* IX, **3**). It did not become a major political issue, however, until the second half of the present decade. The reason was not that the issue had become more important but that the Welsh and Scottish nationalists obtained increasing representation at Westminster at a time when their votes were badly needed to support both the Conservative and the Labour minority governments. Both major parties had therefore to take the issue seriously (*see* **7, 8**).

(*f*) *Electoral reform.* Like devolution this has long been a matter of major importance to a minority group (the Liberal Party). The manifest inequalities of the present system of election were brought sharply into focus in the two general elections of 1974 and the prospect of direct elections to the European Assembly caused some public debate as to the form that they should take. The "Lib-Lab" pact in 1977, by which the Liberal Party enabled the Labour government to continue in office, meant that the Liberals were at last able to have their pleas for electoral reform considered more favourably (*see* IX, **16**).

POLITICAL PARTIES

3. Political parties. The essence of the party system is that the party, or combination of parties, which obtains the most seats in Parliament forms the government. The other parties form H.M. Opposition. In British politics there have been two major parties for over 200 years, together with a number of smaller ones. For the past fifty years the main focus of the struggle has been between the Labour and Conservative parties, with first one and then the other forming the government.

4. The Labour Party. The Labour party owes its origin to a meeting called by the T.U.C. in 1900 to consider how the various socialist bodies which formed the Labour movement could best be represented in Parliament. As a result of that meeting the Labour Representation Committee was formed and, at the general election of 1906, some twenty-nine M.P.s were elected. At that stage they called themselves the Labour Party and they have been known by that name ever since. The first Labour government was formed in 1924 but it was only in power for ten months. Labour was returned to power for two years in 1929 but it was the 1945 election which really saw the start of its rise to power. At that election Labour won 393 seats, giving them a majority over all other parties of 146 seats.

(a) *Structure.* The management of the Labour Party is entrusted to a National Executive Committee (N.E.C.), elected by
the annual party conference and answerable to that body. It has
great influence on the parliamentary Labour Party, i.e. Labour
M.P.s, but has no formal authority over the way they carry out
their parliamentary duties. It has twenty-nine members, twelve
of whom are elected directly by the trade unions. The Leader and
Deputy Leader of the Parliamentary Labour Party are members
of the N.E.C. but are elected by their fellow M.P.s. The other
members are elected by either trade unions, constituency parties
or a combination of both. Decisions of the Labour Party conference are binding on the N.E.C. and frequently form the basis
of party policy as set out in manifestos. If, however, a Labour
government decides to pursue a policy at variance with that of
the N.E.C. it can and does do so.

(b) *Policies.* The Labour Party stands for socialist ideals, although some socialists would claim that the ideals have been so
diluted as to be unrecognisable. Its central theme, underlining
all its policies, is that of equality. The emphasis is on a classless
society in which all have equal opportunities and in which gross
inequalities of wealth and opportunity are removed. Labour
governments were concerned with such legislation as the Education Act 1944 and the National Health Service Act 1946. Current
amendments to these Acts include moves to introduce comprehensive education throughout the public educational system and
the phasing out of private beds in the N.H.S. hospitals (*see*
XVI).

(c) *Current position.* In the general election of October 1974
the Labour Party polled 39.3 per cent of the votes cast and obtained 319 seats. This initially gave it a majority over all other
parties but the majority was reduced by by-elections and was no
longer sufficient to maintain a stable government. In 1977 the
Liberal Party agreed to throw its weight behind the Labour
government to enable it to continue in office. This arrangement
(the Lib-Lab pact) allowed the Liberals to curb what they saw as
extremism on the part of the Labour government.

5. The Conservative Party. The Conservative Party were the
Tories of the seventeenth and eighteenth centuries. During the
period between 1886 and 1922, when the question of Irish Home
Rule was a major political issue, they were known by their full
title, the National Union of Conservative and Unionist Associ-

ations, and this is still the correct title for the confederation of local associations. In general, however, they are now known as the Conservative Party.

(*a*) *Structure.* The internal structure of the Conservative Party is not so monolithic as that of the Labour Party. There are, in fact, two separate structures. The National Union is in some respects similar to the Labour Party in that it has an annual conference at which workers express their views on Conservative policy. Control of the party is however more effectively in the hands of the Conservative Central Office which represents the party leadership. The Conservatives do not accept that conference decisions are binding upon M.P.s although, of course, any member who consistently defied the express wishes of his fellow party members would have difficulty in finding a constituency prepared to adopt him when he wished to contest a subsequent election.

(*b*) *Policies.* The Conservative Party, as its name suggests, sees its function as conserving that which it considers best in Britain. It does not believe in "change for the sake of change" and it is opposed to the idea that policies should be imposed in the interest of some ill-defined "will of the majority". This does not mean that it is opposed to change, merely that a good case must be made out for it and that any change should be seen to be of benefit to the development of the individual. Private enterprise is seen as an important element in the social structure and any infringement of man's freedom must be justified. Conservatives resisted the Reform Act of 1832 but subsequently initiated a programme of reform largely carried out by Peel's government of 1841 to 1846 which included a great deal of legislation to improve the conditions of women and children in factories and mines. The opposition to the Reform Act of 1832 gradually abated and the second Reform Act of 1867 was largely the work of Disraeli's Tory administration. More recently, the Conservatives, as part of a coalition government, shared the responsibility for the social reforms of the 1940s but they countered Labour's proposals for greater reforms in these areas by advocating the encouragement of direct grant schools in 1970, and by proposing amendments to the Social Security Act 1966 so that the Act would be more effective against those whom they saw as "scroungers". Both these measures were in line with their policy of encouraging individual effort rather than state support wherever possible (*see* XV).

(c) *Current position.* In October 1974 the Conservatives polled 35.8 per cent of the votes cast. This gave them 276 seats and the status of H.M. Opposition. Even with the combined votes of the other parties however they could not muster sufficient votes to defeat the government on a major issue. As the Opposition however they have a number of important functions, amongst them the following:

(*i*) they are seen as the alternative government and, should they win the next election, their leader would become the Prime Minister and their shadow cabinet become the Cabinet;

(*ii*) they are to some extent a moderating influence as they may call upon the government to justify its policies.

6. The Liberal Party. The Liberal Party owes its foundation as a political movement to the philosopher John Locke (1632–1704) and, in particular, to his views on the social contract (*see* III, 4). Whigs (Liberals) and Tories contended for power throughout the eighteenth and nineteenth centuries but is was the period between 1830 and 1865 in which the Whigs, largely representative of the land-owning aristocracy, became transformed into the Liberal Party which we know today. The repeal of the Corn Laws in 1846 split the Tory Party and, as a result of that split, a number of Conservatives joined the opposition and formed the present Liberal Party.

The Liberal Party, like the two major parties, has a history of social reform. The Parliament Act 1911 was a Liberal measure, as was the early legislation on old-age pensions. The Liberal Party has also traditionally had an interest in free trade, profit-sharing, and industrial and electoral reform. The last is particularly understandable when one considers that in the 1974 general election 18 per cent of the votes gave them around 2 per cent of the seats. Basically it is now a "middle-of-the-road" party whose complaint, frequently apparently justified, is that the two major parties have taken over its electoral programme.

7. The Scottish National Party. The Scottish National Party (S.N.P.) has existed in its present form since 1932. Its main concern, as its name implies, is the achievement of self-government for Scotland. Scottish Nationalists are careful to point out that this is not the same as devolution. Self-government involves the recognition of Scotland as a free and equal nation within the British Commonwealth and it points to a number of other countries which are either smaller in size (like Belgium) or have smaller populations (the Scandinavian countries) all of which are recognised as free and independent nations. It stresses that the way to achieve independence is by constitutional means and its party programme includes a detailed written constitution and plans for a national assembly.

On broader issues it sees a case for a change in Britain's economic policies, more particularly of course because the discovery of oil in the North Sea would, if the claim were conceded, give Scotland great natural resources. The S.N.P. did not have any seats in Parliament until 1970, when it won one seat (in the Western Isles). Since then their progress has been remarkable and in the general election of 1974 they won no less than eleven seats, which represented about 30 per cent of all Scottish votes.

8. Plaid Cymru. Welsh nationalism is much older than Plaid Cymru, the party which is now its main spokesman. The party was formed in 1925 committed to "full national status" for Wales. Both Labour and Liberal M.P.s who had represented Welsh constituencies prior to that date had advanced the specifically Welsh interests of their constituents but it was Plaid Cymru, with its strong emphasis on Welsh culture and traditions and, in particular, its insistence on the importance of the Welsh language, which was seen as truly representative. It only became an independent parliamentary party in 1974 (on St. David's Day appropriately enough) but by the election of October of that year it was able to capture three seats and, by 1975, it had seen the publication of the Labour government's proposal for a Welsh Development Agency.

9. Ideological (minority) parties (*see* V, **9**). There are a number of small parties, most of whom have not yet succeeded in returning a member to Parliament but which are, nevertheless, significant because they represent the more extreme ends of the political spectrum. The list below is not exhaustive and is ranged in order, approximately from "left" to "right".

(*a*) *The New Left* is not a party but a number of groups frequently at odds with each other but united in a common belief that society should be governed by an élite. Regimes, except those which they specifically support, are seen as corrupt and the only way to change the system is by violent means. They include the Trotskyists (members of the International Marxist Group), Maoists, who accept that the Chinese version of communism is the correct one, and anarchists (who share most of the above views but do not see violence as the way to achieve their aims). Members of such groups tend to be young, frequently well-educated and may achieve results disproportionate to their numbers. The universities of California, the Sorbonne and the London School of Economics have all, in their time, been centres of New Left activity. The link with the student population can be seen as evidence either of young idealism or of gullibility, depending upon one's point of view. Many left-wing splinter groups, e.g. the Socialist Workers Party, boast a high proportion of young people in their ranks.

(*b*) *Communism* is a world-wide movement and forms the government of several countries. In Britain the Communist Party regularly contests parliamentary elections but no Communist candidate has been elected since the Second World War. The British Communist Party was formed in 1920 and claims its origin directly through the Russian revolution of 1917 and, indirectly, to the Levellers of the time of Oliver Cromwell. It is concerned with the "class struggle", as a result of which all workers will eventually control the means of production. It sees this struggle as a political one and is very active in the trade union movement, where a small group of dedicated workers can exert an influence out of all proportion to its numerical strength because of the apathy of the majority. It is controlled by a national congress which meets every two years and its newspaper, the *Morning Star*, has a circulation of over a million copies. It is, incidentally, the only daily paper in Britain owned by a political party.

(*c*) *The National Front*. This is a fascist organisation but it should be noted that "fascist" is a descriptive, not a pejorative, term. It merely defines "right-wing" groups (*see* V, 9(*c*)). The movement is small but, like the Communist Party, it wields an influence out of proportion to its size. Like the Communist Party the National Front has no representation in Parliament although it regularly contests elections. It is a nationalist party, concerned to "keep Britain British", and its successes are mainly due to its opposition to the government's immigration policies and its demands that immigrants should be repatriated. Its candidates tend to be younger than those of the main political parties and it has been described as a "lower middle-class backlash" comparable to McCarthyism in America or Poujadism in France. Its supporters are predominantly poorly educated youngsters with working-class backgrounds.

It claims to be gaining ground and, interestingly, in areas where there is a high proportion of the population with immigrant backgrounds it is particularly successful. In the Ladywood area of Birmingham, for example, it contested the seat in the by-election of 18th August 1977 and came third. This result is indicative, rather than typical, since the N.F. candidate only polled 888 votes, as compared with the winner's 8,227 votes, and the poll was less than 43 per cent (an average poll for a by-election would be of the order of 60 to 70 per cent).

(d) *The National Party* is a small group which broke away from the National Front. It has similar aims and a comparable, though smaller, membership.

POLITICS AND SOCIAL CLASS

10. Politics and social class. Social class, one's position in society, can be defined in a number of ways. Education is important, so is income and occupation. Since one's income and occupation are frequently determined by one's education a grading which takes these factors into account can be used as a rough approximation of social class. The Registrar-General uses such a grading for census purposes and by using either this estimate, the socio-economic group, or some other definition it is possible to say something about the effects of social class on voting patterns and about the class composition of Parliament.

11. Social class and political attitudes. There is considerable evidence that social class and political attitudes are closely related. This does not mean that all working class voters are socialist, nor that all Tories are middle or upper class. There is of course a strong correlation of that nature, but the working-class conservative is a well-known phenomenon, as is the middle-class radical. The working-class conservative was the subject of a book, published in 1968, entitled, *Angels in Marble: Working-class Conservatives in Urban England*. The authors of that book (R. McKenzie and A. Silver) recognise two types of working-class Tory whom they call "deferentials" and "seculars". Deferentials are those who tend to see the Conservative Party as being innately superior to other political parties and more representative of the nation as a whole. Seculars, on the other hand, are pragmatic. They vote for the Conservatives because they judge that Tories know how to govern. This group includes a high proportion of the higher-paid of the working-class Tories, a finding which was confirmed by another study in 1968 called, *The Affluent Worker: Political Attitudes and Behaviour*, by J. H. Goldthorpe *et al.* (Cambridge University Press, 1968). The book *Class* by R. Mabey (Blond, 1967) contains an analysis by M. Abrams of the other "deviant" group, the middle-class radicals. Such people, he says, were to be found predominantly at two ends of the middle-class spectrum. They tended either to be those with "considerable experience of higher education" or those with low work status. His explanation of this finding is that the better-educated people tended to be university graduates in what may be called the "caring professions"; that such people may well have adopted radical views when they were at university as a result of which they gravitated towards these types of jobs. Experience at work then tended to reinforce their previously held left-wing theories.

Social class is important in another aspect of our political life in that it is said that there are very few working-class politicians, even in a Labour government. There is certainly some evidence that numbers are declining but then the unskilled and semi-skilled workers, who are usually defined as "working-class", have also declined as a proportion of the population (*see* V, 10–12).

PROGRESS TEST 6

1. What is a political issue? Give some examples. (1, 2)
2. Write brief notes on the Labour, Conservative and Nationalist parties. (4–8)
3. What do you understand by an ideological party? Give examples. (9)
4. What is the relationship between politics and social class? (10, 11)

PART TWO

INSTITUTIONS

CHAPTER VII

The Legal System

LAW, MORALITY AND CUSTOM

1. Law. Law may be defined as the rules which are imposed on a society for the guidance of its members.

Legal rules are different from other rules in that:

(*a*) they can be enforced by the use of sanctions: if you disobey the law you are liable to be punished;

(*b*) they are codified. Britain does not have a written constitution but all laws and the precedents which form the basis of judges' decisions are written. The Law Commission Act 1965 has started a general codification of all laws, statutes and rules;

(*c*) they are applicable to specified areas. Thus the laws of the United Kingdom are applicable throughout England, Northern Ireland, Scotland and Wales. Some laws relate only to a specific part of the United Kingdom, e.g. the Social Work (Scotland) Act 1968 and some, e.g. the European Communities Act 1972, have a much wider application (which is specified in the Act);

(*d*) laws properly enacted cannot be declared invalid by the courts. This is the position in Britain and may be compared with the position in the United States where the Supreme Court can declare a law invalid if, for example, it violates the principles of the constitution.

2. Custom. Custom, on the other hand, is what people have been used to doing. Certain practices have taken place over a sufficiently long period of time to have become traditional. There is nothing either right or wrong about them, neither is there anything legal or illegal, they are just the accepted ways of doing things in a particular society.

3. Morality. Legality and morality are not synomymous. What is right may not necessarily be in accordance with the law, neither may what is legal be seen by all as right. Thus opponents of the National Front consider it right to disrupt their processions, by violence if necessary (*see* VI, **9**(*c*)), but the law says that the use of violence for this purpose is illegal. There is, on the other hand, nothing illegal about adultery but many people would say that it was wrong.

4. The relationship between law, custom and morality. Whilst law, custom and morality are separate concepts there must clearly be a relationship between the three. A law which conflicts violently with either custom or morality will be a bad law and, if disobeyed frequently, will bring the law itself into disrepute. The historical basis of law is, in this sense, custom. When rules were made for the guidance of society they took account of the normal customs of the society. Similarly when laws are made they take account of what is generally thought of as right in the society. This does not mean that all laws are so based, merely that most people would agree that acts like murder, stealing and fraud are wrong.

However, concepts of right and wrong change over the years and the law may need to be brought up to date. Because the law is slow-moving such changes tend to be delayed. It is still illegal, for example, in Britain for public houses to be open except during specified hours; few people would consider it wrong for them to be open all day. Sometimes, of course, the law is altered in advance of public opinion because Parliament sees it as its duty, on occasion, to give a lead (*see* V, **15**).

THE RULE OF LAW

5. The rule of law. The concept of the rule of law embodies the idea that all people in Britain are subject to the law. There is not "one law for the rich and another for the poor", although it may well be true that the rich man is better able to use it for his purposes. The concept is still valid and one of the purposes of the introduction of legal aid was to make legal services available to those who previously had not been able to afford them. Dicey's work, *Introduction to Study of Law and Constitution* (Macmillan, 1961), has long been regarded as the definitive work on the subject and he laid down a number of criteria by which the rule of law could be judged.

(*a*) *Laws must not be arbitrary.* They specify what can and cannot be done: nobody can be punished by the law except for infringement of the law. Since people are entitled, at the time that they are doing something, to know whether what they are doing is in accordance with the law there is a strong case to be made against retrospective legislation.

(*b*) *Parliament recognises only one body of law.* Although Britain derives its law from many sources (*see* 7) and has a large and growing body of administrative law it forms a united whole. France has two bodies of law, constitutional and administrative, dealt with by separate bodies. British "constitutional lawyers" are specialists in one branch of the whole body of law.

(*c*) *The rights of the individual are to be respected.* This is the basis of the legal principle that a person is innocent until proved guilty. It also means that the rights given to an individual cannot be withdrawn except by legal process. There are occasions on which some rights are restricted "in the national interest" but such infringements are hotly debated in Parliament and the restrictions are removed as soon as the situation which gave rise to them is passed. The Emergency Powers Act 1939 was repealed after the war and the Prevention of Terrorism (Temporary Provisions) Act 1976 is under constant review. This Act contains three special provisions which override the normal processes of the rule of law:

(*i*) it enables terrorist organisations to be proscribed;

(*ii*) it contains powers to ban people who are believed to be liable to enage in acts of terrorism;

(*iii*) it provides special powers in relation to the arrest and detention of suspected terrorists.

6. Is the rule of law still valid? It is clear from the foregoing that the law can, on occasion, appear to be arbitrary. There is in addition a mass of delegated legislation (*see* XIX, 4) which enables tribunals to exercise a judicial function so that, although all law originates in Parliament, there is more than one kind. The rights of the individual are associated with the concept of equality before the law, but there are a number of groups who are unequal. Ambassadors, diplomats, foreign embassy staff and foreign heads of state resident in this country are not subject to its laws, nor are children under the age of ten. Judges are immune from the processes of law when acting in their official capacity and a number of people including the police and factory inspectors have special rights not granted to all citizens. The police might well claim that they do not have special rights but only an enhanced version of the rights of all citizens (*see* **17**). All these exceptions may be justified as due to special circumstances. The question, however, remains open.

SOURCES OF ENGLISH LAW

7. Sources of English Law. English law has its origins in the ancient customs that existed before the Norman invasion. Historical sources, religious beliefs, theories of natural justice and the opinions of learned men formed part of its earliest foundations. Custom is the source of what has become common law and precedent of what has become case law. Beginning with the Normans, the Anglo-Saxon customs have become codified to form statute law. Statute law was later supplemented by the principle of fairness or "equity".

William the Conquerer introduced the idea of a national system of law, applicable throughout the land. Until that time the law had been administered locally, by shire courts, hundred courts and franchise courts. With the coming of a national system of law there developed the idea of sovereignty (*see* V, **12**); the sovereign's law was derived from Parliament which represented the will of the people. This law was supplemented by the writings of men of authority, statutes and law reports.

The following paragraphs relate specifically to English law. Scottish law, although it shares some of the English origins, has developed differently.

8. Common law. The King's Council (the *Curia Regis*) was a body of noblemen who were appointed as judges to hear disputes by the king's subjects. Initially they were concerned with taxation but as time passed the disputes reflected other grievances. In 1273 the first Chief Justice was appointed, responsible for hearing cases in the Court of Common Pleas. This court survived until it was superseded by the Judicature Acts of 1873–5. Until the reign of James I (1603–25) this represented the main body of English law.

9. Statute law. Legislation passed by Parliament can override common law and, in many instances, parts of common law have now been replaced by statutory rules. Statute law has the disadvantage that different Acts of Parliament relating to the same subject may well be passed at different times and, although most

Acts nowadays stipulate what legislation they either amend or repeal, it is difficult for the layman to be completely familiar with them. Consolidating legislation is becoming more common. Thus the Health and Safety at Work etc. Act 1974 superseded earlier Factory Acts, parts of which however remain in force. The Law Commission (*see* **21**(*c*)) will, it is to be hoped, eventually succeed in consolidating various related Acts. Delegated legislation (*see* XIX, **3**) is usually enacted by means of Statutory Instruments which also form part of statute law.

10. Equity. Common law served Britain well for some centuries but, as the population increased and laws became more complex, it became increasingly difficult for the common man to obtain justice. The king's secretary, the Chancellor, was therefore charged with the responsibility for seeing that justice (equity) was done. His court, the Court of Chancery, became the place to which subjects looked for the king's justice and, from the fifteenth century onwards, chancellors would hear cases and deliver judgments. They were not bound by common law and were thus able to "fill in gaps" where the law apparently offered no redress.

The most common complaints were:

(*a*) that common law was defective, e.g. that it was undeveloped;

(*b*) that common law remedies, i.e. damages, were inadequate;

(*c*) that the defendant was too powerful; a humble villager would not expect to get justice if his opponent was important;

(*d*) that common law courts lacked jurisdiction.

The Court of Chancery was abolished by the Judicature Acts of 1873 and 1875 and its work was taken over by the Supreme Court of the Judicature, comprising the High Court of Justice and the Court of Appeal. The High Court now administers both common law and equity and, in the event of a conflict between the two, equity prevails. The Lord Chancellor is still technically head of the courts but in practice his work is done by a Vice-Chancellor, a post created in 1970.

11. Case law. Case law is simply what judges have decided in the past. Records of these precedents have been kept in *Year Books* since the sixteenth century. The application of judicial precedent is binding. That is to say that if a lawyer can convince a judge that the facts of his case are analogous to an earlier case then the decision given in the earlier case will apply. This rule is not invariable however since a higher court may disregard a precedent if, in all the circumstances, it appears right for them to do so; and thus a new precedent is created. In general, however, the highest court in the land (the House of Lords acting in its judicial capacity) accepts the principle of the precedent. Decisions of higher courts are held to be binding on lower ones.

12. Canon law. Prior to the Norman Conquest the Church had wide jurisdiction, not only over the clergy but over a large area of what would today be called family law. King William I separated the lay and ecclesiastical functions of the courts and left canon law to deal with matters relating to the clergy and with wills other than those relating to land. In 1857 their jurisdiction in the matter of wills was transferred to the probate court and that relating to divorce, a carry-over from the time in which they were responsible for jurisdiction concerning the validity of marriage, was transferred to a divorce court. Since that time their sole responsibility has been for church matters such as the discipline of the clergy.

13. Other forms of law. There are a number of other forms of law which, although not as widely known or as important as the foregoing, are equally part of the legal system.

(*a*) *Mercantile and maritime law.* These are both specialised subjects, dealt with by particular courts, the Commercial Court in the case of the former and the Admiralty Court in the case of the latter. Both these courts are parts of the Queen's Bench Division (*see* **15**(*d*)).

(*b*) *Local custom.* A local rule, observed by the inhabitants of a particular area over a long period, may be upheld in a court of law even though there is no relevant legislation, and indeed this may be so even though the custom is at variance with common law.

(*c*) *Treaties.* Britain's entry into the Common Market has brought with it certain legal obligations (*see* X). These obligations may well take precedence over common law and statute law.

THE COURTS

14. Classification of the law. The main division of the law is between civil and criminal law. The way in which the various courts deal with the two divisions is described below.

(*a*) *Civil law* is concerned with disputes between individuals. It includes such matters as contracts and their enforcement; torts, which may be defined as civil wrongs; family law, that branch of the law which deals with the rights, duties and responsibilities of members of the family (husbands and wives, parents and children); and the laws of succession and property.

(*b*) *Criminal law* deals with offences against the state. Such offences do not necessarily violate any private right and, although a private citizen may bring a criminal prosecution, it is more usual for such actions to be brought by the police or the Director of Public Prosecutions, a legal Civil Servant appointed by the Home Secretary. The D.P.P. institutes legal proceedings on behalf of the Attorney General and advises the police on the adminstration of criminal law.

15. The courts. The structure of the system of courts remained basically unchanged from the passing of the Supreme Court of Judicature Acts 1873 and 1875 until the Courts Act 1971. By that time the higher courts had become unable to deal with the increasing number of cases and the new structure, which included certain provisions for Scotland and Northern Ireland, was designed to spread the load more evenly.

(*a*) At the apex of the judicial system is the House of Lords which is the final Court of Appeal for both civil and criminal cases in Britain and Northern Ireland. As a Court of Appeal it consists of the Lord Chancellor and the Law Lords (the Lords of Appeal in Ordinary and others who have held high judicial office).

(*b*) The Judicial Committee of the Privy Council is composed of all privy councillors who hold, or have held, high judicial office. Normally only three members of the committee hear a case but if it is an important one the number will be increased to five. Its main concern is to hear appeals from those Commonwealth countries which have retained the right of appeal. It does not give judgments in the same way as an ordinary court but, instead, it advises the Queen as to how the issue should be settled. The Queen then makes an Order in Council incorporating this advice. A decision on appeal from a colony is binding on the courts of that territory.

(*c*) There are two Courts of Appeal in addition to the House of Lords, one for civil and one for criminal cases. The civil division is presided over by the Master of the Rolls and the criminal division by the Lord Chief Justice. Both have a staff of judges to help them and the function of both is to hear appeals from the lower courts (*see* Fig. 2).

(*d*) The High Court of Justice consists of three parts.

(*i*) Queen's Bench Division combines the old Admiralty Court and the new Commercial Court. In addition it deals with all civil cases not assigned to other courts and hears appeals from lower courts. It also supervises the work of some lower courts and tribunals (*see* XIX). Its president is the Lord Chief Justice.

(*ii*) Chancery Division is composed of the Lord Chancellor, the Vice-Chancellor and seven lesser judges, called *puisne* judges. Its duties are those of the old Court of Chancery, with the addition of certain matters like bankruptcy.

(*iii*) The Family Division is headed by a president and deals with matters relating to legislation affecting the family. It hears appeals from lower courts on matrimonial matters.

(*e*) Crown Courts were created by the Courts Act 1971 to replace the Assize and Quarter Sessions. The country is divided into six circuits, each of which has a number of Crown Courts. They are superior courts, that is they exercise criminal jurisdiction. There are three types of Crown Court judge and, broadly speaking, the higher his status the more serious will be the cases he tries. The types of judge, in order of importance, are:

(*i*) High Court judges;

(*ii*) Circuit judges;

(*iii*) Recorders.

(*f*) Magistrates' Courts are sometimes called petty sessional courts and are responsible for both civil and criminal jurisdiction. Their civil responsibilities include the licensing of public houses, betting shops etc., public health and matrimonial matters. Their function is to deal with civil cases; in criminal matters they act as "court of first instance" to decide whether there is a case to answer. If there is a case it will sometimes be dealt with by the magistrates or, if it is a serious charge, it may be referred to a higher court to be tried by a jury (*see* **16**). Some 98 per cent of criminal cases are dealt with by magistrates. The magistrate, or Justice of the Peace to give the correct title, is usually an unpaid layman (there are about 19,500 of them) or, in a busy court, a full-time paid lawyer called a Stipendary Magistrate. Stipendaries number about fifty and there are about 900 magistrates' courts in England and Wales, the larger ones being served by legally qualified justices' clerks.

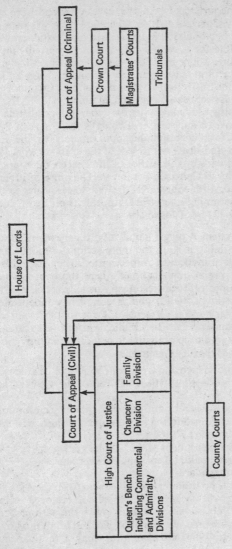

FIG. 2   *Appeals from lower to higher courts.*

(*g*) County courts deal with civil cases only and were created by the County Courts Act 1846. There are over 400 such courts presided over by about 100 judges, called circuit judges, who are each responsible for a certain district. Judges usually sit alone but can empanel a jury in special cases. Each court has a registrar, a solicitor of at least seven years' standing, whose function is mainly administrative, although he may himself try minor cases.

(*h*) Tribunals exercise a quasi-judicial function (*see* XIX, 6).

(*i*) The Scottish judicial system is separate and distinct from the English one. Its supreme civil court is the Court of Session. The Sheriff Court corresponds approximately to the English County Court and deals with most of the criminal work. Minor cases are dealt with by the Justice of the Peace Courts at county level and by Burgh Courts in the towns. The office of Procurator Fiscal has no English equivalent; his function is nearer to that of the French examining magistrate. Appeals from Scottish courts are to the High Court of Justiciary.

16. The jury system. A jury is a body of ordinary men and women whose responsibility it is, in the more serious criminal cases, to decide the guilt or innocence of the accused. They are not lawyers and need no special qualifications except those based on residence and the electoral register. A jury usually consists of twelve people (fifteen in Scotland) and is completely independent of both the judiciary and the executive. Prior to 1967 their verdict had to be unanimous but the Criminal Justice Act of that year made majority verdicts permissible in certain situations.

Advantages of the jury system are:

(*a*) "twelve good men and true" are thought to be able to reach a common-sense decision which will reflect the views of society as a whole;

(*b*) the process whereby the case for the prosecution and for the defence is explained to the jury ensures that justice is not only done but may be seen to be done;

(*c*) juries are independent of the judicial system;

(*d*) jurors are unpaid, except for certain expenses;

The disadvantages are:

(*a*) juries have no training to enable them to do their job;

(*b*) they may be swayed by prejudice, oratory, misplaced sympathy and, occasionally, threats and intimidation. Such intimidation is, of course, a criminal offence but is not unknown;

(*c*) in a long trial the individual jurors may suffer financial loss.

POLICE

17. Status. The status of the policeman is ambiguous. On the one hand, the traditional view of writers like Dicey is that he is a citizen in uniform whose powers, though more specialised than the citizen's, are of the same order. Both have power to use reasonable force to prevent a crime, both can arrest without a warrant and both can sue in a criminal case. On the other hand, the policeman's powers of arrest are more generally recognised and he has other powers, such as search and seizure, which far exceed those of the ordinary citizen.

Although ordinary citizens can sue in criminal cases they do not usually do so and, whilst one citizen may obstruct another engaged in "police" duties, it is only an offence to do so if the person obstructed is a policeman. The ordinary citizen is not called upon to investigate crimes, nor to regulate traffic. In these and countless other ways the policeman is far more than just a citizen in uniform.

The constable's status is ambiguous in other ways. He is a public officer but not, in the normal sense, a Crown servant. Though he upholds "the Queen's peace" he is paid by the local authority but answerable only to a chief constable, who is himself largely independent. Although the Home Secretary can and does take responsibility for police forces generally, his influence, deriving from the Police Act 1964, is largely indirect.

18. Functions. The police have many functions, from looking after the occasional stray dog to attending road accidents and organising crowd control. These are, however, incidental to their main functions which are:

(*a*) to keep the peace and maintain public order;
(*b*) to prevent crime;
(*c*) to provide protection for life and property;
(*d*) to detect and apprehend criminals.

19. Organisation. Police forces, except the Metropolitan Police in London, are the responsibility of local authorities and the Home Secretary (in Scotland, the Secretary of State for Scotland) has overall responsibility for law and order throughout the country. There are forty-three separate forces in England and Wales and a further eight in Scotland, a total of some 118,000 officers. In London the Commissioner of the Metropolitan Police Force is directly answerable to the Home Secretary but, in the other forces, a chief constable is appointed by a police authority, called either a police committee or a watch committee. The Royal Commission on the Police in 1962 considered the idea of a national police force but rejected it in favour of some rationalisation of the existing system.

In addition to the ordinary police there are a number of special forces such as those employed by the Ministry of Defence and those responsible for policing the docks and the royal parks. The police are financed jointly by local and central authorities, each of whom pays half the cost. The government's contribution is conditional upon the efficiency of the local force. It can be, and occasionally is, withheld if the Home Secretary (or Secretary of State for Scotland) is dissatisfied.

20. Complaints against the police. The Police Act 1976 made some alteration to the procedure for handling complaints against the police. The most important of these was the setting up of a Police Complaints Board with lay members to consider complaints against the police. Such complaints still have to be made to, and are investigated by, the police themselves. The investigating officer in such cases does not come from the same force as the officer complained of and if the complaint is found to have some substance after it has been investigated, the offending officer will be dealt with, either by reference to the Director of Public Prosecutions or, in less severe cases, by the Police Complaints Board. The law also requires that all complaints are properly recorded and investigated; the record is inspected regularly by H.M. Inspectors of Constabulary. There were 22,738 such complaints in 1976, 124 of which led to criminal proceedings and a further 124 to disciplinary proceedings. (*Hansard*, 5th December 1977.)

LEGAL REFORM

21. Legal reform. It will be seen from the foregoing that the legal system in Britain is cumbersome and complex. Suggestions as to how it can be reformed are occasionally made and there are a number of standing bodies charged with this responsibility. Parliament itself may take the initiative and there are, from time to time, Royal Commissions and reports on specifically legal matters. There are three permanent bodies charged with keeping the law under review.

(*a*) The Law Reform Committee, set up in 1952, is concerned with matters referred to it by the Lord Chancellor. Its recommendations have resulted in a number of Acts, such as the Law Reform (Husband and Wife) Act 1962.

(*b*) The Criminal Law Revision Committee is to criminal law what the Law Reform Committee is to civil law. It is a standing committee set up in 1959 which reports to the Home Secretary. A number of its reports have been directly responsible for changes in the law, e.g. its *Report on Theft and Related Offences* resulted in the passing of the Theft Act 1968.

(*c*) The Law Commission was set up by the Law Commission Act 1965 to review English law as a whole. It is composed of lawyers and reports annually to Parliament. Its brief is to consolidate and revise statute law and, among other things, has been responsible for a proposal to codify the law on contracts.

22. A Minister of Justice. The suggestion is sometimes made that there should be a Minister of Justice. Jeremy Bentham (1748–1832) was only one of a number of people who felt that such an appointment would be of value. A number of European countries (France, Italy, Switzerland and West Germany) have such a minister.

The arguments for a Minister of Justice include the following.

(*a*) Law reform is the province of lawyers and they tend to move slowly. They are also judges in their own case and would be less than human if they did not advocate most strongly those reforms which benefitted the legal profession.

(*b*) Those responsible for the administration of justice should be directly answerable to Parliament and, indirectly, to the electorate.

(*c*) The proliferation of administrative tribunals (*see* XIX, 6) throws an increasing burden on the legal system, with which it cannot adequately cope.

(*d*) Those countries which have a Minister of Justice find that the post is a useful one.

(*e*) The Parliamentary Commissioner for Administration (*see* XIX, 14) serves a useful purpose and such work as he undertakes may well expand (a local authority ombudsman and a Health Service Commissioner have already been appointed). The Minister of Justice would be the logical person to expand and co-ordinate these services.

The arguments against a Minister of Justice are, to a large extent, the reverse of the arguments set out above.

(a) Law reform is the province of lawyers and a minister who was not himself a lawyer would be in an invidious position;

(b) Administrative tribunals function adequately under the present system;

(c) Those countries which do have Ministers of Justice have different problems and different traditions.

(d) The Parliamentary Commissioner is independent. He should remain so, as should any commissioners who may be appointed subsequently.

(e) If the Minister of Justice were responsible for the police, and this would appear logical, then the theory of the separation of the powers (see I, 20) would be violated. An independent judiciary is an important guardian of liberty. The present system, where the work is shared by the Lord Chancellor, the Attorney-General and the Home Secretary, works well in practice.

23. Justices of the Peace. It is sometimes said that the British system of appointing lay magistrates is archaic and should be abandoned. The reasons for this are as follows:

(a) they are not learned in law, although since 1966 they have received training on appointment;

(b) they may not be impartial, e.g. a country landowner who is also a J.P. may be harsh on poachers;

(c) they tend to come predominantly from one section of society (the middle-aged to elderly middle classes) and are predominantly male.

However, those who support the present system point out that:

(a) it has stood the test of time and has produced a host of dedicated men and women who have dispensed a swift, efficient and cheap justice which has, on the whole, been very fair;

(b) the cost of paying all J.P.s would be considerable.

(c) The Magistrate's (Democratic Selection) Bill, designed to ensure that "each Bench is broadly representative of the community which it has to serve", received its second reading on 15th July 1977.

PROGRESS TEST 7

1. Describe the relationship between law, custom and morality. **(4)**

2. What is the rule of law and is it still valid? **(5, 6)**

3. Write brief notes on (a) common law, (b) statute law, (c) equity and (d) case law. **(7–10)**

4. Distinguish between civil and criminal law and describe the courts set up to deal with them. **(14, 15)**

5. List the advantages and disadvantages of the jury system. **(16)**

6. In what way is the status of a policeman different from that of the ordinary citizen? **(17)**

7. How are complaints against the police dealt with? **(20)**

8. State the functions of the Law Reform Committee, the Criminal Law Reform Committee and the Law Commission. **(21)**

9. Why is it not considered necessary to have a Minister of Justice in Britain? **(22)**

CHAPTER VIII

Local Government

BACKGROUND

1. Why have local government? It could be argued that, in a country so small and comparatively homogeneous as Britain, all the functions of government could be carried out by central government. J. Harvey and L. Bather, in their book, *The British Constitution* (Macmillan, 1964), suggest six reasons why local government is important.

(*a*) It allows for differences in government to meet the needs of different localities, a point also made by John Stuart Mill many years earlier.

(*b*) It utilises abilities and interests in the community (but fewer people vote in local elections than in national ones).

(*c*) It is said to produce a continuity of policy in favour of local interests because local politics tend to be less party-political than national politics. This statement is now less true than it was ten or fifteen years ago.

(*d*) It allows people to be more involved in the government of the country. This too is debatable, since it may be just as difficult to exert legitimate influence on a local councillor as it can be to influence one's Member of Parliament.

(*e*) The "power struggle" which occasionally takes place between local and national government may well keep national government on its toes.

2. Evolution of local government. The history of local government is long and fascinating, but outside the scope of this book. It covers the early parish government, the formation of boroughs, the office of Justice of the Peace and the widespread social and economic changes which accompanied the industrial revolution.

The more recent history of local government starts with the Reform Act 1832. This, and subsequent reform acts, by extending the franchise, created a more lively interest in local as well as in central government and led to the setting up of a Royal Commission into the defects of the most important urban unit of local government, the borough. The resulting legislation, the Municipal Corporations Act 1835, may be said to be the basis of modern local government. But, it was not until the Local Government Act 1888 that equal emphasis was placed on the government of rural areas.

This Act still perpetuated the division between town and country authorities with its sixty-one county councils based on the old shires but rapid developments in the first half of the twentieth century made such divisions unrealistic and, although some twenty new county boroughs were created prior to the outbreak of the Second World War, it was clear that the system laid down in 1888 was no longer adequate.

The spread of urbanisation between the wars, and the explosion of social legislation in the 1940s emphasised two of the greatest weaknesses of the system of local government at that time. One was that, although new communities had grown up and old communities had altered and, in some cases, died, the system of local government, and the boundaries of local government areas, had not always been adjusted to take account of the new situation. The second reason was that increasing legislation had altered the balance between the responsibilities of local and central government and some authorities were too small to undertake the tasks they were required to perform.

For these reasons the period from 1940 to 1970 was one of discussion. Local authorities, Royal Commissions, White Papers, consultative documents, conferences, discussions etc., all contributed their particular point of view. A White Paper, *Local Government in England and Wales during the Period of Reconstruction* (Cmnd. 6579), resulted in the setting up of a Boundary Commission in 1946; but it only lasted for three years and it was dissolved in 1949. The problem was that its terms of reference restricted it to the boundaries of local authorities and the members of the Commission could not therefore discuss local authority functions. It is, of course, very difficult to discuss one without the other if the discussion is to have any practical outcome.

3. Proposals and counter-proposals. The demise of the Boundary Commission revitalised the arguments about local government and resulted in a further spate of proposals and counter-proposals. As a result of these discussions three White Papers were published in the 1950s. They were: *Areas and Status of Local*

Authorities in England and Wales (Cmnd. 9831), *Functions of Local Authorities in England and Wales* (Cmnd. 161) and *Local Government Finance (England and Wales)* (Cmnd. 209). The result of the publication of these three White Papers was the Local Government Act 1958 which provided for a review of local government organisation in England and Wales, with particular emphasis on the problems of conurbations, and wide-spread consultation particularly on the problems of Wales. The immediate result of all this was the creation of:

(a) two new counties: Huntingdonshire and the soke of Peterborough, and Cambridge and the Isle of Ely;

(b) six new county boroughs: Luton, Solihull, Torbay, Teeside, Hartlepool and Warley.

A new system of local government was proposed for Tyneside but was rejected.

THE REDCLIFFE-MAUD REPORT

4. Terms of reference. A Royal Commission was set up in 1966 under the chairmanship of Sir John, later Lord, Redcliffe-Maud. It was to consider the structure of local government (excluding London) and to recommend alterations, both in the structure and the functions of the local government system. The Commission was set up because of a general, and increasing, feeling that the system which had remained basically unchanged since 1888 was inadequate for the second half of the twentieth century. In particular it was felt to be inadequate as a vehicle for vigorous, participating, local democracy. The Commission took three years to produce its report. During that time it took evidence from a wide range of sources (2,156 witnesses) and covered a wide spectrum of opinion. When the report was finally published in 1969 it was in two parts: the majority report, *Royal Commission on Local Government in England* 1966–69 (vol. 1); and the *Memorandum of Dissent* (vol. 2) (Cmnd. 4040). In the event neither report was accepted in its entirety and the resulting legislation, the Local Government Act 1972, followed the publication of two subsequent White Papers (*see* 7).

5. The Redcliffe-Maud proposals. The existing structure of local government was to be replaced by sixty-one new areas (excluding London) and in fifty-eight of these areas there would be a single authority responsible for all services. The three largest areas,

Birmingham, Liverpool and Manchester, would have a two-tier system of metropolitan authorities and metropolitan districts. All sixty-one areas, plus London, would be grouped into eight provinces, each with a provincial council. These changes in structure would reflect new functions and would, it was hoped, increase local democracy by giving people more say in the conduct of local affairs, since the new units of local government were to be "all-purpose authorities".

6. The minority report. Mr. D. Senior, in his *Memorandum of Dissent*, did not accept that the system proposed in the Report would necessarily be more democratic, nor did he think that the suggested new authorities were the right size for the tasks they would be called upon to do. He therefore proposed:

(*a*) that there should be a two-tier system of local government comprising:

   (*i*) regional authorities (35), financed by local taxation;

   (*ii*) district authorities (148), financed by rates;

(*b*) that both regional and district authorities would be directly elected and the regional authorities would have major responsibilities some of which were then being undertaken by central government;

(*c*) that responsibilities which were shared between district and regional authorities would be dealt with in two ways:

   (*i*) delegation to district authorities of personal social services;

   (*ii*) concentration of major responsibilities in the hands of the regional authorities;

(*d*) that parishes and similar "grass-roots" authorities would be replaced by common councils which would act as a sounding board for local opinion and would have more power, but fewer duties, than their predecessors;

(*e*) that elected provincial councils would be responsible for long-term planning. There would be five such councils or, alternatively, twelve to fifteen "sub-provincial authorities".

THE REFORM OF LOCAL GOVERNMENT

7. The White Papers. The Reports were accepted by the Labour government and a White Paper, *Reform of Local Government in England* (Cmnd. 4276), was issued in 1970. A general election followed soon afterwards and the new, Conservative, government put forward its own proposals in 1971 in a White Paper entitled, *Local Government in England: Proposals for Reorganisation* (Cmnd. 4584) and a consultative document for Wales. The White Paper set forth four aims:

(*a*) a new pattern of local authority areas;
(*b*) more power to be given to local authorities;
(*c*) the number of local authority areas to be reduced;
(*d*) operational authorities were to be complemented by provincial and parish authorities.

8. Reformed local government. The Local Government Act 1972 came into effect on 1st April 1974. It owes something to the Redcliffe-Maud Report, something to Mr. Senior's minority report and something to the discussion which followed the two White Papers. It altered the names of some authorities, changed their status and redistributed their functions. The Act itself gave local authorities some flexibility in the way that it was to be implemented and what follows is, therefore, a general view of the new structure, modified by changes since 1974, rather than a precise description of it.

There are currently fifty-three county authorities containing 369 district authorities both of which are elected. The six most heavily populated counties are called "metropolitan" authorities and have populations of from 1.2 to 2.8 millions. Non-metropolitan authorities vary in size from the Isle of Wight, which has a population of about 111,000, to the larger counties with around 1.4 million. District authorities may have anything from 75,000 to 1.1 million population. Greater London and Scotland were not included in the Act and have their own local authority system. Below the county and district councils are the parish councils (community councils in Wales). They now have limited powers but serve a useful purpose in acting as a focus for local opinion.

9. Water services. The Water Act 1973 recognised that the supply and distribution of water was a national, not a local responsibility. It therefore removed responsibility for water from local authorities and gave it to ten regional water authorities, nine in England and Wales and a Welsh National Water Development Authority (Scotland and Northern Ireland have their own arrangements which, like those of England and Wales, have removed the responsibility from local authorities and given it to other bodies).

The majority of the members of water authorities are appointed by the Secretary of State for the Environment but most authorities also have members appointed by the local authorities of the areas in which they operate. Water authorities are responsible for the supply and distribution of water, and for the planning, research and amenity aspects of water; a national water authority, integrating these functions, was proposed in a consultative document in 1976.

10. Why create a new structure? In the late 1950s and early 1960s there was a growing recognition that the existing system of local government was out of date and inadequate. The reasons for this dissatisfaction can be grouped under four headings.

(*a*) It was anachronistic. Local authority areas had grown up piecemeal, there had been some minor alterations to boundaries but the populations contained within those boundaries had altered. The rigid distinction between urban and rural areas was no longer valid, but it was still reflected in the fact that authorities were based on the old shires and hundreds.

(*b*) It was undemocratic. The essence of democracy is the idea that those who are governed should have some say in their government. A local authority structure based on historical accident made proper representation more difficult.

(*c*) It was unresponsive to local needs. Again the fault was chiefly the result of size. Counties, county boroughs and boroughs of various sizes and with differing traditions had grown up to be increasingly subject to central government control, and the control exercised by central government took little or no account of such differences.

(*d*) It was inefficient. The growing administrative complexity of local government, the economic aspects (local government spending now represents about a third of all public spending) and the increasing recognition of the importance of efficient administration all underlined the fact that a basically nineteenth-century structure of local government was inadequate to deal with the problems of the twentieth century.

11. The new structure. Prior to the Redcliffe-Maud Report there had been a tendency to see the function of elected councillors as being to devise policy and for officials to carry out that policy in a way similar to that in which M.P.s and Civil Servants decided and carried out national policy. The division was no more clear-cut in local politics than theorists would claim was the case in

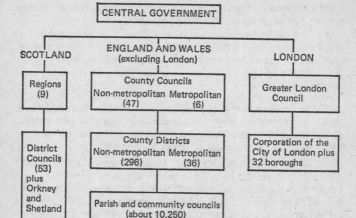

FIG. 3   *The present pattern of local government.*

national politics. There were overlapping areas of interest, in both local and national government, where elected representatives and paid officials had to work together. Nowhere was this more true than in the committee work which represented so much of the business of local government.

The Bains Report (1972) looked at the work of councillors, officials (particularly chief officials) and committees and made a number of recommendations, the bulk of which have been implemented. They were as follows.

(*a*) The council, i.e. the elected members, should do more than simply decide policy; it should be a debating forum.

(*b*) A Policy and Resources Committee should be formed of the chief officers, chairmen of other committees and, where possible, members of the Opposition. Its job should be to provide "co-ordinated advice", i.e. advice representative of all major aspects of the council's work, to the council.

(*c*) A subcommittee of the Policy and Resources Committee should be responsible for day-to-day control of finance.

(*d*) Other committees of the council should be serviced by appropriate specialists.

(e) Committees should be encouraged to consider alternative proposals about any matter which came before them.

(f) Committee chairmen should be carefully chosen.

(g) Working groups should be formed from subcommittees. Such groups should work informally.

12. Corporate management. The "managerial revolution" heralded by the Bains Report has not been without its difficulties. Some of the larger authorities appointed a city or town manager, a new post in some respects equivalent to the town clerk; but he was invariably a lawyer and his responsibilities were as much legal as administrative. The new breed was to be a manager pure and simple and other chief officers, whatever their profession, would be answerable to him.

One such authority was Newcastle-upon-Tyne, where the city manager, an ex-executive of the Ford Motor Company, was appointed in 1965. As senior officer of the council he was responsible to a special committee of the council covering a whole range of local authority activities. This new structure was not always successful however. The chief education officer of Avon resigned in 1976 because he said that corporate management had dissipated his authority among so many committees that he no longer felt that he had any control over educational matters.

THE FUNCTIONS OF LOCAL GOVERNMENT

13. Functions. The first and most important point is that local authorities have no functions at all except those specified by Parliament. If they fail to exercise these functions, exceed their powers or carry out functions not specified by law they can be called to account. Four legal concepts are particularly important.

(a) *Certiorari.* (To be more fully aware of something.) This calls for cases dealt with by a lower court to be reviewed by a higher one and can be used in cases which concern the powers of a local authority.

(b) *Prohibition.* An order which forbids a lower court to deal with a case, on the grounds that the case is properly the responsibility of a higher court.

(c) *Mandamus.* This type of order compels a person or body to do its duty. Thus if a statute places the responsibility for housing homeless persons on the local authority and a complainant alleges that they have neglected this duty an order of *mandamus* may be applied for.

(*d*) *Ultra vires* (literally, "beyond the powers"). This is used in cases where the local authority may have exceeded its powers. For example, the money raised by rates can only be used for specific purposes (except for the product of a 2 pence rate which is allowed, under the provisions of the Local Government (Financial Provisions) Act 1963, to be used for general purposes). Any council which used more than the product of a 2 pence rate for general purposes could find itself facing an *ultra vires* charge.

14. Allocation of responsibilities. The functions performed by local councils following the Local Government Act 1972 remain basically unchanged. What has altered has been the allocation of such functions between county and district councils. The major functions and the allocation of local authority responsibility following the 1972 Act are shown in Table IV. An asterisk in both columns indicates that the responsibility is shared.

15. The relationship between central and local government. The relationship between Whitehall and town hall is a changing one. Strong central government prefers to control a host of activities which the enthusiastic local councillor will claim are better dealt with locally. In the end, of course, power rests with Parliament and the courts. Local authorities can do nothing except in the exercise of powers delegated to them by Parliament.

Some matters, traditionally seen as local concerns, may be better administered centrally. Thus public health, in all its aspects, was traditionally seen as a local matter but the spate of legislation, following the Second World War, produced the National Health Service Act 1946 which not only introduced ancillary services, such as health centres, but also transferred control of local hospitals to central government. In this particular instance the government delegated the responsibility to county councils and county borough councils whose responsibility it remained until the National Health Service Reorganisation Act 1973 (and comparable Acts for Northern Ireland and Scotland) set up a nationally administered organisation.

Education, although locally administered, is still the responsibility of central government and H.M. Inspectors of Schools are government appointees, not servants of the local authority. Within their sphere of delegated authority local authorities are free to administer the various Acts as they think best, but they are sub-

TABLE IV.   FUNCTIONS OF PRINCIPAL LOCAL
AUTHORITIES IN ENGLAND AND WALES

Function	County	District
Consumer protection	*	
Education	Non-metropolitan areas only	Metropolitan areas
Environmental health	Animal diseases	
Fire services	*	
Housing	Reserve powers	General provision
Libraries	Non-metropolitan areas only	Metropolitan areas
Museums and galleries	*	*
National parks	*	
Parks (other than national parks)	*	
Personal social services	*	*
Police	*	*
Public health	*	*
Refuse	Disposal	Collection
Roads	Construction	Maintenance
Sewerage		*
Town and country planning	Major development	Local plans
Transport	Metropolitan areas – passenger transport	Non-metropolitan areas – subject to county policy
Water	(For water authorities *see* 9)	

ject to central direction in the form of circulars which, although
they do not have the force of law, may well be difficult to circum-
vent.

The example of Tameside metropolitan district council education authority in Manchester is interesting. Tameside's Labour-

controlled council agreed, in 1975, to set up a system of comprehensive education in line with a Labour government directive. A local election put the Conservatives in power and they decided to defer the proposed changes, at least temporarily. The Labour Secretary of State for Education insisted that they should proceed with the plan. They refused to do so and the Secretary of State applied for an order of *mandamus* (*see* **13**(*c*)) to compel them to do so. The case was fought in the High Court, the Appeal Court and finally the House of Lords. In the event the council won; but it was a hollow victory as subsequent legislation compelled them to introduce comprehensive education.

LOCAL AUTHORITY AND THE COMMUNITY

16. Local authority elections. The Representation of the People Acts 1949 and 1969 give almost universal adult suffrage similar to that for parliamentary elections, with the additional qualification that the intending voter must be on the register of electors. The register is kept by a registration officer, whose responsibility it is to keep it up to date. The register is compiled annually and elections are held either annually or at such other intervals as may be decided. Councillors for different types of local authority are elected at different intervals.

(*a*) County councillors are elected every four years and all councillors serve for this period. The same rule applies to parish councils.

(*b*) District councillors also serve for four years. They may either retire en bloc or, if the council so decides, a proportion may retire annually. In this case an annual election will be held and one third of the council will retire.

(*c*) Special arrangements apply to London where both the Greater London Council (G.L.C.) councillors and borough councillors serve for three years. Elections are held triennially.

17. Participation. It has already been said that all qualified electors may take part in local elections and it has also been noted (*see* **1**(*b*)) that the poll for local elections is invariably smaller than that for national elections. It may also be noted that there is some evidence that voters in local elections tend to vote for the party currently in opposition in Parliament. Thus if a Labour government is in power the Conservatives may do better in local elections, and vice versa. The intrusion of party politics into local government is of comparatively recent origin and may be attributed to the rise of the Labour Party, which regarded local councils as proper channels for social legislation. Since "political" candidates represented one major party it was natural for the other party to provide "opposition" candidates; the Liberal Party had, in any case, long stressed the importance of local democracy.

The arguments for local party politics are:

(*a*) independent candidates make for fragmented local government;

(*b*) party groups can put forward clear policies, with a reasonable chance of their being adopted if that party has a majority;

(*c*) national problems are reflected locally. If there is a case for party government at a national level the same argument applies at a local level.

(*d*) a great deal of the work of local councils is concerned with the implementation of central government policy and local views on this are likely to be in line with those of the national parties;

(*e*) decision-making is likely to be quicker if a local party leader can speak on behalf of a group of councillors.

The arguments against party politics in local government are:

(*a*) party groups frequently hold meetings before council meetings to decide "the party line". This means, in effect, that decisions are not always made in full accordance with the democratic processes;

(*b*) voting along party lines may be in national, rather than local, interests.

(*c*) chairmen of committees may frequently be appointed by the majority party. Although a chairman should be impartial he is still in a position to wield considerable influence;

(*d*) the work of a local councillor is different to that of an M.P. He is responsible to his constituents in a more personal way.

18. Voters and councillors. Volume III of the Redcliffe-Maud Report contains a number of research reports, including one on *The Local Government Elector*. This research underlines one possible explanation of apathy in local elections, namely ignorance. It established, for example, that people knew little about borough councils and less about county councils. Those in rural districts and in London knew less than people in other parts of the country. Women tended to be less well-informed than men and older people less than younger ones (except for the youngest group interviewed (aged 24–34); but this group was more aware of its ignorance and more disposed to rectify it). In F. W. G. Benemy's book *Whitehall—Town Hall* (Harrap, 1960), we read that, "The councillor is, or usually should be, a local 'worthy', like the country gentleman who used to administer the parishes three hundred years ago". It is debatable whether a councillor should be like a country gentleman of three hundred years ago. However, the preponderance of male middle-aged, middle-class citizens who take part in these affairs is undeniable. Evidence before the Redcliffe-Maude Committee showed that in a survey of 4,000 councillors, 54 per cent were over 55 years old, only 19 per cent "blue-collar" workers and only 12 per cent women. The electorate, on the other hand, was distributed as follows: aged over 55, 34 per cent; "blue-collar" workers, 57 per cent and women, over 50 per cent.

There are a number of possible explanations for this state of affairs. The age of councillors may be due to the fact that only those who are retired or nearing retirement have time for council activities, some of which take place during the day when the working man may lose time by attending (the allowance which he can claim may not adequately compensate for loss of earnings). The traditional social structure is such that the white-collar worker, particularly if he is a business or professional man, may find it easier to get time off than the blue-collar worker and may well retire earlier. The small proportion of women elected as local councillors also owes a lot to tradition. The position of women in society has changed drastically in the last fifty years but this change is not yet reflected in local authority elections.

19. Local Ombudsmen. The office of Parliamentary Commissioner (Ombudsman) has been in existence for some years (*see* **XIX, 14**) and in 1976 three Commissioners for Local Administration were approved, one each for England and Wales and one for Scotland (in Northern Ireland the office is held by a Commissioner for Complaints).

The Commissioner's responsibility is to help local authority councillors to protect the interests of their constituents. As with the Parliamentary Commissioner, the Commissioner's first responsibility is to the elected representative, not to the elector. He can only deal with a complaint which has been submitted by a councillor and then only if he is satisfied that the normal machinery for dealing with complaints has proved inadequate. He (or she, since Baroness Serota was one of the first of such appointments) has no power to order a local authority to take any action which appears to be needed to rectify maladministration but, as with the Parliamentary Commissioner, any "advice" that is given is treated with respect.

The Commissioner's terms of reference, however, are concerned with "maladministration" and he cannot deal with a complaint against a local authority decision unless maladministration is involved. Maladministration is not defined.

LOCAL AUTHORITY FINANCE

20. Sources of income. Local authorities are responsible for a wide range of services (*see* Table IV) and the money to provide these services comes from three main sources:

    (*a*) rates: about two-fifths;

    (*b*) central government funds: about two-fifths;

    (*c*) income from investments, council house rents, etc.: one-fifth.

21. Rates. Rates are charges levied by local authorities based on the value of property. They are, in a sense, a local form of taxation and the Green Paper, *The Future Shape of Local Government Finance* (Cmnd. 4741, 1971), considered their advantages and disadvantages.

The advantages of rates as a source of local authority finance are as follows.

    (*a*) Their yield is "substantial, certain and predictable".

    (*b*) Because they are related to property the revenue stays within a given area and there is little scope for evasion.

    (*c*) The administrative costs of collection are low.

The disadvantages are as follows.

    (*a*) They are regressive. This means that, since they are based on the value of property, those with smaller incomes will pay a higher proportion of their income than others. This is obviated to some extent by rate rebates (*see* XIII, 10).

    (*b*) Those whose income depends upon fixed property and plant will pay more rates.

    (*c*) The amount of rates collected depends partly upon the valuation of property, but revaluations lag behind inflation.

22. Audit. The Local Government Act 1933 set up a number of audit schemes, the most important of which was the introduction of the district auditor. He had wide powers and, if he was satisfied that council funds were improperly spent, could levy a surcharge; i.e. local councillors could be held financially responsible for money which had been improperly disbursed.

The Local Government Act 1972 replaced the compulsory district auditor and the surcharge with either a district auditor similar to the previous one or an "outside" auditor whose appointment had to be approved by the Secretary of State for the Environment. Such auditors were, however, difficult to find, since this type of audit is highly specialised and most suitably experienced auditors were already fully occupied. Whilst the old-style auditor considered the interests of the public as a matter of convention, the new Act now made this consideration a statutory duty.

23. Central government funds. Grants towards expenditure are made to local authorities in the form of rate support grants, introduced by the Rating Act 1966. They are made both as revenue and for specific services. The basis of the grant is threefold: the needs of the authority in relation to the size of its population; the resources element which relates the rateable value of its property to that of other authorities; and the domestic element which compensates for its rates rebate schemes. The Local Government Act 1958 reintroduced the block grant, by means of which local authorities received a grant-in-aid based on local needs and resources which enabled them to use government funds for a range of services. Some services are known as "approved expenditure", e.g. police, and are funded by percentage grants in which the local authority pays one-half of the cost and central funds pay the other. Percentage grants were the normal form of government grant from about the middle of the nineteenth century until 1929. They were thought to be too restrictive and were replaced, apart from some continuing ones for special services, by block grants until 1948. The Local Government Act 1948 then reintroduced percentage grants up until 1958 when these were again superseded except for specific services.

Since local government is so dependent upon central government for funds it follows that central government must have some say in their allocation. The extent to which central government should be involved is debatable, but a number of general principles can be stated (*a*) the growing amount of social legislation has increased central government's involvement in local services. Central government should therefore recognise its share of the cost;

(*b*) local authorities should, however, be directly concerned with the financial aspects of any schemes they have to administer;

(*c*) any system which is devised should provide:

(*i*) freedom for local initiative;

(*ii*) adequate central control so that standards are maintained; and

(*iii*) flexibility to meet local needs.

24. The Layfield Committee. The Layfield Report, *Local Government Finance: Report of the Committee of Enquiry* (Cmnd. 6453, 1976), was commissioned at a time of great (and increasing) local authority spending and it exposed a number of weaknesses in the system then in operation. The Committee stated at the outset that it was not concerned with interim measures to overcome these weaknesses, but with long-term proposals for the construction of a financial system. It looked at two directions in which change could be made. The present system could either go in the direction of more local control or towards more control from central government. There were arguments for and against both tendencies and the recommendations considered both.

(*a*) *More local control.* This was a long-term goal and related partly to local accountability and partly to the possibility of a local income tax (*see* **25**). Given improved accountability and an assured income, local authorities could have more discretion in the way in which funds were allocated. The rating system should continue for the time being but some modifications could be made:

(*i*) valuation of property could be on its capital value;

(*ii*) crown properties, which do not at present pay rates, could be rated;

(*iii*) agricultural land and buildings, also not rated at present, could also be rated.

(*b*) *More central control.* This could be introduced fairly quickly and would involve assessment of the expenditure plans of each authority so that grants could be based on prescribed figures. Audit should be divorced from both central and local authority and should be the responsibility of an independent official.

25. Local income tax. The Layfield Committee recognised the increasing trend towards local self-government and felt that this could be encouraged by allowing local income tax (L.I.T.). Whether such a tax should be introduced would depend upon a number of factors.

(*a*) The cost was estimated to be of the order of £100 million per year and the Inland Revenue would need to employ some 12,000 more staff to deal with it. This must be set against the intangible benefits of more local independence.

(*b*) Government grants depend upon the ability of local authorities to persuade the government to pay more: L.I.T. depends upon the ability of local authorities to persuade the taxpayer to pay more.

(*c*) A decision has to be made as to where the responsibility lies for taking decisions which affect people's lives and livelihood. Should this be undertaken by elected national governments who can administer the country as a whole, or by local authorities with less scope but more immediate contact with those affected by the legislation?

(*d*) The committee did not make a firm recommendation. On balance they felt that the increased cost of L.I.T. was justified but that it was for the government to decide.

PROGRESS TEST 8

1. How and why did local government evolve? **(1, 2)**

2. What were the main proposals of the Redcliffe-Maud Report and the minority report? **(5, 6)**

3. What were the important features of the new structure introduced by the Local Government Act 1972? **(8–12)**

4. What is meant by *certiorari*, prohibition, *mandamus* and *ultra vires*? **(13)**

5. Describe the allocation of local authority functions following the Local Government Act 1972. **(14)**

6. List the arguments for and against local party politics. **(17)**

7. What are the characteristics of local councillors? **(18)**

8. What are the restrictions placed on the work of the local ombudsman? **(19)**

9. List the advantages and disadvantages of rates as a form of local authority finance. **(21)**

10. What is meant by a surcharge? **(22)**

11. What was the purpose of the Layfield Committee? **(24–25)**

CHAPTER IX

Decentralisation and Devolution

BACKGROUND

1. History. Until the ninth century England was a collection of small, independent states each ruled by its own king and frequently warring with each other. The Saxons united England but Ireland remained a separate kingdom until the thirteenth century and Wales until the fourteenth century. It was not until 1603 that Scotland and England became united under King James VI of Scotland (James I of England). This unity was, however, only dynastic and it was not until the Act of Union of 1707 that the Parliament of Great Britain linked the two countries "forever united into one kingdom".

The Irish had their own Parliament which they retained until the Act for the Union of Great Britain and Ireland (1800). In 1920 the Government of Ireland Act gave Northern Ireland its own Parliament to deal with domestic affairs. At the same time, however, Parliament at Westminster reserved to itself the right to deal with major matters like defence. In 1922 the twenty-six counties of Southern Ireland were declared a republic with no residual control from Westminster. This situation continued until 1972 when, owing to the situation in Northern Ireland, the powers of the Northern Ireland Parliament were suspended and Northern Ireland was ruled directly from Westminster. There have been since then a number of attempts to set up a form of government which would be generally acceptable.

Britain is technically one state, the United Kingdom of Great Britain and Northern Ireland, within a commonwealth of nations. Within that state however there are:

(*a*) different Parliaments, Britain and Northern Ireland (the functions of the Northern Ireland Parliament are suspended, not abrogated);

(*b*) different laws, Scottish law is different in a number of respects from English law;

(*c*) different levels of government, national government, local government and degrees of devolved government, e.g. as in Wales;

(*d*) different government departments. The Secretary of State for Scotland is responsible for a number of Scottish departments with headquarters in Edinburgh (*see* XVII, **19**(*d*));

(*e*) dependencies. The Channel Islands and the Isle of Man both have their own Parliaments and their own courts. The government of the United Kingdom is, however, responsible for matters like defence and international relations which concern the dependencies.

2. Centralisation. Up to the end of the Second World War a number of important functions, e.g. the relief of poverty, education and health services were provided by local authorities. The post-war legislation on social issues imposed a national pattern on the provision of these services. Local authorities still had some responsibilities but the direction came from Westminister. This had some advantages. It enabled a more equitable distribution of funds so that poorer areas, with a higher proportion of social problems and, frequently, a lower income, were enabled to deal more effectively with them. It had disadvantages as well. Areas like the North-East, which traditionally have always had problems of high unemployment, found that national remedies were not always adequate for their needs. The solution would appear to be a compromise, units of government which were larger than most local authorities but smaller than a national government.

Such an idea was not new. A number of ministries developed a regional structure during the Second World War, partly so that the functions of government could continue in the event of a serious disruption in any part of the country. Such developments were not, however, centrally planned or co-ordinated. Some ministries, like the then Board of Trade and the Ministry of Housing and Local Government, worked mainly from central London headquarters. Others, like the Ministry of Labour and National Service, had a regional structure and a network of local offices as well as a London headquarters. Others, again, like the Ministry of Transport, relied chiefly on a network of regional offices with a comparatively small central headquarters. Nearly all government departments, however, had a central headquarters but the emphasis in the 1940s and 1950s on greater local participation suggested that both the legislature and the executive might do well to devolve some of their responsibilities.

DEVOLUTION

3. Reasons for devolution. Devolution may be defined as the delegation of some executive functions of central government to other bodies. It is not a complete separation into separate states but a sharing of the power of the state in which national government remains responsible for major matters of common concern, such as defence, while the federated states are free to legislate on other matters. Advocates of devolution put forward the following arguments.

(*a*) *Cultural*. There are a number of different cultures in Britain. The Scots, Irish and Welsh cultures are well-known and widely recognised. The Cornish culture too is justifiably claimed to be similarly distinct. The Cornish National Party, Mebyon Kernow, has made such claims for many years.

(*b*) *Historical*.

(*i*) The question of Home Rule for Ireland was a major political issue in the late nineteenth and early twentieth century. It was resolved, critics would say unsatisfactorily, by the creation of the Republic of Ireland and the separate constitutional arrangements for Northern Ireland.

(*ii*) The Scots have an equally valid claim to historical independence and the victories of the Scottish National Party in the elections of 1970 and 1974 were based on appeals to Scottish nationalist sentiments.

(*iii*) Plaid Cymru (the "Party of Wales") was formed in 1925 but Welsh nationalism is much older than that. Both the Welsh Liberal Party and the Independent Labour Party campaigned for many years for recognition of the historical importance of the Welsh tradition.

(*c*) *Economic*. The economic imbalance between various regions in the United Kingdom has already been mentioned (*see* **2**). In 1964 the Labour government set up a new department, the Department of Economic Affairs with six (later eight) economic planning boards to work alongside local authorities in matters concerned with economy, transport and housing. Two separate boards were set up for Scotland and Wales and all were to work on a regional basis.

(*d*) *Administrative*. Those matters which were too large for local authorities to deal with unaided, but too closely related to local conditions to be capable of solution by central government, might be better dealt with by a second tier of government some-where between the local and national structures.

(e) *Political.* Given the increasing demands for regionalism in some form or another, by the early 1970s the question of regional government had become a political issue; indeed the Labour, Conservative and Liberal parties all mentioned the matter in their manifestos in the elections of 1974. They disagreed about the exact form which it should take but were agreed about the principle of decentralisation.

(f) *Weakness of local government.* Studies of local government in the 1950s and 1960s suggested that it was not as effective as it might be. One of the reasons for this was the quality of the elected representatives. J. P. Mackintosh, in his book, *The Devolution of Power* (Chatto and Windus, 1968) suggested that this was perhaps because local authorities did not have enough power to attract the right sort of people and that this was one reason for the low turn-out of voters for local elections.

SOME ALTERNATIVES

4. Territorial devolution. The country could be divided into a number of regions (in the 1939–45 war there were twelve of them), each of which would have its own parliament. Regional parliaments would have limited responsibility but the national Parliament would retain its sovereignty. Matters like education and the administration of the personal social services would gain from economies of scale which cannot be attained under the present split of responsibilities between local and national govern-ment. Regional needs and aspirations could be catered for and the legislative strain on central government would be consider-ably reduced. Local taxation could be raised for certain purposes. Such a system would, of course, need a careful consideration of the allocation of responsibilities and would, in all probability, involve a written constitution.

5. Functional devolution. The Fabian Society (*see* II, **13**(b)) looked at this idea which was put forward originally by one of its members, Sidney Webb (Lord Passfield). It was that those parlia-mentary functions which were carried out by professional men and women should be delegated to such professionals. Thus doctors would be responsible for the health service, lawyers for the administration of justice and so on. Quite apart from the im-practicability of the suggestion it would, in the case of the judiciary, be contrary to the theory of the separation of the powers (*see* I, **20–23**) and it begs the question whether professionals already have too much say (because they have strong and highly respected pressure groups) in the functions of government which affect their interests.

6. Administrative devolution. This form of devolution would leave the power in the hands of central government but would recognise that certain services—airports, ambulances, police and water authorities have been suggested (R. N. Punnett, *British Government and Politics*, Heinemann 1971)—should be dealt with regionally. Such devolution would not, however, meet the claims of the nationalists for more independence. Since Punnett's book was written a considerable amount of administrative devolution has taken place. The Secretary of State for the Environment, the Secretary of State for Wales and the Ministry of Agriculture, Fisheries and Food have accepted responsibility for a national policy for water in Britain (*see also* VIII, **9**) and the Secretary of State for Trade for civil aviation throughout the country. Ambulance services are provided by Area Health Authorities, i.e. by a larger unit than most local authorities. Only the police have no national centrally controlled organisation. The present number of police forces, forty-three in England and Wales and eight in Scotland, means that they are organised in larger units than would be provided by a local authority but they are by no means large enough to be considered to have a regional structure, except in Scotland where the Scottish Home and Health Department is responsible for all functions relating to law and order.

7. Scotland. Scotland is the one part of Britain which currently has something akin to regional government. It does not have its own parliament but it does have its own laws and government departments. Even where it shares legislation with England and Wales it still retains some autonomy. The Ministry of Social Security Act 1966 is administered through a series of local and regional offices. Scotland is not part of any region; it has its own Central Office (as does Wales). When matters affecting Scotland are debated at Westminster there are special arrangements to protect Scottish interests. The Scottish Grand Committee, comprising all Scottish M.P.s, debates Scottish estimates, and the committee stage of Scottish legislation is dealt with by a special committee.

These special arrangements do not, however, constitute independence and the more ardent Scottish Nationalists see proposals for devolution as the first step to that end. A large body of opinion, both within Parliament and outside it, sees devolution as an end in itself and regards any further development of regional independence as destructive of the concept of a United Kingdom.

8. Wales. The pattern of government in Wales is different from that of both England and Scotland. The Secretary of State for Wales is a Cabinet Minister and has complete responsibility for matters of social welfare. He has shared responsibilities for matters like agriculture and the administration of urban grants to areas of social deprivation. Although there is a Welsh Office there are no other separate government departments as there are for Scotland. A group of Welsh and Scottish Liberal M.P.s introduced private member's Bills in Parliament in 1967 with the object of securing "Home Rule" for Wales and Scotland, in much the same way as that granted to Ireland, but the Bills were defeated.

THE KILBRANDON REPORT

9. The Majority Report. The Royal Commission on the Constitution 1969–73 vol. 1 (Cmnd. 5460), the Kilbrandon Majority Report, advocated what it called "legislative devolution" for both Scotland and Wales. A Minority Report, also recommending legislative devolution, but for regions in England as well, is dealt with in **11**. All members of the Commission agreed on the need for some form of devolution and advanced three reasons for it.

(a) *Centralisation*. Both Westminster and Whitehall, where all the growing volume of legislation is enacted and the major administrative decisions are taken, are in London. Many provincial leaders, and indeed national politicians, believe that these decisions should be taken nearer to the area which they will affect, so that the allocation of funds can be organised to take closer account of regional priorities. Public opinion shares this view (*see* IV, **5** for an account of research into public opinion which was undertaken by the Kilbrandon Commission). The main area of disagreement among supporters of devolution is the amount of power which should be devolved and the areas in which it would be exercised.

(b) *Weakening of democracy*. Voting for a Member of Parliament every five years or so no longer provides sufficient outlet for democratic expression. The growth of delegated legislation (*see* XIX, 3) increases the gap between the people and their government while the increase in legislation has created a situation in which it is felt that government had developed a momentum of its own, unaware of, or at least unsympathetic to, the views and feelings of the electorate.

(*c*) *National feeling*. Whilst only a small proportion of Scottish and Welsh nationalists favour complete independence, there is a large and growing body in both countries which feels that they are not at present independent enough. The administrative devolution which existed at the time the Commission was sitting was felt to be inadequate and in any case not widely understood or appreciated. In particular, it was felt that economic policies for the United Kingdom as a whole were inappropriate for Scotland and Wales.

10. The limits of devolution. The Commission rejected both separatism, giving the regions complete autonomy, and federalism, creating separate states within the United Kingdom but leaving Parliament sovereign. The preferred solution, for the majority of the Commission, was legislative devolution for Scotland and Wales.

The arguments in favour of legislative devolution for both were that:

(*a*) the feeling of geographical remoteness would be overcome while a focus of political interest would revitalise both Scotland and Wales;

(*b*) transfer of "full responsibility for policy and legislation on prescribed matters" is the only realistic course to adopt if they are to be more than just advisory bodies;

(*c*) it is more democratic;

(*d*) the Scots and Welsh have some advantages, e.g. Secretaries of State to look after their interests. A new scheme must not give them less than they already have.

The main arguments against such devolution were that:

(*a*) there is not really scope for distinctively different regional policies and that this tendency will become more marked as the effects of Britain's membership of the E.E.C. come to be felt;

(*b*) assemblies might use their powers to adopt policies incompatible with those in other parts of the United Kingdom;

(*c*) although Parliament would, theoretically, have power to overrule regional assemblies this power could, in practice, be difficult to exercise.

11. The Minority Report. Lord Crowther-Hunt and Professor A. T. Peacock issued a *Memorandum of Dissent* (vol II of the Report) in which they claimed that the Commission had interpreted its terms of reference too narrowly, concentrating too much on the particular problems of Scotland and Wales and underestimating the likely consequences of Britain's membership of the Common Market. The solutions proposed by the majority would, they felt, give an unfair advantage to the Scots and the Welsh and would not reduce the burden of central government. They saw five major trends in the British system of government:

(*a*) the increasing burden of legislation has involved every aspect of national life and the number of Civil Servants had increased ten-fold since the turn of the century. In the same period the number of ministers had doubled;

(*b*) the power of Parliament was declining;

(*c*) local government was losing both responsibilities and representatives (the local government reorganisation of 1974 reduced the number of elected representatives from 37,510 to 23,950);

(*d*) many local authority functions had been given to *ad hoc* bodies who were nominated rather than elected, thus diluting the element of democratic control;

(*e*) major government departments now have their own regional and local structures.

12. The minority proposals. Regionalism would apply to England as well as to Scotland and Wales. There would be seven regions— Scotland, Wales and five in England. Regions would be responsible for a range of functions, including those currently performed by local and regional offices of central government departments and by the *ad hoc* bodies. They would also supervise some aspects of industry and commerce and would have residual responsibility for any functions not specifically reserved to central government. They would have independent revenue-raising powers and their own civil services. They would have their own assemblies, consisting of about 100 members elected by single transferable vote (*see* **19**(*a*)), for a period of four years. Other minority proposals were as follows:

(*a*) assemblies would make "ordinances" to endorse or adapt United Kingdom legislation and to exercise their own powers;

(*b*) members of Parliament, being relieved of some of their responsibilities, would be free to devote time to other matters;

(*c*) the Secretaries of State for Scotland and Wales would remain and a third Secretary of State would be appointed to represent the interests of the English regions.

THE GOVERNMENT'S APPROACH

13. The White Paper. A White Paper, *Our Changing Democracy: Devolution to Scotland and Wales* (Cmnd. 6348) was published in 1975. This advocated a middle course, taking some of the proposals of the majority report and some from the minority report. It also added one or two new ideas which had arisen in the course of public discussion of the subject. The White Paper became the basis of a Bill presented to Parliament in November 1976. This Bill was probably too contentious to succeed in the 1976/77 session of Parliament and was reintroduced, with amendments, in the 1977/78 session (*see* **15**). The Bill (the Devolution Bill) as originally proposed, advocated the following changes.

(*a*) Scotland and Wales were to have their own assemblies, members of which would be elected in the same way as for general elections. Membership would be for a fixed term of four years and there would be 150 members in the Scottish Assembly and eighty in the Welsh.

(*b*) The Scottish Assembly would be a law-making body in its own right but the Secretary of State would have power of veto if:

(*i*) the Scottish law was incompatible with international obligations of the United Kingdom (including obligations to the E.E.C.); or

(*ii*) it was *ultra vires* (*see* VIII, 3(*d*)). In this case the question would be referred to the Judicial Committee of the Privy Council;

(*c*) Scotland (but not Wales) would have a separate executive accountable to the Assembly but neither would have a separate Civil Service.

(*d*) Finance for the assemblies, and for the projects which they undertake, would come from a substantial block grant from the exchequer. A proposal in the White Paper, that they should raise revenues by means of levies on the rates, was dropped.

(e) Devolved powers would include matters of agriculture, education, environment, housing and industry.

(f) An ombudsman would be appointed for both Scotland and Wales.

14. The English dimension. It will be noted that the Devolution Bill makes no mention of the English regions nor of the proposal, by the writers of the Minority Report, that there should be some form of English regional government. The omission was deliberate. The Labour government was at pains to emphasise that the Bill was intended to preserve a United Kingdom and to assure the Scottish Nationalists, who saw it as the first step towards complete independence, that this was not the intention. Debate on the Bill was lengthy and, at times, heated and, at the end of the debate on the second reading, the government announced that there would be a referendum in both Scotland and Wales before the schemes for devolution were implemented.

This still did not deal adequately with the problems of English devolution and a consultative document, *Devolution: The English Dimension* (H.M.S.O., 1976), was issued in December 1976. This rejected the idea of devolution for England, on the grounds that it might result in marked differences in policy on a number of issues. Such differences would be heightened by the fact that the English regions, if they existed, would be close to each other and could not claim, as could Scotland and Wales, that they were remote from the centre of power. This view was contested in a number of regions, particularly the North-East, where it was said that the government already knew more about Scotland and Wales (because of the existence of the Secretaries of State) than about the problems of the English regions.

15. Political aspects. The question of devolution is not a clear cut party-political issue. Although the Devolution Bill is a Labour measure it does not command full support in the Labour Party, and although Margaret Thatcher leads a Conservative opposition to it she too cannot rely on the whole-hearted support of her party. Rebels in the Tory ranks have included not only Edward Heath, ex-Prime Minister, but also Alec Buchanan-Smith who resigned his post as shadow Scottish Secretary in protest. The Scottish nationalists, on whom the 1977 Labour government relied for support, regarded it as a first step to independence, a view which, as has already been explained, is without foundation. Plaid Cymru, as might have been expected, drew attention to the

more favourable terms given to Scotland and could see no justification for not giving equal advantages to Wales. In spite of their
reservations, however, they supported the government.

On 26th July 1977 Michael Foot, Leader of the House of
Commons, made a statement on devolution in which he said that
the government would bring forward proposals to the next
session of Parliament which would introduce two Bills on devolution, one for Scotland and one for Wales. They were to be
similar to legislation (set out in **13**) and any question of interpretation of the Bills was to be resolved by the Judicial Committee of the Privy Council.

The Bill for Scotland would include the following:

(*a*) the Assembly would be given more power than had previously been envisaged;

(*b*) arrangements would be made for a dissolution of the
Assembly on a vote of two-thirds of the membership;

(*c*) some specific powers relating to rents, rates and rebate
schemes were to be modified, as were pension matters relating to
teachers.

The Welsh Assembly would have a statutory duty to review
arrangements for local government within its area and the question of teachers' pensions would be dealt with by Westminster.

A White Paper would be published giving revised proposals
for the financing of assemblies and joint councils would be
formed for both Scotland and Wales. The Bills, for both Scotland
and Wales, would contain provision for an advisory referendum
to be held after the legislation had been enacted (*Hansard*, 8th
November 1977).

ELECTORAL REFORM

16. Why electoral reform? The present system of electing M.P.s
is sometimes referred to as the "first past the post" system. It has
worked reasonably well but it creates anomalies and is manifestly unfair on smaller parties. The party which wins the majority
of seats forms the government although, as with the 1974 Labour
government and a number of previous administrations, they may
not in fact have the majority of the votes. Minority government
of this kind tends to be the rule rather than the exception today.
A different system of election, for which the Liberal Party has
been campaigning for decades, would produce a different pattern
of parliamentary representation. Is such a change desirable?

In October 1975 the Hansard Society set up a Commission with the following terms of reference: "To examine the existing and any alternative systems of election to the House of Commons and possible systems of election for any devolved legislative assemblies that may be established within the United Kingdom and to report". *The Report of the Hansard Commission on Electoral Reform* (Hansard Society, June 1976) came to the "fundamental and unanimous" decision that there should be electoral reform. The exact nature of the reform would be decided by Parliament but it recommended either the single transferable vote or an additional member system (*see* 19).

17. For and against the present system. Before considering possible alternative systems the Commission looked closely at the present system of electing M.P.s and found as follows:

The case for retaining the present system is that:

(*a*) it works;

(*b*) the in-built bias against the smaller parties makes for strong government;

(*c*) where there is a coalition involving the smaller parties (as in the 1977 Lib-Lab pact) the smaller party has an undue advantage;

(*d*) M.P.s represent constituencies, not parties;

(*e*) Britain's problems do not derive from its electoral system;

(*f*) the cost of introducing a reformed electoral system would be considerable.

The case for a change in the electoral system can be summed up thus:

(*a*) stability of government (*see* (*b*) above) is more apparent than real. There have been two elections within eighteen months on three occasions since 1945;

(*b*) the present system is grossly unfair to smaller parties;

(*c*) adversary politics, in which the Opposition simply opposes and then reverses the previous government's decisions when in power (*see* XII, 3), leads to instability;

(*d*) the present system is said to be unpopular;

(*e*) direct elections to the European Parliament (*see* X, 18) recognise other, better, systems.

18. Alternatives. There are thought to be about 300 different electoral systems which might be used. The Hansard Committee considered the main ones and the context in which they were used before making its recommendations.

(*a*) *Alternative vote.* Candidates are numbered in order of preference. The candidate with the lowest number of votes is eliminated and his votes transferred to the next choice. The process continues until a clear winner emerges. Used in Australia.

(*b*) *Double-ballot.* A candidate with an absolute majority of at least 25 per cent of the number of electors can be declared the winner. If no candidate has this number of votes a second ballot is held. Candidates with less than 10 per cent of the votes are eliminated from this election. Used in France.

(*c*) *Block vote.* Each elector has one vote for each seat. Used in multi-member constituencies in British local government elections and in Greece, Turkey and New Brunswick.

(*d*) *Limited vote.* Electors have less votes than there are seats. Minority parties, by putting up as many candidates as there are votes, ensure that votes can be cast for all their candidates. Used in Gibraltar and Japan.

(*e*) *Cumulative vote.* Each elector has as many votes as there are seats but can use them as he wishes, i.e. he can give them all to one candidate or can divide them between the candidates. The system was used for school board elections in Britain and is currently used in Illinois.

(*f*) *List systems.* There are a number of systems of proportional representation used in various countries and sometimes advocated for Britain. The basis of all these systems is the party list. Votes are for parties rather than individuals and, in a multi-membered constituency, members are elected on the basis of the number of votes cast for the party.

(*g*) *The West German system.* The system is complicated and involves two different methods of election. Half the seats are directly elected and the other half elected by a system of proportional representation. A variant of this system was suggested by the Conservative Action for Electoral Reform group.

(*h*) *Mixed systems.* A number of suggestions were made which incorporated elements of both the existing (first past the post) system and the single transferable vote system (*see* 19). These were rejected as impracticable.

19. The recommended systems. After considering all the alternatives the Commission recommended two systems for Britain which would also apply to Scotland, Wales and Northern Ireland.

(a) *Single transferable vote* (S.T.V.). In multi-member constituencies each voter has a single vote which can be transferred to other candidates. The elector numbers his choices and, if his first choice does not receive sufficient votes, the vote is transferred to the second choice and so on. The system is said to ensure a fairer vote but this depends upon a number of factors, like the size and distribution of constituencies.

(b) *Additional member system.* This system involves two different elections. The Commission recommended a House of Commons of 640 members: 480 of these would be elected by the present method and the other 160 would be "additional" members. These additional seats would be allocated by a variant of the party list system.

20. Advantages of proportional representation. The Hansard Society Commission felt that any reformed system of elections should incorporate certain features and that the two systems they proposed would meet these requirements.

The requirements of a reformed electoral system are that:

(a) governments should not be able to pursue policies which are against the wishes of the majority of the electorate;

(b) elected government should be able to govern effectively;

(c) minority groups should be adequately represented;

(d) any revised system must be acceptable to the electorate.

The advantages of the proposed reformed systems of election are that:

(a) both systems would prevent minority rule whilst at the same time tend towards single party government;

(b) sizeable minority groups would be catered for;

(c) parties with "considerable but not majority support" would be represented;

(d) the additional member system would allow members not representing constituencies to represent some other interest, territorial or regional;

(e) a Single Transferable Vote (S.T.V.) would more accurately represent party support in the House of Commons;

(f) an additional member system would involve fewer changes in the electoral system than S.T.V., but S.T.V. constituencies, being larger, would return more members;

(g) under both systems the voting would more accurately reflect the wishes of the electorate.

PROGRESS TEST 9

1. The United Kingdom is said to be a single state but it has some unusual features. What are they? **(1)**

2. Give the reasons for devolution. **(3)**

3. Name some alternative forms of devolution. **(4–8)**

4. What did the Kilbrandon Majority Report advocate? **(9, 10)**

5. List the proposals set out in the *Memorandum of Dissent*. **(11, 12)**

6. Describe briefly the government proposals for devolution following the Kilbrandon Report. **(13–15)**

7. Set out the arguments for and against electoral reform. **(16, 17)**

8. List some of the systems of electoral reform and describe that which the Hansard Society recommended. **(18–20)**

CHAPTER X

Supra-National Government

NATURAL LAW

1. Natural law. Supra-national government, that is government by a body larger than the individual state, is not a new idea. It can be traced back to the Roman Emperor Justinian whose *Code*, written in A.D. 529–34, set out the *Jus Gentium*, the law of nations: "that law which natural reason has established among men is maintained equally by all nations, and is called the law of nations, as being the law which all nations adopt".

A theory of natural law founded on this belief was propounded by a fifteenth-century lawyer named Grotius. He saw man as a rational animal, social by nature and endowed with reason. Natural law was self-evident to such a man and was the basis of all national laws. He thus anticipated a form of international law, in that all nations, using the same basis for their laws, would subordinate the laws of their individual nations to the basic law of nature. However, there was not then, and is not now, a complete system of international law, although treaty obligations and international legal bodies now cover certain areas of common legal interest (*see* **2**).

The seventeenth century was a time of great political consciousness and both Hobbes and Locke were, in their own ways, natural law theorists. Hobbes saw man as a desiring animal in conflict with his desires. He needed rules to guide his conduct if he was to live amicably with his fellow men. These rules would be provided by natural law and governed by the social contract (*see* III, **4**). Without this contract he saw the life of man in society as "solitary, poor, nasty, brutish and short". Locke did not take so dismal a view. For him man's natural state was one of moral order with a high degree of co-operation. Man had natural rights and the function of governments and legal systems was to safeguard those rights.

2. Practical application. International law is a twentieth-century phenomenon. There were, of course, treaties and recognised obligations between nations before this time but it was the Hague

Conventions of 1899 and 1907 which produced the Permanent Court of Arbitration to settle disputes between nations. The International Court of Justice was not established in its present form until 1945.

Jurists are divided on whether international law actually exists. There are courts and sanctions for infringements of international law it is true; but no nation can be compelled to submit to the arbitration of an international court unless it agrees to do so. There is no accepted procedure for changing international law other than by treaty. Even the Universal Declaration of Human Rights has no legal standing and is, perhaps, better seen as a statement of moral principles.

The United Nations Organisation, set up in 1945 to replace the League of Nations, was seen by many as a first step towards world government. This was never its intention, however, and it soon became clear that, although it has an important role to play in the preservation of world peace and is able to exert considerable influence from time to time, its object was to encourage co-operation between national governments, not to supplant them.

3. European co-operation. Since the Second World War there has been a rapid growth in the number of international organisations which have been set up to foster co-operation between the nations of Europe. Sometimes this has been for reasons of defence, e.g. N.A.T.O. (*see* (*b*)) but more frequently the reason has been economic.

(*a*) The Brussels Treaty between Benelux, France and Britain set up the Organisation for European Economic Co-operation in 1948 to administer American aid. It widened its scope and changed its name to the Organisation for Economic Co-operation and Development (O.E.C.D.) in 1961. Its members now include most of the Western European nations and the U.S.A., and two of its major goals are a high level of economic growth, and the co-ordination of aid to the developing countries.

(*b*) The North Atlantic Treaty Organisation (N.A.T.O.) was set up by twelve nations for defence purposes in 1949.

(*c*) In 1951 the European Coal and Steel Community (E.C.S.C.) was formed and it was the first of the supra-national organisations with France, West Germany, Italy, Holland, Belgium and Luxembourg (the "Six") as participants. It set up a High Authority to run its affairs and a Court of Justice to adjudicate on its laws (*see* **5(*c*)**).

(*d*) The Western European Union (1954) was formed to co-ordinate military planning, largely because its predecessor, the European Defence Community, failed when France refused to join it.

(*e*) Two important treaties, usually referred to jointly as the Treaty of Rome, were signed in 1957 and came into effect the next year. They provided for the setting up of two bodies:

    (*i*) the European Atomic Energy Community (often called Euratom) which was formed to explore the peaceful uses of atomic energy and

    (*ii*) the European Economic Community (Common Market), a customs union, which Britain first applied to join in 1961.

(*f*) The European Free Trade Association (E.F.T.A.) was formed in 1959 by Britain and other European countries who at that time wished to remain outside the E.E.C. Its aim was to establish free trade in industrial goods between its members.

(*g*) In 1967 Britain, together with Ireland and Denmark, submitted formal applications to join the European Economic Community. General de Gaulle, President of France, objected to Britain's entry and it was not finally agreed until 1971. The Treaty of Accession was signed in 1972 and Britain finally became a member in 1973. Even then the story was not ended. The British government sought to re-negotiate the terms of her entry to E.E.C. in 1975 and, as part of these negotiations, a referendum (the first in Britain's history) was held on 5th June 1975. It was decisively in favour of Britain's continued membership of the E.E.C.

THE EUROPEAN COMMUNITY

4. The European Community. Britain joined the European Community on 1st January 1973 and in doing so became a member of three separate, but related, organisations.

(*a*) The European Coal and Steel Community (E.C.S.C.) (*see* 3(*c*)) abolishes trade restrictions in coal and steel transactions between Community members. It provides funds for capital investment and job creation schemes as well as research programmes and training and redundancy schemes.

(*b*) The European Atomic Energy Community (Euratom) is responsible for the development of the peaceful use of atomic energy. It provides a market for all nuclear materials and is responsible for legislation in relation to nuclear matters. It too has a comprehensive research programme, the latest addition to which was a four-year programme agreed in February 1973.

(c) The European Economic Community (E.E.C.), possibly the best known of the three communities, exists to promote the continued and balanced expansion of members' economies by their progressive harmonisation and integration. Measures to achieve this aim include the creation of a customs union, the removal of barriers to trade, the establishment of external tariffs and the development of a common agricultural policy. Overseas countries which have special links with Community members (e.g. the Commonwealth) may themselves become associated with the E.E.C. and thus obtain some of the benefits available to full members of the Community. Agreements of this nature were signed with some twenty-one members of the Commonwealth and came into effect in 1975.

5. European Community Institutions. The Community consists of nine countries, the original six (*see* 3(c)) plus Britain, Denmark and the Republic of Ireland. It forms a trading area of some 250 million people and accounts for about 40 per cent of the world's trade. Such an organisation must clearly need a number of institutions to regulate various aspects of its work and there are a number of specialised agencies which deal with specific subjects.

(a) *The Council of Ministers.* This is the body which takes the final decisions on all major matters affecting the Community. The Foreign Secretary normally represents Britain on this Council but another senior minister may serve as representative if the subject which the Council is to discuss is in his sphere of interest.

(b) *The Commission.* This is the executive arm of the Council of Ministers. It also formulates policy proposals for submission to the Council and has the responsibility of trying to reconcile the various national differences which occur during policy-making discussions.

(c) *The Court of Justice* adjudicates on measures taken by the Council or Commission and on matters referred to it by the courts or member states. Since its rulings are binding on member countries its functions can be said to infringe national sovereignty (*see* **14**).

(d) *The Assembly* (or European Parliament) has 198 members of whom 67 represent Britain. The Assembly debates major policy issues affecting the Community and may question the actions of either the Council or the Commission. The issue of elections to this Parliament is dealt with in **18**.

6. Finance. The work of the Community is financed by its members, partly from customs revenue and partly from the proceeds of value added tax. The full financial provisions of the Treaty of Accession will come into effect in Britain in 1980 but, in the intervening period, Britain's contribution is based on a proportion of her gross national product, currently about 19 per cent. Part of the case for the re-negotiation of the terms of Britain's entry into the Common Market was that these arrangements were felt to be unreasonable.

IMPLICATIONS OF COMMUNITY MEMBERSHIP

7. Treaty of Accession. The European Communities Act 1972 made two important and far-reaching decisions for Britain.

(*a*) It laid down the terms and conditions for Britain's membership of the Community.

(*b*) It gave the force of law to Community law. This meant that in some cases detailed legislation, which the British Parliament had not approved, had to be accepted in Britain. Other legislation, which Britain could debate but which in the end it might have to accept, would have equal force of law with that passed by Parliament.

8. The implications of these decisions were set out in the *Royal Commission on the Constitution 1969–73, vol. 2, Memorandum of Dissent* (Cmnd. 5460, 1973). The dissenters considered that, at the time that Britain decided to join the European Community, insufficient thought had been given to the constitutional issues involved. It set out the issues as it saw them and suggested methods of dealing with them.

(*a*) The overriding consideration was the question of the sovereignty of Parliament (*see* **14**) which was considered to have been dangerously eroded.

(*b*) Ministerial responsibility (*see* V, **15**) was also in danger since ministers could not be held accountable for decisions made in Brussels.

(*c*) The thirty-six M.P.s who were also members of the European Parliament would have a considerable, if not impossible, burden placed upon them. Part of this burden could be relieved by the creation of a select committee to scrutinise Community legislation.

(*d*) Even with a scrutiny committee there would be such a mass of legislation, the bulk of it delegated, that most of the power would be in the hands of bureaucrats both in Brussels and in London. This would weaken still further the concept of ministerial control.

(*e*) The European Parliament sitting in Luxembourg and Strasbourg has practically no power to override decisions made by the Commission in Brussels.

(*f*) The House of Commons Select Committee on Procedure concluded its report on the European Communities as follows, "the entry of Britain into the Communities presents a profound challenge to many of the established procedures of Parliament *which, if not adequately dealt with, could leave Parliament substantially weaker vis-à-vis the executive*".

9. The White Paper. A White Paper, *Membership of the European Community: Report on Re-negotiation* (Cmnd. 6003) was published in 1975. This recognised the effect of membership of the European Community on the principle of parliamentary sovereignty and set out the government's views. It should be remembered that the White Paper followed the general election of October 1974 in which the Labour Party had undertaken, if returned to power, to hold a referendum on the issue of the terms of Britain's membership of the Common Market.

(*a*) *British law and Community law.* Britain's laws and the laws of the Community would both be applicable in Britain and, in the event of a conflict with national legislation, Britain would be required to give priority to Community legislation (para. 133).

(*b*) *Sovereignty* (*see* **14**). Since Parliament, by the European Communities Act 1972, authorised the application of Community law in Britain it could be argued that Parliament is still supreme because our obligation still depends upon the continuing assent of Parliament (para. 135).

(*c*) *Delegated legislation* (*see* **XIX, 3**). M.P.s take part in the discussions of the European Parliament and are answerable to the British Parliament. The important point, therefore, is that Parliament should have adequate opportunity to make its views known to its thirty-six representatives in Strasbourg (paras. 136, 137).

(*d*) *Scrutiny Committees* were set up in both the House of

Lords and the House of Commons. These committees have the status of select committees and are responsible for examining proposals for delegated legislation, including legislation from the European Parliament, and for advising Parliament of those items which they consider should be debated (paras. 138, 139).

(*e*) *Scrutiny Committee activity.* During its first year of office the Commons Scrutiny Committee examined 366 documents and the Lords Scrutiny Committee examined 397. They recommended that a total of seventy-nine of these should be debated and, at the time the White Paper was published, forty-six of these had been debated (para. 140).

THE REFERENDUM

10. The referendum. The Labour government, having made a political issue of the terms of Britain's membership of the European Community, was pledged to re-negotiate those terms if re-elected. Whilst the re-negotiation was in progress they published a White Paper, *Referendum on U.K. Membership of the European Community* (Cmnd. 5295, 1975) in which they referred to their election promise to "let the people decide" whether to remain in the Common Market. This decision was to be by means of a referendum, itself an innovation in Britain, but a recognised constitutional process in a number of European Community countries. Because of the strong views which had been expressed both for and against remaining in the European Community by leading members of all parliamentary parties it was decided to have a free vote. This meant that, once the government had made its recommendation, members of the government, including cabinet ministers, would not be bound by the convention of collective responsibility and could campaign against the government recommendation.

Although Britain's membership of the European Community was an event of profound significance, affecting the lives of every person in the country, and although the debate had been in progress for some fifteen years there was still a surprising amount of public ignorance and apathy. This was due partly to a tendency of politicians, in the early days, to play down the implications of membership and partly to a lack of interest in complex economic issues.

A popular version of the White Paper was delivered to every household, together with two other documents, one setting out the views of those who believed that Britain should remain in the European Community (pro-marketeers) and one setting out the opposing view (anti-marketeers). Both documents had a statement of the case to be made for their particular point of view and both had the same set of questions to which there were, of course, two sets of answers.

A government information unit was set up to disseminate additional information on the issues involved and to answer queries on the interpretation of the re-negotiated terms.

11. Finance. The government undertook to pay for the popular version of the White Paper, the publication and distribution of the two documents setting out the opposing views and the setting up and running of the information unit. It also promised to consider financial assistance to both pro-marketeers and anti-marketeers to propagate their views.

12. The poll. The question of who should vote on this issue, and how the voting was to be organised, was decided by the simple expedient of making the arrangements basically the same as those for a general election. That is to say that all who were on the electoral roll would be allowed to vote (together with peers in these particular circumstances) and the result would be decided by a simple majority.

13. The question. The exact wording of a question in a poll of this sort can have a decisive effect on the answers and the government gave some thought both to the exact wording and to the problem of the number of questions to be asked. It could be argued, for example, that a single question on a matter of this complexity would be unrealistic, that it simply cannot be answered by a plain "yes" or "no". Equally, it would be impossible to devise a set of questions which would be understood by all sections of the public but which would at the same time produce a clear, unambiguous answer. The government therefore decided that the poll should be restricted to one question, the form of which would be incorporated in the Bill which would be produced as a result of the referendum. The final form in which the question was asked was:

The Government have announced the results of the recent re-negotiation of the U.K.'s terms of membership of the European Community. Do you think that the United Kingdom should stay in the European Community?

PARLIAMENTARY SOVEREIGNTY

14. Sovereignty. It is an established constitutional principle that Parliament is sovereign. This means that it, and it alone, is the supreme legislative body. Acts of Parliament are superior to other forms of law and Parliament itself (the House of Lords) is the highest court of appeal. The principle has been enunciated by constitutional lawyers for many years.

Lord Chief Justice Coke, in the seventeenth century, defined parliamentary sovereignty as follows: "The power and jurisdiction of Parliament is so transcendent and absolute that it cannot be confined, either for causes or persons, within any bounds".

Sir William Blackstone, in his *Commentaries on the Laws of England 1765–1769*, said that Parliament had the power to do "everything that is not naturally impossible".

15. Sovereignty and the European Community. The Treaty of Rome (*see* 3(*e*)) set out its ultimate aim as the achievement of economic and political unity, and such an aim can only be achieved at the expense of a loss of autonomy on the part of the nations which comprise the Community. Does this mean that Britain retains its sovereignty? The answer can be either "yes" or "no", depending upon the extent to which one is prepared to concede that sovereignty is a reality.

(*a*) *Yes.* Britain entered freely into the Common Market and is theoretically free to withdraw at any time she wishes. It has long been held that "Parliament cannot bind its successors" and legislation passed by one administration has, on occasion, been reversed by subsequent governments. The nationalisation, denationalisation and re-nationalisation of iron and steel (*see* XII, 3) is a case in point. Further, the Common Market legislation to which Britain is subject is decided by the European Parliament in which Britain is a full partner and any legislation passed by that body is no more a violation of the principle of sovereignty than is the mass of delegated legislation which Parliament already accepts.

(*b*) *No.* Treaty obligations of one sort and another have already eroded the concept of parliamentary sovereignty. The idea that Parliament cannot bind its successors is a myth. The treaty obligations involved in the Common Market negotiations are, in any case, different in kind to previous treaty obligations. They affect Britain's basic economy and their ramifications are so widespread that a simple withdrawal from the Community is unthinkable. International law, however imprecise as a concept, is a fact and where British legislation conflicts with international law the latter has priority (*see* 9(*a*)). Advocates of the view that Britain cannot retain its sovereignty point out that the transformation of the British Empire into the British Commonwealth gave *de facto* recognition to independent members of the Commonwealth. S. A. de Smith, in *Constitutional and Administrative Law* (Penguin, 1971), quotes the Mauritius Independence Act 1968 which says, "No Act of the Parliament of the United Kingdom passed on or after the appointed day (i.e. independence day) shall extend, or be deemed to extend, to Mauritius as part of its law", and asks "Is Parliament competent simply to resume its legislative sovereignty over Mauritius tomorrow?"

16. Practical limitations. Governments generally pass that legislation which they consider important. The importance may depend upon ideological considerations (a socialist government will attempt to put through socialist measures) or on electoral promises or expediency. But governments, like individuals, must accept from time to time that they are unable to carry out their wishes. In the context of this particular subject they may have to accept that parliamentary supremacy can only be achieved at a price and the price may be too high.

Treaty obligations can be abrogated on the grounds that no government can bind its successors; but to do so, and certainly to do so often, would give Britain a reputation for unreliability and dishonesty such that it would be unable to make future treaties. Further, when Britain approached international bodies for help, as it approached the International Monetary Fund for aid in 1977, such help would not be forthcoming. The offer of aid was, on that particular occasion, dependent upon the Chancellor of the Exchequer agreeing to implement severe fiscal and economic measures.

Constitutional convention (*see* IV, 6) demands that a government must not, in general, exceed the mandate which it receives from the electorate. This does not mean, of course, that it can never do anything other than those things which it promised when it was elected. It does mean that major constitutional changes can only be introduced in a way in which the electorate has a chance to make its views known. This may be by means of a general election, as in the case of the reform of the House of Lords in 1911 (*see* I, **11**), or it may be by some other means, such as a referendum.

Legislation must be capable of enforcement. A law which is widely disregarded is a bad law and will almost certainly be repealed or modified after the next general election. In any event, to become law, a party's programme must be supported by the majority of the party, even though they may consider that the electorate itself is not really ready for it, e.g. the abolition of capital punishment.

17. Public opinion. A final point to be made is that although public opinion has no legal standing and is hard to measure and to define (*see* II, **7**), it is, nevertheless, a fact of political life and is frequently voiced by powerful pressure groups whom no government can afford to ignore. When, therefore, there is a clear public demand for a certain course of conduct by the government the government may, if it can, seek to change public opinion. If it cannot do so, however, then Parliament may find itself bound to enact measures it does not like. Such a situation is incompatible with absolute parliamentary sovereignty.

DIRECT ELECTIONS TO THE EUROPEAN ASSEMBLY

18. The Green Paper. In 1976 the government published a Green Paper, *Direct Elections to the European Assembly* (Cmnd. 6399, 1976). It set out the questions which needed to be decided before Britain could devise a suitable scheme for electing its members to the European Assembly. It had been intended that these elections should be held by 1978 but failure to reach agreement on several major matters has resulted in delays.

(*a*) *Number of members.* Article 138 of the Treaty of Rome 1957 laid down that Britain should be represented by thirty-six members. A draft convention in 1975, which has still to be ratified, increased the number to sixty-seven. This was based on a formula (*see* (*b*)) which is still unratified.

(*b*) *Size of the Assembly.* The proposals on the size and composition of the Assembly have been agreed by the British government but smaller countries, e.g. Luxembourg, may not be adequately represented and final details have not, therefore, been ratified. At present the proposals are as follows:

(*i*) up to one million inhabitants, six seats;

(*ii*) between one and two million inhabitants, six more seats;

(*iii*) up to five million inhabitants, a further seat for every 500,000 inhabitants;

(*iv*) between five and ten million inhabitants, one extra seat for every 750,000 inhabitants;

(*v*) between ten and fifty million inhabitants, one extra seat for every additional million (or part of a million) inhabitants;

(*vi*) over fifty million inhabitants, one extra seat for every 1.5 million inhabitants.

(*c*) *System of election.* The Assembly is to be elected by direct universal suffrage. The actual system of voting, i.e. whether "first past the post", proportional representation, etc., is to be decided by member countries in accordance with the way they normally elect their own parliaments. Britain has opted for the "first past the post" system.

(*d*) *Timing of elections.* Elections could be held for all member nations at the same time or different nations could elect their members at different times. The government favours elections at the same time and makes two further recommendations.

(*i*) Elections should not be held on Sundays.

(*ii*) Elections should, if possible, be held in May so as to co-incide with local elections in Britain.

(*e*) *By-elections.* If a by-election was necessary it would be held in accordance with the normal rules which applied in the state in which it was to be held.

(*f*) *Powers of the Assembly.* When members of the Assembly are directly elected it is intended that they should have greater powers. The nature and scope of these powers has still to be decided.

(*g*) *Membership of national parliaments.* If Assembly members are also members of their national parliament they may well be overburdened. If they are not also members of their national parliament they may well be out of touch with national thinking etc. It should, therefore, be left for individual nations to decide. A dual mandate would appear to be the solution and would be consistent with the following rules of eligibility.

(*i*) Members may not hold office in the government of their country.

(*ii*) As members of the Assembly they would automatically be ineligible for certain positions within the Community. This rule is similar to that which prevents M.P.s in Britain holding an office of profit under the Crown (*see* I, 22).

(*h*) *Status.* Members of the Assembly would have special privileges and immunities, details of which have still to be decided. Members would be accredited and individual states would decide what constituted appropriate credentials. There would be an appeal to either the Court of Justice or to the Assembly itself in cases of doubt.

PROGRESS TEST 10

1. What is meant by "natural law"? (1)

2. List the organisations set up since the Second World War to foster co-operation between European nations. (3–5)

3. What are the implications for Britain of membership of the European Community? (7–9)

4. Why was the re-negotiation of the terms of Britain's entry into the E.E.C. made the subject of a referendum, and what arrangements did the government make to ensure that the issues to be decided were understood by the electorate? (10–13)

5. How is parliamentary sovereignty affected by Britain's membership of the E.E.C.? (14–17)

6. Write a brief note on the questions which were considered in the Green Paper, *Direct Elections to the European Assembly.* (18)

PART THREE
POLITICAL ISSUES

CHAPTER XI
Education

THE PURPOSE OF EDUCATION

1. What is education for? There is, of course, no definitive answer to this question. It depends on many things, personal views, educationalists' ideas, society's demands on its educational system and so on. Above all it is, in the broadest sense, a political question. A general political view of the aims of society, and how it should be governed to achieve those aims, is essential if one is to consider education as an issue in British politics. The basic differences between the Conservative and Labour Parties in the past thirty years have stemmed as much from their differing views of the purpose of education as from detailed arguments as to how policies should be implemented.

The 1977 Green Paper, *Education in Schools: A Consultative Document* (*see* **15**) looked at the ways in which schooling was related to the society which provided it and recognised that one of the functions of education was the preparation of children for their working life when they left school. This emphasis was not accidental. It followed a period of public debate about standards of literacy and the protracted enquiry into the running of the William Tyndale Junior School in London in 1976. The progressive headmaster there had exercised such lax discipline that some local parents refused to let their children attend his school because, it was claimed, they did not even learn how to read and write. Industrialists, too, were complaining that the products of the 1970s educational system were bereft of even the most basic academic skills.

2. Training for industry. The Robbins Report on *Higher Education* (Cmnd. 2154, 1963) laid great stress on scientific and technological studies and was warmly greeted by the Conservative government of the time. In 1964 Labour returned to power and, whilst they accepted the need for technological training, they disagreed with the way it should be provided. Critics claimed that Robbins had concentrated too much on the education of an élite and pointed out that the majority of school-leavers would not go on to higher education. However true this may be, it is hardly fair to Robbins, since his terms of reference were, "To review the pattern of full-time higher education in Great Britain". Those children who did not proceed to higher education were, however, catered for to some extent by the Industrial Training Act 1964 which encouraged those children who had left school without qualifications to study for them during their working hours, with employers paying a levy to help with the cost.

3. Training for life. The view that education is designed to fit a person for his place in society, and that its aims should be to provide for the needs of industry and commerce, is a legitimate one and has many supporters of all shades of political opinion. But it is not the only view. In the 1960s and 1970s an alternative view increased its support. This was that education had been too narrowly defined; that it was in fact about the whole business of living, and that to teach children and young people only the purely academic subject was not enough. This view found expression in a number of ways. For example, liberal studies became an accepted part of the curriculum of most schools and formed the only compulsory paper in a number of otherwise technical courses. The foundation of the Open University in 1970 put the possibility of a university education before large numbers of people who, until that time, had had no opportunity to enjoy education at that level. In 1973 the Russell Report was published. This dealt with adult education which, the report stressed, should be a lifelong process, "broad enough to meet the needs of the adult in our society". The report stressed the importance of the voluntary organisations in the provision of adult education and recommended that much more money should be spent, both in helping these organisations and in providing far more facilities linked to local communities. The report was welcomed by the government but public expenditure cuts soon afterwards found adult education as one of the first casualties.

SCHOOLS AND TEACHERS

4. Selection. The Education Act 1944 had not set out specifically to impose a tripartite system of education but most local education authorities' systems tended to stress the distinctions between primary, secondary and tertiary (further or higher) education. The primary schools for junior and infant children did not present any problems of selection, but when children reached the age of eleven a decision had to be made as to the form that their secondary education should take. Although in theory the three forms, secondary-modern, grammar and technical, had "parity of esteem", in practice it was different. Grammar schools had long been regarded as better than the other two forms and the method used to select children, the eleven plus exam, favoured middle-class children at the expense of those of working-class parentage.

Although in theory it was possible to transfer from one type of secondary school to another at a later date, this rarely happened in practice. What is more, the selection procedures worked as a self-fulfilling prophesy. Children who failed the eleven plus (and educationalists, it should be noted, disapproved of the word "failed" in this context) started life at a disadvantage. The eleven plus relied heavily on I.Q. tests and in 1957 a report from the British Psychological Society threw grave doubts on the validity of such tests. The National Foundation for Educational Research disagreed but, whether the tests were valid or not, there was still a case for abolishing selection at eleven plus. The Labour Party therefore included the abolition of the eleven plus in its manifestos from 1955 to 1966 and, eventually, succeeded in doing so when they were returned to power in 1966.

5. Comprehensive education. The Labour solution to the problem of selection was comprehensive education. All children in the state schools would be transferred to comprehensive schools, large schools containing grammar, secondary and technical "streams", and within these schools children would have a much wider range of subjects to study and would, it was said, have the opportunity to use whatever abilities they possessed. The Conservatives were opposed to comprehensive education partly because there were just not enough buildings capable of housing this type of school but, equally, because they saw it as a "levelling-down" process which deprived the really bright child of a good start in life.

The battle raged for at least ten years. Labour, when in power, sought to advance the spread of comprehensive education and the Conservatives, when the opportunity arose, fought a rear-guard action. In 1965 the Department of Education and Science (D.E.S.) issued a *Circular* (10/65) to local authorities, requiring them to submit plans for (comprehensive) education in their areas. Some, who had no wish to do so, delayed submitting their plans until after the next general election when the Conservatives, true to their election pledges, took steps to halt the movement towards comprehensives. D.E.S. *Circular* 10/70, issued in 1970, also asked for forward plans but did not stipulate that new schools had to be comprehensive. The battle was not finally won until the second half of the decade when, as a result of a D.E.S. *Circular* in 1974, all education authorities accepted that comprehensive education had come to stay (but *see* also VIII, **15**, the Tameside case).

6. Alternatives to comprehensives. The Conservative Party did not just oppose comprehensive education. They put forward positive proposals to ensure that parents had an alternative school to which their children could be sent. They encouraged private education in schools which the English predictably call public schools. They were not part of the state system of education although a proportion of them received help from public funds in return for taking some non-fee-paying secondary pupils. They represent some 5 per cent of all educational provision in Britain and, in 1964, the Labour Party suggested that an educational trust should be formed to integrate the public schools into the state system. The Conservative alternative was the direct grant school. These schools received some help from public funds and were to be encouraged to grow separately alongside the increasing number of comprehensive schools. In the October 1974 election the Labour Party pledged itself to the withdrawal of charitable status from public schools. This would mean that such public schools as survived would find it more difficult to continue.

The debate on the purpose and structure of the educational system went on through the 1960s and 1970s. A group of educationalists opposed to the direction being taken by state education produced a series of Black Papers which were, in effect, replies to the official White Papers. Prominent among the authors of these papers was Dr. Rhodes Boyson M.P., formerly head-master of a comprehensive school and now a Conservative spokesman on education.

7. Teachers. Teachers in state schools are appointed by local authorities through the governing bodies or managers of schools. Throughout the years from 1950 to 1970 the numbers of teachers had been increasing because a reduction in the pupil-teacher ratio was seen as one of the better ways of improving the stand-ards of education which were provided. By 1972 the combined total of full-time and part-time teachers was equivalent to 456,156 full-time teachers. This figure had increased to the equivalent of 520,000 by 1975 and an increasing number of "teachers' aides" were being employed to cope with non-teaching aspects of the work. Both major parties supported the drive for more teachers with better qualifications. Edward Short, Secretary of State for Education in the Labour administration of 1970, set up a select committee to look into the whole question, together with that of the teacher-training institutions.

The next general election put the Conservatives in power and their Secretary of State for Education (Mrs. Thatcher) appointed the James Committee whose Report, in 1972, recommended the pattern of teacher training for the next decade. The findings were, in the main, accepted by the government whose White Paper, *Education: a Framework for Expansion* was published later that year. The main proposals were that the teaching force should by 1981 be expanded to 110 per cent of the 1971 figure, and that teachers should be better trained, leading eventually to an all-graduate profession. Unqualified teachers currently in service were to be given opportunities to gain qualifications and new qualifications, B.Ed and Dip H.E., were to be introduced. There was to be an alteration in the administrative structure of teacher training. This would be expensive but the outlay was considered justified and would reduce the pupil-teacher ratio from 22:1 to 18.5:1 by 1980.

These plans would, it was believed, produce the equivalent of half a million new teachers by 1980 and, given the increases in teachers' pay which had taken place in the late 1960s and early 1970s, it was envisaged that the high drop-out rate from the teaching profession in the first five years would be reduced.

Alas for good intentions. The economic climate of 1976–7 re-sulted in the closure of a number of teacher-training colleges, a reduction in output of others and the situation in which a large number of newly qualified graduate teachers were unable to obtain teaching jobs. In spite of this, the Green Paper in 1977 (*see* 15) talked of improving staffing conditions "as soon as economic conditions allowed". The point was made, however, that new teachers should have experience of employment outside the field of education, so perhaps the newly qualified teachers who were unable to find teaching jobs in 1976–7 may yet be seen as better qualified.

OTHER EDUCATIONAL ISSUES

8. Religious education. Religious education was a contentious issue prior to the Education Act 1944. That Act, broadly in agreement with the spirit of the times, made religious education the only compulsory subject on the curriculum and stipulated that the school day should start with an assembly which included an act of divine worship. The next thirty years saw great changes in society. It became increasingly secular and, particularly in certain areas, the religious background of the children was a non-Christian faith. For growing numbers of people, therefore, the religious element in education seemed out of place.

Interestingly, the main opposition to religious education came almost equally from the churches and the humanist societies, the former because they felt that they were better qualified to provide it and the latter because they saw it as indoctrination and therefore an abuse of the education system. Neither of the main political parties took much notice of the controversy and it was left to head teachers to make their "assemblies" more liberal in outlook than a strict interpretation of the law would justify.

9. Positive discrimination. The intention of the 1944 Act was to give equality of opportunity to all who could benefit from it but, as time went on, it became clear that to give equal opportunity meant giving unequal facilities. The Central Advisory Council for Education produced three reports between 1959 and 1967, Crowther (1959–60), Newsome (1963) and Plowden (1967). In all three they advocated special facilities for various parts of the educational system and in the last, Plowden, they advocated a completely new concept: the Educational Priority Area.

Schools in educationally deprived areas were to be given better facilities than other schools. They would be given priority in the provision of new buildings. Teachers at such schools would be paid higher salaries. Classes would be smaller and a greater proportion of "teachers' aides" would be employed. At the other end of the scale, the small proportion of highly gifted children, for whom the state system of education was inadequate, should also receive special treatment. More research should be undertaken into the needs of such children and into the whole question of priorities in education. The research was subsequently undertaken and published as *Educational Priority: E.P.A. Problems and Policies* (H.M.S.O., 1972). It was supported by the then Conservative government but, as with the White Paper, *Education: a Framework for Expansion*, it was not fully implemented because of the economic difficulties of 1976–7.

10. Alternative education. The writers of the Black Papers had made a number of suggestions as to alternative forms of education within the state system. Some critics went further and suggested that the only real alternative lay outside the system altogether. The Schools Action Union, for example, was founded in the late 1960s to establish an educational system in which the schools were controlled by the pupils, teachers and parents. Ivan Illich, a psychologist, went further and advocated de-schooling by which he meant removing education from educational institutions and operating it through "educational webs" (or life experience). Such a process would be life-long and is seen as a rejection of the values of capitalist society.

11. Raising the school-leaving age. The Education Act 1944 raised the school-leaving age to sixteen. This provision was not, however, implemented until 1972 because there were simply not enough buildings or teachers to cope with the increased school population. When the leaving age was raised it gave rise to two problems, one long-term and one short-term.

The short-term problem was what to do with children who were expecting to leave school at fifteen and suddenly found themselves compelled to spend another year in school. Such children could, and did, exert a disruptive influence out of all proportion to their numbers and traditional academic subjects were not really of interest to them. This increased the emphasis on liberal studies (*see* 3) and, incidentally, the truancy rate particularly in "tough" areas.

The long-term problem concerned patterns of employment. There was a year in which very few children left school, but in subsequent years, when unemployment was increasing, the "school-leavers" formed a significant seasonal addition to the published figures. Rising unemployment may well have had another, unplanned, effect in that if no jobs were available it made more sense for children to stay on at school and gain qualifications which would, it was hoped, improve their chances of a job when they finally left school.

12. School government. For practical purposes state schools are at present governed by the majority party of the local council. This is because local education authorities are responsible for appointing school governors and managers, and such appointments tend to be party political ones. A report, published in September 1977, strongly criticised this state of affairs and recommended a new system of appointing governors and a wider interpretation of their powers. The Report, *A New Partnership for Our Schools* (H.M.S.O., 1977), said that there should be four types of governors who would serve for a period of four years:

(*a*) local authority representatives, appointed by the local authority;

(*b*) school staff, also appointed by the local education authority;

(*c*) representatives of the parents and pupils, elected by an appropriate body;

(*d*) representatives of the community, who would be co-opted by the other governors; the aim would be to ensure that all organisations in a given area who had an interest in educational matters could be considered.

13. The powers of school governors. The Report recommended that the new type of governing body should have much wider powers. The local education authority would still have ultimate authority but it should delegate as much as possible to boards of governors.

(*a*) The curriculum should be decided by governors, not teachers. Teachers would obviously have an important say in such a decision but, since the curriculum is defined as "everything which happens in school", i.e. not just the formal lessons, the responsibility should be shared with parents and the community.

(*b*) Training of governors should be an important part of their service. All new governors should be taught their responsibilities and there should be a regular and recognised series of refresher courses.

(c) Changes in the law would be necessary, both to define the statutory responsibilities of local authorities and to define the status of student-governors. The legislation should take effect within five years.

(d) Boards of government should be mandatory for all schools.

A minority report condemned the Report as impracticable and pointed out that most of the objectives could already be attained by present governors if they chose to interpret their mandate in a different way. Appointment as a school governor, for example, does not have to be a party political nomination.

CURRENT SITUATION AND FUTURE TRENDS

14. Current situation and future trends. There are around 12 million full-time students in Britain. Expenditure in 1976–7 was £7,519 million or over 12 per cent of all public expenditure. This accounts for about 95 per cent of all educational provision. The remaining 5 per cent is provided by non-maintained schools. The educational system in England and Wales is governed by the provisions of the Education Act 1944, that of Scotland by the Education (Scotland) Act 1962 and of Northern Ireland by the Education and Libraries (Northern Ireland) Order 1972. The Scottish and Irish legislation is broadly in line with that of the Education Act 1944.

The Labour Party is committed to a gradual phasing out of the private sector of education and both Labour and Conservative Parties are committed to improvements in the present educational structure when economic circumstances permit. The implementation of a full system of comprehensive education is almost complete and it is unlikely that a future Conservative government would attempt to dismantle the present structure although they have promised, if re-elected, to bring back direct grant schools. A number of pressure groups are concerned with specific aspects of education. For example, the Committee for the Advancement of State Education (C.A.S.E.) is currently concerned with the power of head teachers and advocates that this should be reduced.

15. The Green Paper. A Green Paper, *Education in Schools: A Consultative Document* (Cmnd. 6869) was issued by the Labour government in July 1977. It reiterates the government's intention to complete the process of comprehensive reorganisation and stresses that this is a partnership between education authorities, teachers and churches; all of whom must be held accountable to the communities which they serve. The following points are also covered.

(*a*) *Curriculum.* London authorities should review the curricular arrangements in their areas, to ensure that what is taught in schools is related to the needs of the late 1970s. This review would recognise that we live in a multicultural, multiracial society and includes special arrangements to review the teaching of Welsh in Welsh schools. The National Union of Teachers objected to the review of the curriculum since, in their view, this was the province of the teaching profession, not the administrators.

(*b*) *Standards.* The document recognises the importance of standards and methods of measuring them but rejects what it describes as, "rigid and uniform national tests".

(*c*) *Transition between schools.* The problems which are created when parents move from one educational area to another are recognised and local education authorities are urged to look closely at their procedures to ensure that children in this situation do not suffer educational disadvantage as a result.

(*d*) *Minority groups.* The special needs of ethnic minorities and handicapped children should be investigated.

(*e*) *Teachers.* In spite of a temporary glut of teachers from training colleges who are unable to find teaching jobs the document emphasises the need for more, and better trained, teachers. It sees teaching as an all-graduate profession and urges that new teachers should have had experience of the world outside the classroom. In-service training is not neglected. Some 4,500 teachers took part in such training in 1977, and this figure is to be increased to 18,500 by 1981.

(*f*) *Links with industry and commerce.* Links with industry already exist in some areas. The document suggests that they should be extended and improved so that what is taught in schools is of benefit to school-leavers when they come to find work. This may well involve an increase in the scope of the Careers Service which should be available to school children from the age of thirteen.

(*g*) *Links with the community.* This part of the document is closely linked to the recommendations of the Taylor Report, *A New Partnership for Our Schools* (*see* **12**), and stresses the responsibility of local education authorities for encouraging parental and community involvement.

TABLE V.   EDUCATIONAL LANDMARKS 1944–77

Party in power	Act, report etc.
Coalition	Education Act 1944
Labour	Percy Report (Higher Technological Education) 1945
	Urwick Report (Education for Management) 1947
Conservative	Albermarle Report (Youth Service) 1958
	Crowther Report (15- to 18-year-olds) 1959
	Education (Scotland) Act 1962
	Newsome Report (Secondary Education) 1963
	Robbins Report (Higher Education) 1963
Labour	D.E.S. *Circular* 10/65 (Comprehensives) 1965
	Plowden Report (Primary Schools) 1967
	Report of the Public Schools Commission 1968
	Report (*Youth and Community Work in the 1970s*) 1969
Conservative	Open University founded (1970)
	D.E.S. *Circular* 10/70 (Comprehensives) 1970
	Halsey Report (Educational Priority Areas) 1972
	Education and Libraries (Northern Ireland) Order 1972
	James Report (Teacher Training) 1972
	White Paper (*Education: a Framework for Expansion*) 1972
	Russell Report (Adult Education) 1973
Labour	White Paper (*Education: Disadvantages and the Needs of Immigrants*) 1974
	D.E.S. *Circular* 10/74 (Comprehensives) 1974
	Taylor Report (*A New Partnership for our Schools*) 1977
	Green Paper (*Education in Schools: A Consultative Document*) 1977

16. Summary. Table V summarises the major developments in the field of education between the Act of 1944 and the Green Paper of 1977.

PROGRESS TEST 11

1. What factors need to be taken into account in deciding what education is for? **(1)**

2. How does education train for (*a*) industry and (*b*) life? **(2, 3)**

3. What do you understand by primary, secondary and tertiary education; and how are these related to comprehensive education? **(4, 5)**

4. What alternatives are there within the state educational system? **(6)**

5. What did the White Paper, *Education: A Framework for Expansion* propose? **(7)**

6. What is meant by "positive discrimination"? **(9)**

7. Define "de-schooling". **(10)**

8. What proposals did the Report, *A New Partnership for our Schools* make about school governors? **(12, 13)**

9. List the main points in the Green Paper, *Education in Schools: A Consultative Document*. **(15)**

CHAPTER XII

Industry and Employment

NATIONALISATION

1. Nationalisation (*see* also XIX, **10**). The question of the owner-ship of the means of production is, perhaps, that on which the two major parties are most widely separated. Clause IV of the Labour Party Constitution commits the party to "the best avail-able system of popular administration and control of each in-dustry or service". To most socialists this invariably means con-trol by the government. The Conservative philosphy stresses the encouragement of individual effort and the responsibility of government is to refrain from interference in the lives of its citizens. The issue of nationalisation has therefore figured in every election from 1945 onwards.

If the Labour Party sees wholesale nationalisation as a matter of principle (although this principle seems to have been eroded in recent years), the Conservatives have never claimed such justifi-cation for their opposition. Indeed, the earlier nationalisation measures, such as the creation of the London Passenger Transport Board in 1933, were the work of a Conservative government. Their objection is far more pragmatic: it simply does not work. All managers of nationalised industries have two guiding principles which the opponents of nationalisation claim are incompatible.

(*a*) *Accountability*. The manager of a nationalised industry has day-to-day control but he is answerable to a minister, and thus to Parliament, for major decisions. His accountability to Parlia-ment however differs in kind from that of a director to his share-holders.

(*b*) *Efficiency*. He is required, taking one year with another, to make a profit or at least break even. This may mean that he needs more independence than Parliament is prepared to give him. Dr. Beeching, when responsible for the running of British Rail in the 1950s, was unable to implement some of the changes which he wished to introduce because the railways had a wider function than that of a commercial organisation, namely that of providing a service to the public. It was felt that the cuts which he proposed would unduly restrict the service.

2. Mines. The National Coal Board was created by the Coal Industry Nationalisation Act 1946 in response to Labour's election pledges. There were good historical reasons why the mines were the first to be nationalised. They had borne the brunt of massive unemployment in the 1930s and had long and close ties with the Labour Party, indeed one commentator goes so far as to say that "in some constituencies the National Union of Mineworkers *is* the Labour Party" (R. Rose, *Politics in England*, Faber, 1965). Like subsequent nationalised industries they were required to be economically viable and like them they did not always succeed. In 1967, for example, the Coal Industry Act authorised payment of £47 million to relieve the hardship caused to miners by the decreasing demand for coal. There was no serious demand for the mining industry to be de-nationalised, not even during the general election of February 1974, when the Conservatives made the miners' pay claim an election issue. Labour, whilst not making an issue specifically of the miners, did pledge at the same election, that if they were returned they would extend "public ownership" (which was not necessarily the same as nationalisation) to other sectors of industry.

3. Iron and steel. The nationalisation of the iron and steel industries caused the most protracted fight, not only between the major parties but among Labour supporters and supporters of the industry. The 1945 (Labour) Cabinet was divided between those who felt that a socialist principle was at stake and those who felt that, regardless of principles, there were sound economic arguments for not nationalising. The iron and steel industries were, however, nationalised and the Iron and Steel Corporation took up its duties in 1949.

The fight against nationalisation was not yet over. The British Iron and Steel Federation, representing the companies which had been nationalised, and Aims of Industry, an organisation dedicated to the principles of free trade, mounted a campaign against nationalisation in general and the nationalisation of iron and steel in particular. The election of February 1950 saw Labour returned with a reduced majority. It was sufficient to enable the government to consolidate its position but not enough to convince the iron and steel trades that there was a clear public demand for nationalisation. They therefore refused to suggest names for the new Iron and Steel Corporation and discouraged their members from serving on it. The general election of 1951 brought the Conservatives back into power and the Bill to denationalise the industry became law in 1953 in fulfilment of their election pledges. The Labour Party included the re-nationalisation of the iron and steel industry in their manifestos for the elections of 1955 and 1959 but it was not until they were returned to power in 1964 that they were able to fulfil them.

The Iron and Steel Act 1967 did not re-nationalise the entire industry, however; instead it created the British Steel Corporation from fourteen major companies, leaving the remainder of the industry in private hands. Thus the "mixed economy", partly public and partly private, was reconciled with Labour's aims of the best obtainable system of popular administration and control.

TRADE UNIONS

4. Trade unions and the Labour Party. The relationship between the trade union movement and the Labour Party has always been close; indeed the Labour Party was born of the desire of the trade unions to be adequately represented in Parliament. The unions give a Labour administration a great deal of support but there is a price to be paid. Acting together as the Trades Union Congress (T.U.C.) they can form an extremely powerful pressure group. Some of the bitterest arguments about the relationship have been on what critics describe as the undue influence which trade unions wield in public affairs. The T.U.C. represents over twelve million workers (the Transport and General Workers Union alone has over 1.5 million members) and charges of undue influence are hardly surprising.

One of the major issues of the 1945 election was the right of trade unionists to strike. This right had been severely curtailed by the Trade Disputes Act 1927, a hastily conceived piece of legislation rushed through after the General Strike of 1926. Labour pledged itself to repeal this Act if it was returned to power and the Trade Disputes and Trade Unions Act 1945 completely repealed the previous legislation. This Act gave unions greater autonomy in the ordering of their affairs and appeared to open the door to a wide range of industrial action.

5. The Donovan Commission. Neither the Labour Party nor the Conservative Party were happy with the new status of the unions, although they now had more clearly defined rights to strike and were able to take part in peaceful picketing. The 1960s saw an unprecedented number of unofficial strikes which damaged not only the economy but more effectively the trade union movement itself. The Donovan Report (*Royal Commission on Trade Unions and Employers' Associations* 1968, Cmnd. 3623) was concerned to define the rights and responsibilities of both unions and employers' organisations. Collective bargaining was a particularly thorny problem. Whilst workers and employers could, and did, arrive at collective agreements they were not legally binding. Although the majority of the Commission felt that they should be binding, as was the practice in most western countries, they did not make a specific recommendation to this effect. It was left to the Labour government to produce a White Paper which proposed legislation broadly on the lines suggested by Donovan.

6. The White Paper. The White Paper, *In Place of Strife*, was issued in 1969 and proposed a number of measures by means of which the unions would be encouraged to regulate their affairs in the public interest. Three items in particular were singled out for early legislation.

(*a*) A Commission on Industrial Relations (C.I.R.) was to be set up, together with an Industrial Board.

(*b*) Inter-union disputes would be referred to the Industrial Board.

(*c*) In the case of an unofficial strike the Secretary of State could impose a "cooling-off period" of up to twenty-eight days in order to give the recognised negotiating machinery a chance to work.

A fourth proposal, that the Industrial Board should have power to impose financial penalties on unions, employers or individuals who "broke the rules" did not figure in the original plans for the Bill, neither did two further proposals.

(*d*) In the case of a threatened official strike which appeared to be a threat to public interest the Secretary of State could require the union to ballot its members on the question of strike action before a decision was taken.

(*e*) A registrar of trade unions and employers' associations would be appointed and unions would be required to submit their rules to the registrar, who would decide if they were fair and adequate.

7. The response to the White Paper. Both the T.U.C. and the national executive of the Labour Party rejected the proposals, as did a fairly substantial number of Labour M.P.s. A special T.U.C. Conference in rejecting the government's proposals endorsed an alternative scheme which they called, "Programme for Action". This programme put the responsibility for disciplining trade unions on to the T.U.C., specifically the T.U.C.'s General Council. The Council would have power to suspend from membership of the T.U.C. those unions which did not comply with the rules. Neither the government nor the T.U.C. were happy with this stalemate but they finally worked out a compromise which would have become law had the Labour government stayed in office.

8. The Industrial Relations Act 1971. June 1970 saw the return of a Conservative government pledged to do something about the industrial situation. Their solution was embodied in the short-lived Industrial Relations Act 1971. The Act set up the National Relations Court (N.I.R.C.) which, it should be noted, was a fully recognised legal court specialising in industrial relations matters. It also accepted the idea of a registrar and, a new departure in trade union practice, stipulated that collective agreements would be legally enforceable unless they contained a clause to the contrary. The Act reintroduced the idea of a "cooling-off" period and the compulsory strike ballot. A Code of Practice was introduced and a number of "unfair industrial practices" were defined. Unions which indulged in these practices could be fined by the N.I.R.C.

Reaction to the Act was very strong. The public in general thought that the Act was reasonable and should help industrial relations. The unions generally, and the T.U.C. in particular were opposed to it from the start and, by refusing to register under the requirements of the Act and by "writing in" to agreements that they were not to be legally enforceable, they made it extremely difficult to enforce. Their influence on the Labour Party ensured that repeal of the Act was included in the manifesto and this in fact was one of the first steps to be taken when the Labour Party was returned to power in February 1974.

At the next general election (October 1974) both Labour and Conservatives pledged themselves to "do something about the unions", since public opinion felt that this was necessary. The Conservatives had decided not to try to reintroduce the Industrial Relations Act (politics is the art of the possible) but concentrated instead on the emotive issue of picketing during a strike. Labour for their part had a new measure, the Trade Union and Labour Relations Act 1974, which had been subject to amendment by the House of Lords. Their manifesto promised to complete the work done in the previous Parliament and, incidentally, to curb the power of the Lords still further if, in their opinion, this should be necessary. In the event it was not necessary because the Lords' amendments, although not accepted in full, were considered and some were incorporated in a modified form while others were dealt with by further legislation (*see* 9).

9. Trade Union and Labour Relations Acts. The Trade Union and Labour Relations Acts 1974 and 1976 were in two parts and had two purposes. The principle Act, which was passed in July 1974, repealed the Industrial Relations Act 1971 and restored some of the traditional powers of the trade unions and employers' associations. The amending Act, The Trade Union and Labour Relations (Amendment) Act 1976, was passed in March 1976 and legislated on the thorny question of the "closed shop". The Act also provided for a charter on press freedom, a matter on which the National Union of Journalists, among others, had been pressing for some time. Other provisions included the following.

(*a*) *Peaceful picketing.* This was to be legally permissible so long as it was, "solely in order peacefully to obtain or communicate information or persuade someone to work or not to work" (section 15).

(*b*) *Collective agreements.* Agreements made between December 1971 and September 1974, i.e. when the Industrial Relations Act was in force, would not now be legally enforceable (section 18).

(*c*) *Code of Practice.* The Code of Practice introduced under the Industrial Relations Act 1971 (*see* 8) was replaced by new legislation, the Employment Protection Act 1975, which regulated collective bargining and set up the Advisory Conciliation and Arbitration Service on a statutory basis. It also extended the powers of wages councils and dealt with terms and conditions of employment.

EMPLOYMENT DISADVANTAGE

10. The disadvantaged. There are a number of people who have particular difficulties in getting or keeping work. They rarely become a political issue in the way that trade unions do. They are usually minority groups and their disadvantages may well be taken for granted by society as a whole until something happens to turn the spotlight on them, such as pressure group activity or the effect of changing social *mores*.

11. The disabled. The disabled were one of the earliest groups to have their particular employment problems recognised. The Disabled Persons (Employment) Act 1944 was passed during the spate of welfare legislation which followed the Second World War. There were, of course, some war disabled but they alone would not have been the cause of such legislation. The immediate post-war period was one of economic expansion and full employment. It was practical and praiseworthy, therefore, to make special provision for those who would otherwise be at a disadvantage in their search for work. The main provisions of the Act were as follows.

(*a*) At every employment exchange there was to be a Disablement Resettlement Officer (D.R.O.), a specialist with particular responsibility for the disabled.

(*b*) A quota system was introduced, whereby all firms employing more than twenty people had to ensure that at least three per cent of their employees were disabled people. The scheme lingered on for a number of years but was never effectively enforced, mainly because there were insufficient disabled people with appropriate skills.

(*c*) Certain occupations, e.g. electric lift attendants and car-park attendants, were to be reserved for disabled workers. This provision was rather more successful than the quota system.

(*d*) Industrial Rehabilitation Units (since renamed Employment Rehabilitation Centres) were set up in twenty-five centres of industry throughout the country. They offered some 14,000 places per year and their aim was to help persons who had been unemployed for a long time because of disablement or sickness to regain sufficient general health and fitness for work.

(*e*) Sheltered employment was provided for those whose skills could not command an economic wage in normal industry.

(*f*) Remploy, a government subsidised company, was established to provide employment for disabled persons.

One of the most consistent campaigners for the disabled is a self-help group called Disablement Income Group. Their campaigns have been particularly effective in the field of disability pensions and allowances and they have been aided by a number of M.P.s. Some, like Jack Ashley, M.P. for Stoke on Trent South, are themselves disabled.

12. Ethnic minorities. Ethnic minorities did not really become an issue until the early 1960s (*see* XIV, 1) when increasing numbers of coloured immigrants in certain areas caused a certain amount of social unrest. Some had come into this country with qualifications which they then found were not acceptable. Others had difficulty in getting work because of fear, either by employers or work-mates, of "problems" which would be created. These matters came to a head in 1968 when the Race Relations Act of that year made discrimination on the grounds of colour a punishable offence. The Act provided redress for coloured workers who felt that they had been victimised at work because of their colour. It was not entirely successful because, it was alleged, most discrimination was covert and therefore difficult to prove. There is some evidence that, in spite of further legislation, this discrimination continues, particularly among coloured school-leavers who were grossly over-represented among the unemployed in the 1970s.

13. Women at work. Women have, for many years, comprised about a third of the total work force. Until the outbreak of the Second World War, and for some time afterwards, they tended to be predominantly single women who gave up work on marriage. The needs of war-time production created a demand for more women workers. Nurseries were provided so that married women were able to work. After the war many such nurseries were closed, and places in the remaining ones were in short supply and tended to be reserved for women who needed to work, e.g. deserted wives and unmarried mothers. From 1951 onwards the proportion of married women in the work-force started to increase and, in 1977, nearly half the total number of married women are in employment. Their needs for special arrangements like day nurseries and flexible working hours were, however, only slowly recognised and it was not until the early 1970s that demands for true equality were taken seriously by the politicians.

The Equal Pay Act was passed in 1970 although it did not come into force until the end of 1975. It stipulated that men and women doing the same jobs should be paid the same rate; individuals who felt they were being unfairly treated could complain to an industrial tribunal. An Industrial Arbitration Board (later the Central Arbitration Committee) was set up with power to resolve disputes about collective agreements containing differences in rates of pay between men and women. The effects of the Equal Pay Act on female employment are uncertain. Some employers, faced with the necessity of paying the same rates to men and women, may have preferred to employ men, on the basis that they would be more reliable since they would not need to have time off if children were ill and in similar domestic crises. The idea that men would be more reliable had little basis in fact but it was widely held and probably resulted in a reduction in the number of jobs open to women.

The Sex Discrimination Act 1975 made it unlawful for an employer to treat a woman, on the ground of her sex, less favourably than a man in respect of employment and other matters. As with the Equal Pay Act, individuals who feel unfairly treated can complain to an industrial tribunal. The Act set up an Equal Opportunities Commission charged with working towards the elimination of discrimination and keeping both the Equal Pay Act and the Sex Discrimination Act under review. The Commission also had powers to investigate cases of alleged discrimination and, in certain circumstances, to assist individual complainants. The legislation also covered job advertisements and demanded that they were not to stipulate the sex of prospective applicants, unless this was a relevant factor. A male go-go dancer might well be considered a contradiction in terms but there was no reason, on grounds of sex, why a woman should not drive a lorry. "Man wanted, lorry driver" therefore gave way to "Person wanted, able to drive a lorry". The trend went to ridiculous lengths, for example, "Person Friday" (for an office junior) and "Foreperson" (for a factory supervisor).

The combined effect of the two Acts was to ensure a great deal of ostensible equality. Whether it created an equal society is still an open question. Critics of the social scene point to the rising crime rate, the break-up of family patterns and the increasing instability of marriage as an institution and ask whether these problems are not the unwanted concomitants of a policy of equality.

UNEMPLOYMENT

14. Unemployment. The spectre of widespread unemployment loomed large during the inter-war years. Although it was only

2 per cent at the close of the First World War it reached a peak of 22.1 per cent in 1932 and was still 11.6 per cent at the outbreak of the Second World War. By the time the war had ended the figure was reduced to around 1.2 per cent and it stayed below 3 per cent until after the mid-1960s (figures from *Trends in British Society since 1900*, A. H. Halsey (ed.), Macmillan, 1972). Post-war governments had therefore no need to worry about the problems of unemployment and legislation was concerned with such matters as the special problems of the disabled worker, the various schemes of training and the re-deployment of redundant workers.

The first post-war occasion on which unemployment became an election issue was in 1959 and the unemployment rate at that time was only 2.3 per cent. This however represented a doubling of the rate since the last general election and it was clear, both from election campaigns and from public opinion polls in the late 1950s and early 1960s, that this was becoming an important political issue; indeed it appeared in some guise in every subsequent election. From 1970 onwards it remained a very live issue. By July 1976 the unemployed figure had risen to 5.4 per cent and by July 1977 to just under 7 per cent.

The rates varied considerably between regions. Northern Ireland, Scotland and Wales had a higher unemployment figure, as did the North-east and Merseyside. The south-east of England had a consistently lower figure than the rest of the country.

15. Measures to combat unemployment. By the mid-1970s the problem of unemployment had become an urgent priority. Following are some of the measures adopted to deal with the problem.

(*a*) *European Social Fund.* As a member of the European Economic Community, Britain was able to apply for grants from the European Social Fund, which exists primarily to support schemes connected with employment and training. The fund provided over £45 million in 1973, £25.9 million in 1974, £23.9 million in 1975 and £44.3 million in 1976. All this money was spent, directly or indirectly, on the alleviation of unemployment. In 1976 allocations included:

(*i*) training and transfer schemes for Great Britain and Northern Ireland, £3.9 million;

(*ii*) training of unemployed in assisted areas in Great Britain, £17.9 million;

(*iii*) rehabilitation, particularly amongst the young people, in Northern Ireland, £5.6 million.

(*b*) *Job subsidies.* Small manufacturing firms in areas of high unemployment were able to claim a subsidy of £20 per week for every extra job they could provide.

(*c*) *Job Creation Programmes.* These programmes were administered by Community Relations Councils and financed by the Manpower Services Commission. In 1976/77 the programme provided 231 jobs at a total cost of £260,384.

(*d*) *Job Release Scheme.* Under this scheme the government paid an allowance of £23 per week (raised to £26.50 in November 1977) to anyone within a year of the official retiring age (65 for men and 60 for women) who was prepared to retire early so that their job could be taken by somebody who was unemployed.

Further measures were planned for 1978. They include a Youth Opportunities Programme which would provide jobs for 23,000 young people. A similar programme, the Special Temporary Employment Programme (S.T.E.P.), would provide temporary jobs for adults over nineteen years old who have been unemployed for long periods. S.T.E.P. superseded the Job Creation Programme in 1978.

16. A planned economy. One method of controlling unemployment is by means of a planned economy, and both major parties have accepted that governments have a responsibility for the economic well-being of the country. They disagree fundamentally however on how that responsibility is to be discharged. Broadly the Labour view would be that the state has a right, indeed a duty, to intervene and the Conservative view is that, whilst the state has a responsibility for the economic well-being of its citizens, this responsibility is best discharged by a policy of non-intervention. Public opinion polls in the 1950s and 1960s showed that electors tended to support those parties whose economic policies were thought to be most effective.

(*a*) *Wage restraint.* In 1948 the Labour government persuaded the T.U.C. to accept a policy of voluntary restraint by its members. The policy worked for two years but it then became clear that prices were rising faster than wages and, by 1950, the T.U.C. had abandoned the policy in favour of free collective bargaining. It was a Conservative Chancellor of the Exchequer, Selwyn Lloyd, who introduced the first pay pause (from July 1961 to March 1962) and successive governments have tried, with varying degrees of success, to insist on more government control of wages policies.

(b) *Control of prices.* One of the problems of wage restraint is that it can only be successful if prices are also controlled and the National Board for Prices and Incomes was a Labour attempt (in 1965) to control both. It lasted for five years and it has been estimated that during its lifetime it kept incomes down by about one per cent per year. It was less successful in keeping down prices and was, therefore, disbanded by the Conservative government of 1970. They tried to introduce a policy of wage restraint which was rejected by the T.U.C. The next major development was a ninety day standstill on both prices and incomes (including incomes from dividends) but this measure, introduced in November 1972, was not re-introduced in 1973 because, whilst successful in reducing wage increases, it had done nothing to stem the increase in prices. The Labour government of October 1974 therefore promised to impose tighter controls on price increases and to ensure that the state had a greater say in the running of major industries.

(c) *State control of industry.* Nationalisation has always been socialist policy (*see* 1) but the Labour government of October 1974 proposed a number of other measures to control the economy and thus, it was hoped, reduce the problems of unemployment. These measures included:

(*i*) planning agreements with industry to ensure that industrial development was in the national interest;

(*ii*) the setting-up of a National Enterprise Board and more government control of companies which received government grants. In particular the vast government investment in North Sea oil would be reflected in a greater degree of participation by the government in the running of the enterprise;

(*iii*) strengthening of the role of the National Economic Development Council and of the individual industry economic development committees.

17. Why combat unemployment? The question may seem superfluous but there are critics who maintain that a degree of unemployment is good for the economy because fear of the sack would make workers work better. Karl Marx, for example, believed that a "reserve army of the unemployed" would enable capitalist employers to exploit their workers by paying lower wages. The truth may well be the opposite. Inflation encourages unemployment. Conversely, full employment is a valuable protection against the evils of inflation. The unemployed still need to be maintained and this puts a strain on insurance and supplementary benefit funds. A man out of work for a long period becomes demoralised. His skills may well become out of date and he himself may give up all hope of ever becoming employed again.

PROGRESS TEST 12

1. Why has the issue of nationalisation figured in general elections since 1945?   **(1)**

2. Give an account of the nationalisation of (*a*) mines and (*b*) iron and steel.   **(2, 3)**

3. What was the purpose of the Donovan Commission?   **(5)**

4. *In Place of Strife* produced some criticism and so did the Industrial Relations Act 1971. What were the criticisms and in what way did the legislation set out to answer them?   **(6–8)**

5. What were the provisions of the Trade Union and Labour Relations Acts?   **(9)**

6. List the disadvantages suffered in the field of employment by (*a*) the disabled, (*b*) ethnic minorities, and (*c*) women.   **(11–13)**

7. List some of the measures taken to combat unemployment.   **(15)**

8. In what ways can the economy of Britain be said to be planned?   **(16)**

CHAPTER XIII

Housing and the Environment

THE HOUSING PROBLEM

1. The problem. Housing has been a major political issue throughout the twentieth century. Both major parties have stressed some aspect of it in their manifestos since the Second World War. The problems which arose have changed over the years and the stance of the parties has altered as the problems changed; but the central problem, which has been documented by surveys, statistics and manifestos, was set out by J. Greve in a paper published in 1965 entitled, *Private Landlords in England*. Everybody needs housing:

    (*a*) of a reasonable standard;

    (*b*) at a rent they can afford; and

    (*c*) with security of tenure.

2. Housing of a reasonable standard. Standards vary, both over time and by regions. What might have been acceptable in a prewar rural area is unlikely to be acceptable in a post-war metropolitan area. Property which is officially designated as unfit for habitation may be stoutly defended by those who see it as their home. During the 1930s all local authorities had slum clearance programmes but national statistics were not kept until the *Government Social Survey*, 1947. It was the census of 1951, with its questions about the basic amenities in housing, which first enabled reliable estimates of housing needs to be calculated. Calculating the needs was one matter; meeting them was another. The two major parties differed fundamentally over how this was to be done.

3. Housing needs. In 1945 both major parties stressed the need for more, and better housing at a price that people could afford. The Labour solution was for the local authorities to take over the private housing sector and the Conservative answer was mainly in the encouragement of private building, most of which was destined for owner-occupation. The regulation of rents was tried by both parties, the Rent Acts of 1954 and 1957 being Conservative measures and the 1965 Act being passed by a Labour government. The pre-war (1939) figure for houses scheduled for slum clearance under local authority programmes was around 400,000. During the war there were more important priorities than slum clearance and enemy action had added to the number of houses needing to be replaced. Houses were getting older and, since there had been very little house-building during the war, this backlog had to be added to the slum clearance and replacement figures. The 1951 census produced an estimate of 845,000 slum dwellings out of a total of some thirteen million dwellings; but these replacements would only touch the fringe of the problem since housing standards had risen and pre-war housing standards were no longer seen as acceptable.

4. Housing tenure. The *Social Survey* in 1947 had distinguished three main types of tenure, owner-occupation, renting from local authorities and "other tenures". This last category consisted mainly of those who rented their dwellings from private landlords. There has been a steady increase in the proportion of owner-occupiers and an equally steady decline in the number renting from private landlords (*see* Table VI).

TABLE VI.   PERCENTAGE OF THE POPULATION IN
VARIOUS TYPES OF TENURE

	1947	1975
Owner-occupiers	27	50
Public housing authorities	12	31
Other tenancies	61	19

Source: Annual Abstract of Statistics, 1976.

HOME OWNERSHIP

5. Home ownership. The immediate post-war stock of some thirteen million dwellings was increased to over twenty millions by 1977. Nearly seventeen million of these were in England, a million in Wales, nearly two million in Scotland and the rest in Northern Ireland (figures from *Britain 1977*) and the proportion of owner-occupiers is still increasing. There are a number of reasons for this: the inability of local authorities to provide for all housing wants (which are not, of course the same as housing needs), the declining rate of provision of places to rent in the private sector and the public demand for "a home of one's own" to which politicians must pay heed.

The cost of mortgages fluctuates with the general conditions of the money market and calls for reductions in government expenditure may mean less money available from local authorities for this purpose under the Housing (Financial Provisions) Act 1958. Building societies too may need to be subsidised if they are to provide housing loans at a price that people can afford when interest rates are increasing. The Conservatives were responsible for the 1958 Act but the price of houses doubled between 1963 and 1973 and has been rising steadily since then.

Those hardest hit by these increases are the poorer sections of the community and, in particular, young couples setting up home and buying a house for the first time. The option mortgage scheme introduced by the Labour government of 1968 was designed to help those who were unable to pay the interest on mortgages which, at that time, was about 8 per cent. Under this scheme, instead of receiving income-tax relief on mortgage (which benefits those with sufficient income to pay a fairly high proportion in taxes) they received a subsidy which reduced the rate of mortgage interest which they paid. Whilst this scheme has not been as widely used as had been intended it still accounted for subsidies of the order of £106 million in 1976.

6. Improvement. Slum clearance and similar schemes had helped the housing situation in one way, in that it had improved the quality of the housing which was available. It had aggravated the situation in another way, however, in that it reduced the stock of houses. The government therefore gave some thought to increasing the life of older properties by means of subsidies to the owners.

The White Paper, *Old Houses into New Homes* (Cmnd. 3602, 1968) had indicated what could be done to older properties both to extend their life and to bring them into line with higher standards of housing. Although the Housing Acts of 1957 and 1961 had given local authorities powers to provide grants for the improvement of property in their areas this aspect had not received sufficient emphasis. The Housing Act 1969 implemented some of the proposals of the White Paper, modified the system of grants, and gave local authorities power to declare areas for general improvement. This meant that not only could owners receive grants to enable them to provide amenities in individual dwellings but also the council could provide general amenities in an area which might otherwise deteriorate. Grants were available to cover up to half the cost of providing specified amenities in individual dwellings. These grants enabled owners to install basic amenities like fixed baths, lighting and hot and cold water supplies.

The scheme ran into an unexpected problem in the 1970s when improvement grants came increasingly to be paid to speculators who, having renovated a house or block of flats with the aid of a grant, were able, after an interval, to make a large profit out of the enhanced property. Although one purpose of the Act, that of conserving older property which still had some useful life, was fulfilled, the second purpose, that of providing accommodation to those who could not afford dearer properties, was partially defeated.

The houses built in the immediate post-war years were mainly local authority property (80 per cent of all housing came into this category during the period 1948–52), the majority of it being for letting. Local authorities were subsidised by the government and, until the advent of the Conservative administration in 1951, private building was restricted. The subsidies to local authorities continued until 1956 when the Housing Subsidies Act of that year restricted subsidies to special purposes such as slum clearance and the building of new towns.

RENTED PROPERTY

7. Rent restriction. Private property rents had been frozen in 1939 and remained so for a decade after the war. The Housing Repairs and Rent Act 1954 allowed an economic rent to be charged for new houses but it was not until the Rent Act 1957 that serious consideration was given to the thousands of houses up and down the country which had been allowed to fall into disrepair. Such houses added to the number of slums or potential slums simply because their owners could not afford to pay for repairs out of the rents that they were allowed to charge. The typical owner in the decade 1955–65 was, incidentally, more likely to be an individual than a property company. A study by B. J. Cullingworth in Lancaster, quoted by L. J. Macfarlane in *Issues in British Politics Since 1945* (Longman, 1975), sees the typical landlord of the time as an old lady owning only a very small amount of property, possibly only one house which she had inherited, the rent of which was under 75 pence per week. She had neither the ability nor the interest to maintain it.

The control of rents, and the associated problem of security of tenure, applied to both furnished and unfurnished tenancies. However, both aspects were stressed much more in the case of unfurnished than furnished tenancies. It was not until 1974 (*see* 9) that tenants of furnished accommodation received equal consideration.

8. The Rent Acts 1957 and 1965. The Rent Act 1957 released all but the houses with low rateable value from the rent restrictions which had been imposed during the war. It was hoped that, since landlords would now be able to charge a more economic rent, there would be more houses available to rent in the private sector. It was also anticipated that the charging of economic rents would cause those people who were living in accommodation which was now too large for them (e.g. older people whose families had grown up and left) to find somewhere smaller.

In the event neither of these things happened to any great extent. Landlords found it more convenient and rewarding to sell property with vacant possession as their tenants left and older people in the larger properties tended to carry on living there even though the rent was increased. The Labour Party, unhappy about these effects upon the housing situation, pledged themselves to repeal the Act if they were returned to power. (They also promised to reduce the rate of mortgage interest on new properties, as did the Conservatives. In the event neither party was able to do so.)

The Rent Act 1965 recognised two types of unfurnished tenancies in the private sector. Controlled tenancies were mainly small, low-rated dwellings subject to the earlier Rent Act, while regulated tenancies were the higher-rented properties (but not the highest rents, which remained outside the scope of the legislation) whose rateable value, in 1965, was less than £200 (£400 in London). Rent officers were empowered to determine "fair rents", in consultation with landlords and tenants, and a rent assessment committee could arbitrate if necessary.

9. Furnished tenancies. Whilst furnished tenancies were not subject to the same degree of control as unfurnished tenancies there was provision, under both the Rent Act 1965 and the Furnished Houses (Rent Control) Act 1946 for control of a sort. Tenants with security of tenure had little to fear from landlords but the tenants of furnished accommodation had, up to that time, very little security. The Milner Holland Committee, whose report (*Report of the Committee on Housing in Greater London*, 1965, Cmnd. 2605) uncovered horrific tales of harassment by landlords seeking to evict tenants, added a new word, "Rachmanism", to the language. As a result of this report "harassment" was more carefully defined and stricter penalties were imposed upon landlords found guilty of treating their tenants in this way.

The Labour government's Rent Act 1974 virtually completed the process of giving the tenants of furnished accommodation the same protection from harassment as that enjoyed by those living in unfurnished accommodation by including within its scope all tenancies with a rateable value of less than £750 (£1,500 in London). Such tenancies may now have their rents determined by a rent tribunal and where a landlord wishes to enforce his right of possession he must now obtain a county court order to do so. One of the unforeseen consequences of this act has again been to limit the amount of accommodation available for letting, since some landlords, whilst quite happy to let accommodation on a short-term basis, are not prepared to do so if, when they wish to regain their property, they may find it difficult to do so. Some groups of potential tenants of furnished accommodation, e.g. students during term-time, have thus found themselves unable to find accommodation.

10. Rent and rate rebates. Rent and rate rebate schemes had been in existence in the local authority housing sector in the 1960s, but such schemes were by no means general and were at the discretion of local authorities. The Housing Subsidies Act 1972 extended the idea of "fair rents" to the public sector and also introduced an important new concept. The quality of housing which a person had enjoyed prior to the Act depended upon his ability to pay the rent. The introduction of a general scheme of rent and rate rebates, which covered all unfurnished tenancies and was later extended to furnished tenancies, meant that, in future, housing would depend more upon housing need than upon ability to pay.

The Act was a Conservative measure supported in principle by the Labour Party who, however, objected to the so-called "fair rents" provisions being extended to the public sector. For this reason they undertook, if returned to power, to repeal the Act.

In fact they introduced further legislation. The Local Government Act 1974 introduced a more generous scheme of rate rebates. The Housing Rents and Subsidies Act 1975 and the Housing Rents and Subsidies (Scotland) Act 1975 changed the basis on which local authority rents were calculated. The intention was that council house rents should be calculated in the interests of both the tenants and the ratepayers.

HOMELESSNESS

11. Homelessness. The homeless face one of the major social problems, which is the source of many other problems. Lack of a home may lead to the break-up of a family. Having no settled address may give rise to problems of unemployment (on the other hand it may be useful because, at least in theory, the unemployed homeless person is mobile). Not having a roof over one's head may make a law-breaker out of a previously honest citizen. For these and similar reasons it is surprising that so little is known about the size of the problem. Official statistics derive from local authority figures of numbers in "Part III Accommodation", i.e. accommodation provided under Part III of the National Assistance Act 1948 which charges local authorities with the responsibility of providing temporary accommodation for those who need it. Such figures represent only the tip of an iceberg of unknown size.

Perhaps more than any other political issue the problem of homelessness depends for its definition upon public opinion. For example, official figures for the number of homeless in 1969 were less than a quarter of a million. The housing charity Shelter, in an inspired piece of propaganda put out just before Christmas of that year, put the figure at over a million. The Shelter figures took a different definition of homelessness and they were published after the showing of a now-famous television play *Cathy Come Home*. It should be emphasised that this play was a piece of special pleading. Although it undoubtedly did a great deal of good in forcing the public to recognise the unsatisfactory provisions made for the homeless it also did harm, since a number of people who could have been helped by the services which were provided were said to have been frightened off and would not seek the help which they clearly needed. Both the Shelter publication and the T.V. film stimulated public interest and, as a result, a number of studies in the late 1960s and early 1970s influenced the government and local authorities to reconsider the accommodation which they provided for the homeless.

Until the mid-1960s the main emphasis, almost the only emphasis, was on homeless families. The early 1960s saw a new group, designated "homeless single persons", whose problems loomed larger as the decade progressed. The Ministry of Social Security Act 1966 had placed the responsibility for "persons without a settled way of living" on the newly-formed Supplementary Benefits Commission; but their hostels and reception centres were designed to deal with an older age range than the 1960s single homeless. These came more and more from the younger elements of society and, particularly in big cities like London and Birmingham, they became a growing problem; a problem, it may be said, which could not be solved simply by the provision of accommodation since, even if accommodation had been available, it would inevitably have increased the demand.

One answer to the problem, both from single persons and from homeless families, was squatting. The taking over of empty houses by those with no homes raised a number of issues. Apart from drawing attention to a pressing need it also gave rise to heated discussions about property rights and the morality of "direct action". Some local authorities took a tough line with squatters and either tried to evict them or ensured that empty properties were made uninhabitable. Some authorities co-operated with the squatters and made "short-life property" available to squatting organisations on the understanding that it was made available to the council when they needed it.

THE ENVIRONMENT

12. Environment. The basic question with which the environmentalist is concerned is, "What use should be made of the available land?" This is a question which has exercised governments, of all parties, since before the Second World War. The basis of most of the current legislation, however, can be found in the reports of three committees which met in the early 1940s. They were:

(a) the Barlow Committee on the *Geographical Location of the Industrial Population* (1940);

(b) the Scott Committee on *Land Utilisation in Rural Areas* (1942);

(c) the Uthwatt Committee on *Compensation and Betterment* (1942).

13. Town and country planning. The Town and Country Planning Act 1947 replaced and amended an earlier Act of the same name passed in 1944. Whilst the earlier Act had been a coalition measure, designed to repair the ravages of war, the 1947 Act was a Labour measure with much more positive aims. It set up a Ministry of Town and Country Planning (later the Department of the Environment) and pioneered the idea of development rights for the community. The Central Land Board, which it set up for this purpose, was later disbanded.

14. New towns. The New Towns Act 1946 was one of a series of measures, accepted by both Labour and Conservative governments, as a means of alleviating the immediate post-war housing shortage. It did not become a general political issue, although there were local arguments about the siting of new towns and social problems which the planners had not foreseen. New town populations tended to have a higher proportion of younger people than established towns so that the provision of ante-natal clinics, day nurseries and schools had to be given priority. As the years passed and the populations grew older the towns had the wrong sort of amenities. A higher proportion of adolescents in the new towns gave them an undeserved reputation for lawlessness. The young population of the new towns were not more criminal than the population in general, there were simply more youngsters in the "teenage delinquency" group.

15. The Land Commission. The Land Commission Act 1967 was a Labour measure designed to deal with problems of development. Part of the problem was that speculators could buy up land when it was cheap, hold it for some years and then sell it at a substantial profit when it was needed for building. Whilst this may have made economic sense it created political havoc. The Commission was authorised to collect a "betterment levy" which represented a tax on the increased value of the land. The Conservative Party was opposed to this levy and campaigned against it in the 1970 election. On winning the election they abolished the Land Commission and substituted capital gains tax for the betterment levy.

16. Community involvement. The early 1970s saw the start of a widespread interest in conservation. The idea had been around for a considerable time but it suddenly seemed to become fashionable. There was a growing realisation that all aspects of the environment were related, that the building of motorways, for example, did more than just benefit the motorist. It could, and sometimes did, wreak havoc on people's homes. The question of a third London airport in the 1970s is interesting because of the part which organised and vocal public opinion played in affecting the decision. The original decision to site the airport at Stanstead was taken on sound technical advice which entirely overlooked the social consequences on the local inhabitants of the building of a large new airport in the locality. The objectors made such a fuss and deployed their arguments with such skill that, during the course of the debate, the basic question became changed. What had started as a discussion as to where a new airport should be sited became converted into the question, "Do we need a third London airport at all?"

17. Participation in environmental matters. The Skeffington Report, *People and Planning, Report of the Committee on Public Participation in Planning* (H.M.S.O., 1969), recognised the importance of allowing members of the community to have a greater share in important decisions which could have a lasting effect on their environment. They therefore proposed the creation of a number of community development officers, appointed by local authorities, to represent the local residents to those who governed them. What was probably insufficiently recognised at the time was the tremendous amount of role conflict which this could cause in the individuals concerned. Was their job to represent the views of those who disagreed with the local authority? There were undoubtedly occasions when this was so and the officer was then seriously expected to tell his bosses that they were wrong. Even if his bosses were magnanimous enough not to override him it would be asking too much that they should always be happy at the stand he felt called upon to make.

PROGRESS TEST 13

1. How can housing needs be defined? **(1)**
2. What was the main difference between the approaches of the Labour and Conservative Parties to the question of housing? **(3)**
3. What was the option mortgage scheme? **(5)**

4. In what way did the Housing Act 1969 help the housing problem? **(6)**

5. Describe some of the ways in which legislation affected rented property. **(7–10)**

6. Why is it difficult to establish the number of homeless persons? **(11)**

7. In what way does the government involve itself in problems of the environment? **(12–17)**

CHAPTER XIV

Immigration and Racialism

THE PROBLEM

1. Immigration and racialism. These two subjects are frequently combined and, as frequently, confused. Britain has a long history of hospitality to immigrants, most of whom have settled happily and integrated successfully with the host population. The "immigration problem" of the 1960s was of a different order because the majority of immigrants at that time, and subsequently, were coloured. There is no logical reason why the colour of a person's skin should make any difference to the way he is treated; but societies and individuals do not always either think or act logically. Immigration on the scale of the 1960s and 1970s brought with it racialism. Racialism may be defined as the process whereby one person or group discriminates against another because of racial characteristics. Whether these characteristics are real or imagined is irrelevant, it is sufficient for the "victim" to be seen as a member of the despised group for it to be assumed that he shares the group's characteristics.

2. What makes it a problem? One may enquire why some minorities can be assimilated without trouble whereas others are seen as a threat and treated with fear and suspicion. The answers are complex and involve subjective and emotive judgments. Among the factors used in defining immigration and racialism as problems are the following.

(a) *The relative size of the minority.* There are no accurate figures on which the size of the coloured population can be calculated. This is partly because official statistics do not normally include "colour" but only country of origin. Whilst it is safe to assume that, for example, those who come from India will be Indians this is not necessarily so. Some who came from India in the 1940s were white people, possibly born in India, who left when India gained her independence. Kenyans might be of Indian, Asian, African or British origin. As time goes by the children of immigrants, British citizens born in Britain, will increase the coloured population of the country but will not necessarily appear on any statistics of the coloured population. The best estimate is probably that derived from census figures and, at the time of the 1971 census, coloured Commonwealth and Pakistani immigrants and their families accounted for about 2.5 per cent of the population, i.e. 1.33 million people. A number of critics, including Mr. Enoch Powell, believe that these figures grossly underestimate the true size of the problem.

(b) *Perceived differences.* Pre-war immigrants tended, in the main, to be white. The Irish came during the inter-war years and the European refugees swelled the numbers in the late 1930s. Such people could be more easily assimilated, partly because their numbers were not so great but partly because they were not immediately distinguishable as "different". The coloured immigrants with different languages and cultural backgrounds were less easy to integrate. Even when they spoke English it was not always the same sort of English as was spoken in Britain, e.g. West Indians have a number of different usages and the children of the early West Indian immigrants were frequently regarded as "backward" when, in fact, the problem was one of communication.

(c) *Prejudice.* Prejudice may be defined in this context as a hostile attitude towards a member of a group simply because he belongs to it and is, therefore, assumed to have objectionable qualities ascribed to the group (*see* 4).

(d) *Social conditions.* In a booming economy with full employment a society may well be able to assimilate newcomers and may actively encourage them to come to Britain and make use of their skills. The welfare state of the 1940s and 1950s was such a society. When problems arise, however, there is a tendency to look for a scapegoat. The indigenous, homeless family may well feel that "they" get priority in housing (the reverse is, in fact, the case) or that "they" take the best jobs (this too is not supported by the evidence).

(e) *Subjective views.* Members of the host community may well be prejudiced and may simply not like coloured people, without feeling it necessary to give a rational reason for this dislike. It tends to be overlooked however that the immigrants themselves may be prejudiced. They may have been led to believe that they would be welcome, and then feel that they were rejected. Such feelings lead to resentment and a tendency to take offence. If alleged slights are thought to be because of colour prejudice on the part of the host community it matters little what the truth of the matter really is. Discrimination will be seen as a fact, whether the intention was discriminatory or not.

3. Public and politicians. There is clear evidence, from opinion polls in the early 1960s, that the public showed far more concern with the problems of immigration than the politicians. It may be, of course, that politicians were concerned with the problem but not prepared to say so. In a series of interviews conducted between 1963 and 1970, for example, Butler and Stokes found that over 80 per cent of their respondents felt that too many immigrants had been let into the country (D. Butler and D. Stokes, *Political Change in Britain*, Macmillan, 1969). Gallup and other polls showed similar figures.

Whilst it is true that the Conservative Party had passed the Commonwealth Immigrants Act 1962, which the Labour Party opposed, it was not until 1966 that the Conservatives made the further restriction of immigration a feature of their election campaign; and it was April 1968 before Enoch Powell, then a leading member of the Conservative Party, made his famous speech in Birmingham in which he warned of grave dangers which would face the country if immigration policies continued unchecked. The fact that he made the speech in Birmingham is significant, as is the fact that his own constituency at that time contained a high proportion of coloured inhabitants. One of the salient factors of the racialism problem is that it is concentrated in small, heavily populated areas, which house the most poorly paid and less well educated. Such areas could easily become ghettoes.

On balance the Conservatives were more prepared to take a strong line on problems of immigration than were the Labour Party, but even the Conservatives did not generally publicise this stance. It was evident in constituencies like Smethwick, where it was an important fact of life for the local population, but in the country as a whole there was a tendency to play it down.

4. The role of the media. The mass media, T.V., radio and newspapers, are frequently credited with "creating" public opinion and a study published in 1974, *Racism and the Mass Media*, by P. Hartman and C. Husband (Davis-Poynter, 1974), tried to establish what truth there was in this belief. An important part of the study was a content analysis of four newspapers, *The Times*, the *Guardian*, the *Daily Express* and the *Daily Mirror*, between

1963 and 1970. They found that the coverage of "racial" items doubled during this period and that the way in which items were dealt with changed over the period.

(a) Coloured people were not, as a general rule, seen as an integral part of British society.

(b) There had been during this period a number of instances in which a noteworthy racial harmony could be seen in certain areas. Such instances were not, however, considered newsworthy and the emphasis in the papers was on incidents of hostility and strife.

(c) Stereotypes, by which a majority of people judge members of another race, had been left intact; i.e. any mistaken impressions caused by the use of stereotypes had remained uncorrected.

(d) The media served three purposes:

(i) *definition;* people tended to see a situation in terms of boundaries set by the media;

(ii) *education;* the media made people alive to issues which they would not otherwise have considered;

(iii) *discrimination;* because of the way news about immigrants was presented they were seen as a potential threat.

5. A minority view. The majority view of the problems of discrimination is that they are caused by the inability of the host community to assimilate newcomers. One writer who disputes this view is Dillibe Onyeoma, a Biafran, educated at Eton. He claims that the African, in refusing to adapt to the customs of the host community, has only himself to blame if he feels unwanted. His book, *John Bull's Nigger* (L. Frewin, 1974) does not claim to be scientific in its approach. A writer who does claim scientific backing for his views is the American psychologist Arthur Jensen, who sees American Negroes as genetically inferior to white Americans and of lower intelligence. A similar view was taken in Britain by Professor Eysenck.

6. Smethwick election. The major political parties have differing views on how questions of immigration and race should be dealt with. The differences are, however, more of degree than of kind and neither party is keen to be seen to take an extreme view. To advocate a strong line, to limit the number of immigrants severely and to undertake a programme of repatriation on a large scale might be a popular vote-catching platform, particularly in areas with a large proportion of immigrants.

Although the Conservative Party comes nearer to this approach, and did in fact advocate taking a tough line in the 1970 elections, they had not previously been noted for their stand on the subject. The matter was not on their manifesto until after the 1959 election and it was a party conference resolution in 1961 which led to the Commonwealth Immigrants Act 1962.

Labour, on the other hand, did not include this in their party manifesto even as late as 1964; but in that year one election was fought on the immigration issue. This was at Smethwick, where the moderate Labour ex-Foreign Secretary, Patrick Gordon-Walker, was defeated by Mr. P. Griffiths. The consituency was one in which there was a high proportion of coloured inhabitants and it was thought that the strength of Mr. Griffiths' opposition to further unrestricted immigration gained him the seat.

7. Testing the extent of discrimination. In 1967 the research organisation, Political and Economic Planning, carried out an experiment to test the amount of discrimination against coloured applicants for employment and housing. The findings were published as P.E.P. *Broadsheet No. 547* in September 1974. A group of actors were used. Half of them were white and half were coloured. They answered a series of advertisements for jobs and houses in London and Birmingham. The response to these applications was then examined and it was discovered that:

(*a*) there was still (i.e. after the Race Relations Act 1965) a substantial amount of discrimination against minority groups seeking jobs and housing, although the amount of discrimination in housing was less than it had been;

(*b*) discrimination was related to colour rather than foreign origin (Italian and Greek actors did not experience it to the same extent);

(*c*) discrimination by estate agents against prospective purchasers was initially lower than in other situations;

(*d*) discrimination dealt with by the law, whether by conciliation or the operation of the Act, was only a very small proportion of the total.

The findings were thought by P.E.P. to be an underestimate of the true extent of discrimination since the experiment dealt only with the initial stages of an application for a job or accommodation and there might well have been more discrimination shown at a later stage.

SOME POSSIBLE SOLUTIONS

8. Unrestricted immigration. The immediate post-war era was a period of open entry. The British Empire was still a fact, although the so-called "wind of change" had started to blow. The Commonwealth had fought on Britain's side during the war and its members were all British citizens. They therefore had unrestricted right of entry and, since they posed no threat and some were possessed of skills which Britain required, they were welcome; they made a valuable contribution to the economy. At that time the pattern of immigration was different in that immigrants from certain countries, the Indian sub-continent in particular, did not come to stay indefinitely. A young man would come, spend about five years either studying or working and sending home money to his family, and would then return home and settle down.

Home Office estimates for the number of immigrants entering this country during the period 1955–9 gave an average net increase in population of about 34,000 per year. This was an increase which could be assimilated without difficulty. The figure for 1960 however was 57,700 and it was clear that the pattern was changing. Immigrants coming to Britain at that time began more and more to send for their families and this resulted in a record net increase of some 136,400 in 1961 and a further 94,000 in the first half of 1962. At the same time there were growing demands for a restriction in numbers.

9. Restricted immigration. The passing of the Commonwealth Immigrants Act 1962 brought to an end the period of unrestricted entry. However, unrestricted rights of entry remained for wives and dependants of those immigrants who were admitted.

(*a*) *Conditions of entry*. An immigrant seeking to enter Britain had to satisfy the immigration officer that he (or she) was:

(*i*) in possession of a work voucher issued by the then Ministry of Labour (*see* (*b*)); or

(*ii*) a *bona fide* student; or

(*iii*) a visitor, in which case he was admitted for a limited period providing that he could show that he would be able to maintain himself during that time; or

(*iv*) a dependant. Spouse was broadly defined and included fiancées and "common law" partners of immigrants already settled in Britain. Children could come to join a close relative, not necessarily a parent; and the widows and elderly relatives of those who had already settled could also be admitted.

(b) *Work vouchers.* There were three types of vouchers, valid for six months, and the number and types of vouchers were decided by the Cabinet in the light of the economic situation.

(i) An employer who was prepared to offer a job to an immigrant could apply for a voucher for a specific person to do a particular job.

(ii) Certain skills and professional qualifications were in short supply and immigrants possessing these skills, particularly those with professional qualifications, who wished to come would be provided with a voucher. Such people were however in great demand in their countries of origin.

(iii) Unskilled workers, without specific jobs, could also be granted a voucher; but the number of such vouchers was strictly controlled and they ceased to be issued after September 1964.

10. Repatriation. This solution to the problem has a great deal of emotive appeal. It was advocated by Enoch Powell in 1968 but he at least was careful to stipulate that people should only be repatriated if they wanted to go. He made light of the expense which such a scheme would involve but pointed out that if the problem was serious enough the expense would be seen as justified. The idea is, however, unlikely to result in legislation since, for the second-generation immigrants, "home" is Britain. The Ministry of Social Security Act 1966 enables public funds to be used for such purposes if, in all the circumstances, such a course seems to be the only solution to a particular situation. Very few immigrants have, however, been repatriated by this means.

The National Front and the National Party campaign on a repatriation platform and succeed in arousing considerable feeling, particularly in areas with a high proportion of coloured people in their population. They are seen, however, more as a political threat than as serious political parties and have not so far succeeded in winning a parliamentary seat. It is interesting, however, to recall that the Labour Party devoted most of its party political broadcast in December 1977 to an attack on the attitudes which the National Front represent.

11. East African Asians. Until 1968 the right of Commonwealth immigrants to enter Britain had been comparatively free. The British Nationality Act 1964 gave them the right, if they chose, to retain British citizenship when their own country became independent. The Kenyan and Ugandan governments had, for some years, been pursuing a policy of "Africanisation" in which key posts were increasingly being given to Africans. In late 1967 it became obvious that the Asian community in East Africa had to make up its mind. Either they would have to adapt to the policy of Africanisation or they must leave. About 100,000 of them decided to come to Britain and public opinion in Britain was almost equally divided between those who felt that the Asians had a right to come and should be welcomed and those who saw the mounting racial problem and had no wish to add to it. In the event those advocating restriction won the day and the Labour government hurried through special legislation to meet the new situation. The Commonwealth Immigrants Act 1968 had the following main provisions.

(a) A special annual allocation of employment vouchers was to be issued, restricted to 1,500 per year, so that the immigrants could be absorbed more easily.

(b) Illegal immigration had become an increasing problem at this time and the new legislation tightened up measures for dealing with such cases. Immigration officers had previously had power to detain suspected illegal immigrants for twenty-four hours whilst enquiries were made. This period was extended to twenty-eight days.

(c) Restrictions were placed on the number and types of dependents who would be admitted.

RACE RELATIONS LEGISLATION

12. Race Relations Acts. There have been three such Acts, in 1965, 1968 and 1976. They represent a new departure in British politics, a conscious attempt to ensure that a specified part of the community receives fair treatment and is not subject to adverse discrimination. Critics of these measures argue that, in specifying penalties against racial discrimination, the Acts merely exacerbate the problem which they are designed to solve. The argument is that in creating a special minority group with the right not to be discriminated against you define a majority with no such rights. In any case, such critics would claim, you cannot, by law, compel a man to love his neighbour.

13. Race Relations Act 1965. The Labour government which passed this Act was, it has been argued, going against the wishes of the majority of the electorate. Such an argument cannot be either proved or disproved; but even if it were proved it could be said that this was an act of responsible government (*see* V, **15**) designed to secure what the Home Secretary of the time described as "an atmosphere of mutual tolerance".

(*a*) The Act defined "discrimination" as treating a person less favourably than he would otherwise have been treated, purely on the grounds of race, colour, ethnic or national origin.

(*b*) The stirring up of hatred on the grounds of race, colour, ethnic or national origin in a public place was forbidden, as was discrimination in the sale or disposal of leases on property.

(*c*) A Race Relations Board was set up, together with regional conciliation committees, each with its own conciliation officer, whose responsibility it was to settle complaints of discrimination, preferably without reference to the courts.

(*d*) Penalties of up to £1,000 or two years imprisonment, could be imposed for offences under the Act.

14. Race Relations Act 1968. The working of the 1965 Act had shown some problems, notably that it dealt with discrimination in "places of public resort" and there had been arguments about what constituted such a place. It was also felt to be too narrow in its definition of discrimination. The new Act similarly avoided the problems of definition, but it did at least set out a list of examples of the sort of situation in which discrimination could occur. It extended the provisions of the 1965 Act to cover a wider field, particularly in the areas of housing and employment. It did, however, allow some exemptions to its provisions in the field of employment, in that small employers were able to evade its provisions for two years, after which they were required to comply. It also established a Community Relations Commission to encourage good community relations with immigrant populations and to advise the Secretary of State on race relations matters.

15. Race Relations Act 1976. This Act came into force on 13th June 1977 and repealed the two previous Acts. It also abolished the Race Relations Board and the Community Relations Commission, whose functions were to be taken over by a Commission for Racial Equality with increased powers. It defined discrimination in two ways.

(*a*) *Direct discrimination* consists of "treating a person, on racial grounds, less favourably than others are or would be treated in the same circumstances".

(b) *Indirect discrimination* consists of "applying a requirement or condition which, whether intentionally or not, adversely affects one racial group considerably more than another and cannot be justified on non-racial grounds".

THE FUTURE

16. Future trends. One cannot, of course, predict the future, particularly in a book of this nature. One can, however, distinguish certain trends and speculate where they might lead if they continued.

(a) *Numbers of immigrants*. The Commonwealth Immigration Acts reduced the flow of immigrant workers and this, in a period of rising unemployment, may well be an advantage, but at the same time the proportion of dependents has risen steadily and these, together with the children born in Britain of immigrant parents, means that the proportion of coloured population in Britain will continue to rise. A report issued by the Runnymede Trust, *Census 1971: The Coloured Population of Great Britain* (1973) draws attention to the imbalance between the male and female immigrant population and predicts that if the laws remain the same and that immigrant communities, with a disproportionate proportion of men to women, continue to send for their womenfolk to join them there will be a substantial influx into Britain of immigrant women of child-bearing age.

(b) *Unemployment*. A high proportion of unemployed schoolleavers, particularly in the major cities, are coloured and they tend to remain unemployed longer than their white contemporaries. Whether, as some claim, this is an example of covert colour prejudice remains unproven. It is, however, an undeniable fact in such areas and is a cause of a great deal of local ill-feeling. Whilst the Race Relations Act 1976 permits certain exceptions, for example in the field of special training courses, the Act itself does not permit what is described as "reverse discrimination", i.e. discrimination in favour of a person, or group, on the grounds that he or she has suffered adverse discrimination in the past and should be given an opportunity to "catch up".

(c) *Crime*. Areas of high unemployment, particularly where the unemployed are young, tend to have a high juvenile delinquency rate. It is sometimes alleged that the crime rate among coloured youngsters is higher than that among the white population and the Chief of Police in Brixton, an area with a high proportion of coloured residents, asserted in the early part of 1977 that this was so. A study carried out for the Institute of Race Relations in Birmingham, *Crime, Police and Race Relations, 1970*, pointed in the opposite direction and tended to suggest that crime rates for the coloured population were, in fact, lower than for the white residents in the area.

PROGRESS TEST 14

1. Why is racialism a problem? **(2)**

2. Describe the role of (*a*) politicians, (*b*) the media and (*c*) public opinion on questions of immigration. **(3–7)**

3. Outline some possible solutions to problems caused by immigration. **(8–10)**

4. State the main provisions of the Race Relations Acts of (*a*) 1965, (*b*) 1968, and (*c*) 1976. **(12–15)**

5. Indicate some possible future trends in matters of immigration. **(16)**

CHAPTER XV

Poverty

PROBLEMS

1. Defining poverty. The poor, it has been said, are always with us; and poverty, or the relief of poverty, has been a political issue for many years. The nineteenth-century view was that it was a personal misfortune and that legislation, in so far as it was necessary, should be concerned with discouraging "idleness". By the 1920s and 1930s, with rising unemployment, it became clear that poverty was not simply a personal misfortune, but was directly related to the economy of the country and the state therefore had a duty to relieve it (*see* 12).

But to define poverty is very difficult. All poverty is relative and what might have been an acceptable standard of living for an unemployed man in the 1930s would not be regarded as acceptable in the 1970s. What might be considered a tolerable level in a poor and backward country would not be acceptable in a rich and advanced one. What seems to be needed, therefore, is a "poverty line" which divides the poor from those not needing help. The earliest attempt in Britain to draw such a line was made by B. Seebohm Rowntree in 1901 and described in his book, *Poverty: A Study of Town Life* (Macmillan, 1901). In it he distinguished between "primary" and "secondary" poverty, in other words, between those who needed to be helped and those who, although poor, did not qualify for help according to the standards which were then applied. The standards were, however, extremely low and were fixed at subsistence level, i.e. the minimum a person needed to survive. In a later survey, the results of which were published in 1941 he adopted slightly higher standards. It was this survey on which the income-maintenance parts of the Beveridge Report (*see* 12) were based.

Critics of the present system of income-maintenance claim that the basis of national assistance (later supplementary benefit) is still too close to subsistence level and it has been suggested that the poverty line be drawn at 140 per cent of the existing supplementary benefit level (B. Abel-Smith and P. Townsend, *The Poor and the Poorest*, 1965). This level represents a more generous and humane approach and probably reflects fairly accurately the changes in public opinion as to the treatment of the poor in the latter half of the twentieth century. It should be noted, however, that acceptance of poverty as a "relative" problem creates a Catch 22 situation in that no matter what a government does to alleviate poverty it cannot, by definition, do so. There will always be people at the bottom of the ladder who need help.

2. Changes in the pattern of poverty. At the time of Rowntree's second survey in York in 1936 the two main causes of poverty were low wages and unemployment. By 1950 the pattern had changed drastically and the major cause of poverty was old age. Throughout the 1960s and 1970s the elderly continued to be the main low-income group, but other groups had appeared on the scene. The one-parent family, which was hardly recognised in the earlier York surveys, came to be recognised as a deprived group for whom more needed to be done. The Finer Committee Report, published in 1974, proposed a number of new benefits for this group but economic stringency prevented their full implementation (*see* **20**). The unemployed increased in numbers in 1975–8 and the whole question of the adequacy of wage levels assumed a greater importance. Supplementary benefit could not be paid to those in full-time work and the situation then arose in which low-paid workers would be better off by not working.

3. Universality and selectivity. There are basically two ways in which benefits can be given to relieve poverty. Either everybody can be given benefits so that they are assured of an adequate minimum standard of living, and those who do not need such benefits will pay them back through the tax system; or benefits can be paid only to those who demonstrate that they are in need. The first method, known as universality, tends to be favoured by the Labour Party, and the second method, selectivity, receives more encouragement from the Conservative Party.

4. Universality. A number of Labour thinkers, e.g. B. Abel-Smith, P. Townsend and the late Professor Titmuss of the London School of Economics have argued that selective benefits are unsatisfactory for a number of reasons.

(*a*) The amount spent on income-maintenance should be based on need, not cost, and the more costly universal benefits would ensure that all needs would be met.

(*b*) Inequality is intrinsically wrong. The recipients of selective benefits lose self-respect.

(*c*) Selectivity can only be effective if accompanied by some form of means test, and such tests lead to stigma.

(*d*) The fear of stigma and loss of self-respect will prevent people claiming money to which they are entitled and those most in need may not be helped.

(*e*) Means tests are unpopular and are expensive to administer.

5. Selectivity. The Institute of Economic Affairs and some other groups have argued that there is only a limited amount of money (the language of welfare is the language of priorities) and that it must be distributed where it is most needed. They therefore advocate a pricing policy for all social services, not just income-maintenance services, since people value what they pay for. People should also be encouraged to help themselves as much as possible. There would still be people in need, of course, but in this way the numbers requiring help would be reduced and a means test would then enable the reduced number to be given a larger share of the available resources.

6. Areas of agreement. Both universalists and selectivists agree that:

(*a*) a greater part of the gross national product should be spent on welfare payments;

(*b*) benefits should go to those who need them;

(*c*) the "consumer" should have more say in the services provided for him.

7. Take-up of benefits. Payments to relieve poverty should go to those who need them, and no one in need should be deprived of such benefits. Both major parties accept these statements but, with the formation of poverty pressure groups (*see* **14**), it has become clear that need is not always being met. The reasons why people do not take up benefits to which they are entitled are, of course, personal and subjective and the problem of lack of take-up strengthens the arguments of the universalists (*see* **4**) who can point to a benefit like the retirement pension which is paid to nearly all persons over retirement age. All those who need the money get it and those who do not need it pay it back in tax. Family income supplement, on the other hand, which is specific-ally designed to help poorer families, has not been claimed by anything like the number of people who were estimated to be entitled to it.

8. Reasons for lack of take-up. No one knows for certain why people who appear to be entitled to certain welfare benefits do not claim them. It may be, of course, that, although they appear to be entitled, they know their own circumstances sufficiently well to know that in fact they have no entitlement and therefore they do not claim. Other explanations include the following.

(*a*) *Ignorance*. Official publicity about welfare benefits costs thousands of pounds per year but there is evidence, from surveys and similar sources, that a majority of poorer people get their information about such benefits from friends, relatives and acquaintances rather than from official sources. A "Welfare Rights Project" carried out by the Merseyside branch of the Child Poverty Action Group in 1968 discovered that over 85 per cent of those in poverty knew about supplementary benefits but they suggested that "official" sources seemed remote and that, whilst leaflets and information could be obtained from post offices, social workers, old people's clubs and various recognised sources, the methods of disseminating information were not imaginative enough. They suggested posters in laundrettes, fish and chip shops and market-places. A move in this direction was tried when family income supplement was introduced. Newspaper advertisements publicising the scheme were linked with the name of a well-known columnist, Marjorie Proops.

(*b*) *Pride and fear of stigma*. The welfare state has been in existence for at least three decades, and the nineteenth-century idea that poverty was a disgrace and that supplementary benefits were charity might now be thought unrealistic. Unrealistic or not, if people believe that it is so, they will not claim the benefits which they need.

The Ministry of Social Security Act 1966 tried to recognise this fact by altering the official terminology. The words "national assistance", which were reminiscent of the Poor Law, were no longer used and those who received benefit got either a supplementary pension or a supplementary allowance. They were now called "claimants", not "applicants", and they claimed an "entitlement". The order-books in which supplementary pensions were paid were virtually indistinguishable from those for retirement pensions. Retirement pension books themselves contained a slip advising pensioners that if they could not manage on their pension it could be supplemented.

(c) *Distrust of official procedures and inability to complete forms*. The extent to which those entitled to benefits are prevented from claiming them for this reason is difficult to gauge. Certainly the paralysis which sometimes affects people confronted by officials and officialdom is not confined to the poor or the pensioners; but the official claim forms required no more than the name and address of the claimant. Even this can be dispensed with if a letter is received saying that a person wishes to make a claim. The subsequent form-filling is done by officials.

9. Extent of lack of take-up. In 1974 the Child Poverty Action Group estimated that there were one million old people and ten thousand fatherless families eligible for supplementary benefit but not receiving it (*Poverty*, no. 29, Summer 1974). In the same year, the Department of Health and Social Security produced a figure of one and a half million. The official figures were derived from estimates made from the Family Expenditure Survey but the Department was careful to point out that such figures should be treated with caution because the method of sampling used for the Family Expenditure Survey allowed a wide margin of error. Whatever the true figures may be it is obvious that there are a large number of people who appear to need help from the state and are not receiving it. Both major parties were concerned with this problem and claimed that their particular proposals for improvement of poverty legislation would help to solve it.

10. Cycle of deprivation. This phrase was first used in 1972 by Sir Keith Joseph, the Conservative spokesman on social services matters. He was discussing the situation well known to social workers and similar groups in which families who are poor seem to transmit their poverty to the next generation. Such families are not just poor, they are afflicted by a number of social ills. They have a higher rate of unemployment, they are among the most badly housed, their health is poorer than that of the rest of the community and their educational standards are lower. They used to be called "problem families" and they also had a higher rate of criminal activity than the rest of the community. They therefore represented a great challenge to the whole concept of the welfare state and were among those most likely to fall into the "poverty trap". This was the situation where, because there were a number of means-related benefits (supplementary benefit, family income supplement, rent and rate rebates, free school meals, etc.) it was possible for a person to gain an increase in his basic income which would then be cancelled out by a reduction in means-tested benefits. Neither the Conservative nor the Labour Party had any firm proposals about the solution to this particular problem but the Liberal Party manifesto for 1974, *Why Britain Needs a Liberal Government*, proposed a "social dividend scheme" which would seem to go a long way towards it (*see* also **13**).

11. Payment for strikers. Neither the National Assistance Act 1948 nor the Ministry of Social Security Act 1966 allowed payment for persons engaged in an industrial dispute, but both Acts permitted payment to be made for the wives and children of men on strike. The calculation of such payments took account of any strike pay which was received and was defended on the grounds that to have refused payment would have imposed an unfair burden of poverty on the dependents of men who were, after all, only exercising a democratic, and perfectly lawful right to withhold their labour.

The late 1960s and early 1970s were a period of industrial unrest and, by 1972, the number of workers involved in strikes during the year had exceeded 1.7 million (*Central Statistical Office Digest of Statistics*, July 1977). The strain on union funds was considerable and trade unionists were urged, particularly by the claimants unions (*see* **14**), to use "the biggest strike fund of all", i.e. supplementary benefit. The Conservative Party therefore advocated, in its 1974 manifesto, that the whole question of the power of the trade unions should be examined and, in particular, that the cost of industrial action should be borne by the unions rather than by the tax-payer. The Labour Party, although they shared the Conservative's concern, did not advocate such a drastic step. They did, however, when returned to power, make an amendment to the Social Security Act which meant that when a strike ceased and the men returned to work they would no longer be eligible for supplementary benefit whilst awaiting their first week's wages, except in the form of a loan.

PROPOSALS TO DEAL WITH POVERTY

12. The Beveridge Report. During the Second World War the coalition government began to lay plans for post-war reconstruction. Among the most important of these was the Beveridge

Report, *Social Insurance and Allied Services* (Cmnd. 6404, 1942). Beveridge, an economist, advocated complete welfare coverage, "from the cradle to the grave", for the entire population of Britain. Such coverage would cost a lot of money and could only be effective in conditions of full employment.

It is interesting that at that time he defined full employment as an unemployment rate of not more than 8 per cent, whilst during the high unemployment of the mid 1970s the rate was about 6 per cent. It must be remembered, however, that the immediate pre-war level of unemployment (1938) was 13.5 per cent so that Beveridge's figure of 8 per cent unemployment was, in fact, low by the then contemporary standards.

According to Beveridge complete welfare coverage would be achieved by three different means.

(*a*) There would be a comprehensive system of *national insurance*, to which all workers, and those of the non-employed who were not specifically exempt, would be required to contribute. Benefits would be at a flat rate, i.e. related to contributions rather than need, and there would be additions to the flat rate to provide for the needs of dependents. The scheme would be based on figures supplied by the Government Actuary and the cost of benefits would be covered by contributions.

(*b*) *Family allowances* were to be introduced for all children in the family except the first. This was to be a universal, non-contributory benefit payable at subsistence level. Beveridge's original suggestion was that the rate should be 8 shillings (40 pence) per week. The first allowances were, however, 5 shillings (25 pence) per week and they were not increased to 8 shillings until some years later. The important point about family allowances was that they were paid regardless of the income of the recipients and this meant a very high take-up of the benefits (*see* 7–9). Further, for the lowest paid workers it meant that they would receive at least a small income, related to the size of their family, whether or not they were in employment.

(*c*) *National assistance* was to be provided for those who were still in need despite the existence of national insurance benefits and family allowances (*see* 17). The national insurance and family allowance schemes would cover most of the population, and the intention was that the rates of national insurance were to be such that people would be able to live on their benefit without further help from the state. Since practically everybody was to be included in the scheme there would only be a small minority, e.g. pensioners, who were too old to have contributed to the scheme when it was first introduced, who would need national assistance. In the course of time this group would dwindle and assistance, which was to be means-tested, would deal with the small minority who had slipped through the welfare net. Such was the intention but in the event the standard rates of national insurance were insufficient to meet needs and had to be supplemented in many more cases than expected.

13. Poverty and the political parties. Both major parties, and the Liberal Party, profess concern for the problems of the poor and all advocate various measures to improve the schemes which were introduced by Beveridge (*see* **12**). From 1945 to 1950 there was not a great deal to be said. The general feeling was that poverty had been abolished and that although there was always room for improvement the schemes which had been devised were basically sound, and bore comparison with a number of similar schemes in other parts of the western world. The Labour Party manifesto for 1950 proudly boasted that destitution had been abolished while by 1951 their aim was to "humanise" the national assistance scheme.

By 1955, when Labour were in opposition, they were less sanguine about the claim to have abolished poverty and the Conservative government was becoming aware of the problems of pensioners. This concern was focused by the publication in 1957 of a study of pensioners in Bethnel Green, *Family Life of Old People*, by P. Townsend (Routledge and Kegan Paul, 1957). In that year the Conservatives increased the basic retirement pension and a further increase was given in 1959. Neither of these increases, however, enabled pensioners to dispense with national assistance, they merely reduced the proportion of income which came from this source. The Labour manifesto for 1959 made a strong feature of the need to abolish poverty, and for the 1966 election all party manifestos took this line.

The Labour victory of 1966 enabled them to introduce the Ministry of Social Security Act 1966 (*see* **18**) and in 1967 to increase family allowances. The election of 1970 saw both major parties promising improvements, Labour by undertaking to review the whole social security system and the Conservatives by undertaking to introduce a system of negative income tax or tax credit (*see* **16**). The Conservative government of 1970 in fact introduced a new benefit, family income supplement (*see* **21**) and amendments to the pension scheme (*see* **22**).

The elections in 1974 saw three major proposals in the manifestos. The Labour Party promised to increase retirement pensions to a level which would enable pensioners to live on their pensions and thus not need supplementary benefit. This would bring the whole system of income-maintenance closer to Beveridge's original conception. The Conservative proposal was concerned with benefits paid to strikers (*see* **11**) and the Liberal suggestion was for minimum wage levels throughout the country allied to a social dividend scheme which would rationalise a great deal of the piecemeal legislation which had been passed since 1945 (*see*, **17–19**). In 1977 the Labour government announced a complete review of the social security system.

14. Pressure groups. Pressure groups on the problems of poverty can be divided into two types, those who work on behalf of the poor and those which consist of the poor themselves. The best known of the first type of group is the Child Poverty Action Group, founded in 1965, mainly by academics in the field of social policy. The group produces regular bulletins on matters relating to poverty and is consulted by the Department of Health and Social Security and by party spokesmen on poverty issues. It has produced, or sponsored, a number of researches into problems of poverty and its evidence, together with that of the National Council for the Unmarried Mother and her Child (now the National Council for One-Parent Families) influenced the Finer Committee whose report, *Committee on One-Parent Families* (Cmnd. 5692), was published in 1974.

Claimants unions are, as the name implies, groups of claimants banded together to advance the needs of individual claimants. Their methods and organisation are different from those of the other type of group. Whilst not avowedly political organisations they contain some members who are highly motivated politically. The National Federation of Claimants Unions was founded in 1968, partly as a response to what they saw as the "establishment" mentality of the older groups and partly as an extension of the "community involvement" movement which grew up in the late 1960s (*see* XIII, **16**). Claimants unions have figured less prominently in the poverty lobby in recent years, probably because of the unacceptable militancy of some of their members. A comparable, although more specialised, group is Gingerbread, founded, like the claimants unions, to provide "grassroots" representation, in this case for one-parent families. Like the claimants unions, they considered that the existing pressure groups were not sufficiently in touch with the problems with which they were faced and laid great stress on schemes for mutual help.

15. Political pressure groups. Both the Fabian Society and the Bow Group (*see* II, 13) have, from time to time, made proposals for the relief of poverty. Fabian Tract no. 399, *Paying for the Social Services*, published in 1969, suggested a "poverty clawback", i.e. a system whereby those who did not need benefits paid them back in taxes (*see* 16), and an incomes guarantee. The Bow Group produced a number of papers of their own and one of their members, Russell Lewis, director of the Conservative Political Centre, was a contributor to a symposium on questions of poverty edited by Dr. Rhodes Boyson and published in 1971 under the title, *Down with the Poor*.

16. Poverty and tax. One method of abolishing supplementary benefit would be to use the tax system to meet the problem of poverty. A number of suggestions have been made as to how this could be done and advocates of the schemes stress two great advantages. One is that it would dispense with any form of means test (not quite true because any such system would rely on declarations of means given for tax purposes) and the other is that administrative costs would be considerably reduced. Against this must be weighed the fact that such a scheme could not be as flexible as the present social security scheme. It is difficult to see how any taxation scheme could take account of changes in payments like rent, which has an important effect on a person's supplementary benefit; and it is even more difficult to see how any taxation scheme could be flexible enough to meet the sort of emergency payments which are currently made in special circumstances (in 1975 for example 945,000 payments were made to avoid hardship in cases of special need). The Labour "clawback", the Conservative tax credit scheme and the social dividend plan outlined by the Liberals in 1974 all suffer from these drawbacks.

LEGISLATION

17. National assistance. The National Assistance Act 1948 was a Labour government measure based on Beveridge's proposals and designed to replace the local authority provisions administered by the Boards of Guardians. The Act applied throughout Britain and was financed by the Exchequer. The welfare of applicants was, for the first time, made a statutory duty and the "means test", by which the relatives of the poor were expected to contribute to their maintenance, was virtually abolished. Husbands and wives were still required to maintain each other, and parents were still responsible for children under sixteen. Beyond this, however, there was no requirement on anybody to maintain anybody else. The administration of the scheme was entrusted to a National Assistance Board which was largely autonomous but answerable to Parliament through the Minister of National Insurance.

18. Supplementary benefit. The National Assistance Board represented a great advance on previous schemes for the relief of poverty but by the mid-1960s it became clear that a number of potential beneficiaries were not receiving money to which they would appear to be entitled. This was confirmed by a study carried out in 1965 and subsequently published as *Circumstances of Families* (H.M.S.O., 1967) which suggested that anything up to a third of all retirement pensioners were not getting the assistance to which they were entitled. One of the main reasons was felt to be the label, "national assistance" with its lingering Poor Law associations.

Both the major parties promised, if elected, to improve the income-maintenance scheme. The 1966 Labour government passed the Ministry of Social Security Act 1966. By this time some 77 per cent of all people receiving assistance were also receiving national insurance benefits and the amalgamation of the Ministry of Pensions and National Insurance with the National Assistance Board into one Ministry of Social Security not only made administrative sense, but also blurred the line between contributory and non-contributory benefits. It was hoped to encourage those, particularly the elderly, who needed help and had not claimed it. A Supplementary Benefits Commission was formed to deal with the work previously undertaken by the National Assistance Board and the Commission, like the Board before it, was largely autonomous. The Supplementary Benefits Act 1976 consolidated amendments to the Act which had occurred since 1966.

19. Family allowances. The Family Allowances Act 1945 was the first of a series of Acts, passed by a Labour government and designed to implement the principles of the Beveridge Report. It provided for an allowance of 5 shillings (25 pence) for all children of the family except the first. This amount was raised to 8 shillings (40 pence) in 1952 as a result of a Conservative measure. There were various increases until 1977 when family allowance was £1.50 for each child in the family after the first. It was then replaced by a scheme of child benefits.

20. Child benefits. Criticisms of the family allowance scheme were that it was taxable, it did not include the first child in the family and failed to give special help to those who needed it most, i.e. one-parent families. The child benefit scheme was introduced to meet these criticisms. The Child Benefit Bill reached the statute book in 1975, but the government, finding itself short of money, postponed implementation. In the meanwhile a leak to the magazine *New Society* in the form of an anonymous article entitled "Killing a commitment: the cabinet v. the children" (*New Society*, 17th June 1976) caused a major cabinet rift not only on the question of child benefits but on the whole question of open government (*see* III, **11**). The new benefit was finally introduced in April 1977, later than originally intended but probably earlier than would have been the case if the information had not been leaked. The main points of the new scheme were as follows.

(*a*) The benefit was payable in respect of all children in the family, not just the second and subsequent children.

(*b*) the weekly rate of benefit was to be £1 for the first or only child and £1.50 for subsequent children.

(*c*) It was tax free.

(*d*) One-parent families received £1.50 for all children, including the first.

(*e*) A special interim benefit was introduced prior to the main scheme (in April 1976) to give the increased rates to one-parent families at an earlier date. However, this was limited in its effect because it was taken into account when calculating entitlement to supplementary benefit, and a considerable proportion of one-parent families were receiving supplementary benefit.

21. Family income supplement. The Family Income Supplement Act 1970 introduced a new concept to modern social legislation. This was a major allowance unrelated to contributions which was paid to people in full-time work (defined as over thirty hours a week) whose wages were inadequate. The basic principle of supplementing wages had once before been introduced, by the justices of Speenhamland in Berkshire, in 1795, but was later abandoned because employers used the allowance as an excuse to pay lower wages. By 1970, however, it was felt, probably quite rightly, that conditions had changed and that modern wage legislation would prevent a similar problem.

The basis of the scheme, introduced by a Conservative government, was that people whose wages were less than an amount prescribed by Parliament (the "prescribed amount") would receive up to half of the difference between their wages and that amount. The scheme was for families (including one-parent families) with children and a sliding scale was devised so that the prescribed amount took account of the number of children. Recipients of family income supplement were automatically entitled to certain other welfare benefits. In 1977 the prescribed amount was £39 for a family with one child plus an addition of £4.50 for each additional child.

Critics of the scheme point out that it is a major factor in the poverty trap (*see* **10**) and that, in making up only half of the difference between the prescribed amount and a person's wages, the benefit fails to help those most in need, i.e. the lowest-paid workers. Family income supplement is also one of the benefits which appears to suffer from a low take-up (*see* **7–9**).

22. National Insurance. The National Insurance Act 1946 came into operation in July 1948 and, together with the National Insurance (Industrial Injuries) Act 1946 (which replaced earlier schemes of workmen's compensation), completed the grand design which Beveridge had introduced. National insurance is, briefly, a scheme of contributory benefits designed to cover all the major periods when a worker can expect to be without wages. These include sickness, unemployment, retirement, maternity and death. The scheme includes widows' pensions and other benefits. It worked reasonably well for the first two decades but the *Report on the Circumstances of Families*, 1967 (H.M.S.O.) showed that demographic changes which had taken place since 1945 meant that pensioners, who were increasing in numbers, were continually having to claim supplementary benefit to supplement their pensions.

The Labour government therefore produced a White Paper, *National Superannuation and Social Insurance* (Cmnd. 3883, 1969) which proposed radical changes in the pension scheme. Before the Bill could become law the Labour government had fallen and the Conservative counter-proposal, *Strategy for Pen-*

sions (Cmnd. 4755, 1971) resulted in the Social Security Act 1973. This Act was due to come into force in 1975 but, in the meanwhile, there had been another general election. The incoming Labour government however accepted the broad principles of the Conservative measure, and issued a White Paper, *Better Pensions* (Cmnd. 5713, 1974) keeping the basic Conservative plan but adding their own amendments.

The resulting legislation, the Social Security Pensions Act 1975, came into effect on 6th April 1978 and was designed to ensure that pensioners are given a greater share of the rising standards of living. For this reason the new pension scheme, as well as being related to the pensioner's previous earnings, will also include a protection against inflation. Employers whose own pension schemes are as good as, or better than, the government scheme will be allowed to opt out.

PROGRESS TEST 15

1. Outline some of the problems of poverty. (1–11)
2. How did the Beveridge Report propose to deal with poverty? (12)
3. How did the major political parties propose to deal with poverty from 1950 onwards? (13)
4. What is the basic difference between the approach of the Child Poverty Action Group and claimants unions to problems of poverty? (14)
5. How are poverty and tax related? (16)
6. What was the distinctive feature of the National Assistance Act 1948? (17)
7. What was the point of blurring the line between contributory and non-contributory benefits in 1966? (18)
8. Write brief notes on (*a*) family allowances, (*b*) child benefits and (*c*) family income supplement. (19–21)
9. What is the main purpose of national insurance? (22)

CHAPTER XVI

Health

THE DEVELOPMENT OF THE HEALTH SERVICE

1. The pre-war situation. Before the Second World War there was a Minister of Health, but he had no control over national policy as a whole. The health services were controlled by three groups of people, those responsible for hospitals, the general practitioner (family doctor) services and the local authorities who dealt with matters like public health, maternity and child welfare services. The exigencies of a major war called for a more unified service and an emergency medical service was set up as a war-time measure. The Beveridge Report in 1942, saw the need for a comprehensive health service, serving the whole community and complementary to the other services which were proposed for post-war Britain.

2. The National Health Service. The post-war Labour government can claim the credit for the National Health Service Act 1946 which accepted, in the main, the proposals put forward by Beveridge. In fairness it should be said that the Conservative Party was not opposed to the creation of a national health service but their plans were not so comprehensive as those of the Labour Party. The main credit for the introduction of the scheme in its final form probably belongs to the then Minister of Health, Aneurin Bevan. It was he who conducted the long and difficult discussions with the British Medical Association and other interested bodies. The doctors feared that a state medical service would be salaried and they would lose their autonomy (*see* **12**).

3. Principles of the health service. Four basic principles were to guide the new health service and the principles, although not the structure which supported them, still apply.

(*a*) The traditional doctor-patient relationship was to be retained. The family doctor, general practitioner or, as he is now officially known, the community physician, was to remain the first point of contact for most patients and to provide the link between the individual and the various medical services.

(b) The patient was to be free to choose his own doctor and the doctors retained the right, in certain circumstances, to choose their patients.

(c) Doctors were to be given autonomy in medical matters.

(d) The service was to be free to all who needed it. Generally this is still so since, although certain charges are now made (see 5), those who cannot afford them can have them refunded.

4. Structure. The service was intended to prevent, as well as to cure, illness and the tripartite system which evolved owed much to the pre-war origins. The three branches were linked in a number of ways but they were, and remained for some thirty years, separate but related systems.

(a) *Hospital and specialist services.* In 1948 when the National Health Service started, there were some 2,800 hospitals with about 500,000 beds. The Secretary of State appointed fifteen Regional Hospital Boards who in turn appointed hospital management committees responsible for a group of hospitals. The services provided by the hospitals were:

(i) care and treatment;

(ii) specialist services such as child guidance;

(iii) ancillary services, e.g. X-ray services and the supply and fitting of surgical appliances.

(b) *Practitioner services, family doctors, dentists, opticians and chemists.* The doctors were not salaried, as they had feared, but instead their remuneration was based on the number of patients registered with them, plus additions for certain services. This part of the service was also administered by appointed local committees.

(c) *Local authority health services.* These services included the ambulance services, ante- and post-natal clinics, midwifery services, health visitors and a number of related services which were concerned more with social welfare than medical need. The home help service, originally a permissive measure under the National Health Service Act, was made a statutory responsibility of the local authorities under the Health Services and Public Health Act 1968. Local authority health services also included the provision, equipment and maintenance of health centres. This particular provision was only implemented gradually and the first twelve years saw the provision of only fourteen centres.

5. The 1950s. The period between 1948 and 1952 was mainly one of consolidation. The general feeling was that the National Health Service had made a valuable contribution to the welfare state and that, although it was costing more than had been envisaged, it still gave good value for money and did not need drastic alteration. There had been some excesses initially. In the first year about 187 million prescriptions were dispensed and there was a huge demand for free spectacles and deaf aids. Some of this demand was almost certainly due to the fact that poorer people, who in the past had needed such aids but could not afford them, now made use of the free services provided. The provision of a full range of free medical services also gave rise to charges of malingering, and concern was expressed about the number of foreigners who were alleged to be coming to Britain to take advantage of the facilities provided; but these were minor criticisms of a scheme which, on the whole, was seen as a valuable social service.

The Conservatives were particularly concerned with what they saw as abuses of the scheme and, on their return to power, they imposed a nominal charge on all prescriptions dispensed under the health service regulations. The charge was not excessive, one shilling (5 pence), but it was sufficient to justify charges that the principle of a free health service was at stake. Opponents of the prescription charge pointed out that the main sufferers were likely to be the chronic sick and the poorest sections of the community (although in fact the National Assistance Board had power to refund such charges to those who could not afford them).

The Labour Party campaigned in 1955 for the abolition of the charges but were unsuccessful and a Report in 1956 seemed to support the Conservative's case. The Report of the Guillebaud Committee of Enquiry into the Cost of the National Health Service (Cmnd. 9663) was in favour of retaining the prescription charge. It recognised that the health service had cost more than had originally been estimated but said this was not due to maladministration but to the increasing costs of wages and specialists fees. It could have said, but did not, that another reason was that the original estimates were based on a false assumption. The architects of the health service had assumed that, with a comprehensive scheme and a "backlog" of cases to be dealt with initially, the scheme would be expensive in the first few years. After that, since the general level of health would have improved, the cost of running the service should not increase. What happened, of course, was that as the health of the nation improved so the health service became more specialised and therefore more expensive.

6. The 1960s. The Labour Party continued to press for improvements in the health service. Aneurin Bevan had opened a "showpiece" health centre at Harold Hill, near Romford, in 1954 and health centres, it will be remembered, had been a feature of the original Act. Very few had been built and it was calculated in 1960 that it would cost up to £150 million to provide sufficient centres to meet the needs of the population.

The Porritt Report of 1962 was the work of a committee of doctors. Whilst it appeared uncertain about health centres in their present form it endorsed the principle of doctors working in some form of group practice. In this it foreshadowed community care, that is the range of agencies: doctors, voluntary bodies and self-help schemes, which between them provide hospital, day centre, residential and domicillary support. The report also raised again the question of the way in which general practitioners were paid. As a result a new system was introduced in which the capitation fee was supplemented by what was called a basic practice allowance which took account of such factors as seniority, training, ancillary staff, working hours and cost of premises.

7. The Labour government, 1964–70. During their years in opposition the Labour Party had been critical of a number of aspects of the Conservative handling of health service matters. Surveys had shown that it was Labour rather than Conservative supporters who continued to regard improvements in the health service as an important political issue. On their return to power, therefore, it was only to be expected that the Labour Party would make a number of changes, such as the reintroduction of free prescriptions.

However in 1968 the government reimposed charges, although the disabled and long-term sick were excluded from such payments and those on supplementary benefit could, as before, have the charges refunded. By the late 1960s, the average cost of prescriptions had risen to 75 pence and the number to around 250 million. The National Health Service (Family Planning) Act 1967 allowed contraceptive advice and supplies to be provided to a wider range of people (*see* **11**). The Sainsbury Committee of

Enquiry into the Pharmaceutical Industry (1967) had reported on the profits (which they considered excessive) which had been made from the supply of drugs for the National Health Service.

Other developments in the 1960s included the Abortion Act 1968 which was a private member's Bill moved by David Steel, later to become leader of the Liberal Party. The vote was an open one and neither the Conservative nor the Labour Party saw it as a party matter (*see* 10). The year 1968 also saw the publication of the Seebohm Report, *Local Authority and Allied Personal Services*, mainly concerned with local authority social services, but having important implications for the future of the National Health Service.

8. The 1970s. By the middle of the 1960s it was clear to both major parties that a reorganisation of the National Health Service was called for. The Redcliffe-Maud Report (*see* VIII, 4) had resulted in the alteration of local authority boundaries and the Seebohm Report (*see* 7) had altered the responsibilities of local authorities. A Green Paper published by the Labour government, *The Administrative Structure of Medical and Related Services in England and Wales* (H.M.S.O., 1968) and a Conservative Green Paper, *The Future Structure of the National Health Service* (H.M.S.O., 1970), both pointed to the need for a major reorganisation. The Conservative government therefore introduced the National Health Service Reorganisation Act 1973 which took effect in April 1974, just after the Labour government was returned to power. Its main features were as follows.

(*a*) The three separate services: hospitals, general practitioner services and local authority services, were amalgamated in an integrated management structure.

(*b*) Regional hospital boards, hospital management committees, boards of governors of hospitals, executive councils and local health authorities were replaced by a two-tier structure.

(*i*) Regional health authorities (R.H.A.s) were set up, with chairmen appointed by the Secretary of State.

(*ii*) Area health authorities (A.H.A.s) formed the second tier and were, in the main, appointed by the R.H.A.s.

(*iii*) Although both R.H.A.s and A.H.A.s were appointed, not elected, the Act stipulated that certain bodies, including representatives of trade unions and voluntary organisations, were to be consulted.

PROBLEMS

9. Euthanasia. Euthanasia is defined as, "gentle and easy death; bringing this about especially in the case of incurable and painful disease" (O.E.D.). It is clearly more of a moral problem than a political one but, since Parliament has to legislate for the National Health Service, it becomes a political issue if it is proposed that it should be allowed in state hospitals. It is at present illegal in any circumstances but a private member's Bill in 1970 proposed that it should, in certain circumstances, be legal. The Bill was defeated but the question still remains. The Euthanasia Society has for many years campaigned for what they call "mercy-killing" while a number of religious groups, particularly the Roman Catholic Church, have resolutely opposed it. The arguments for and against are summarised in the report of a symposium in 1972 which was published under the title, *Care of the Dying* (H.M.S.O., 1973).

(*a*) Advocates of euthanasia claim that:

(*i*) it is already practised and the fact should be recognised;

(*ii*) given adequate safeguards it is a kindness to terminal patients in the throes of a painful and incurable illness;

(*iii*) more than half of all deaths take place in hospital and over two-thirds of such deaths are old people; if they were allowed to choose to die the hospital and nursing services would be relieved of an intolerable strain;

(*iv*) a person should be allowed to die with dignity if he or she asks to do so and is of sound mind at the time;

(*v*) the cost of the health service is excessive; if those who wished to die were allowed to do so the money which would have been spent to keep them alive could be used elsewhere.

(*b*) Opponents of euthanasia use the following arguments.

(*i*) No one is ever justified in taking another's life.

(*ii*) To legalise killing could open the floodgates and could result in the killing of people who were considered "inconvenient". Some critics point to Hitler's extermination of the Jews as an example of what can happen if killing is legalised.

(*iii*) Modern methods of treatment mean that "incurable" illnesses may yet prove curable.

(*iv*) The responsibility placed on doctors in this situation is more than they can be expected to bear.

10. Abortion. The grounds for legal abortion were restricted, prior to the National Health (Abortion) Act 1967, to the situation in which abortion was necessary to prevent a threat to the physical or mental health of the mother. There was increasing evidence, however, that more and more women were having "back-street abortions" which were costly, dangerous and, in some cases, fatal. For obvious reasons it is impossible to estimate the exact size of the problem but it is closely related to the problem of family planning (*see* **11**) and, in 1968, the chief medical officer of the Department of Health estimated the number of unwanted pregnancies as being of the order of 200,000 per year.

The Abortion Act 1968 extended the grounds on which legal abortion could be given. The Act was the culmination of a long campaign by the Abortion Law Reform Society and led to the formation of a counter organisation in 1967. It was called the Society for the Protection of the Unborn Child and aimed to halt what it saw as the dangerous erosion of the rights of unborn children.

The medical profession too had reservations about altering the law on abortion. They agreed that some reform was called for but both the British Medical Association (B.M.A.) and the Royal College of Obstetricians felt that the proposals were unsatisfactory. The B.M.A. pointed out that doctors with moral objections to abortion might find themselves called upon to carry out what they considered an immoral operation. A "conscience clause" enabling them to refuse to perform such duties would not be the answer since their promotion prospects might be damaged thereby. It would be difficult in the case of a doctor with known objections to abortion and who had been passed over for promotion to prove that his lack of preferment was in no way associated with his known views. The Royal College of Obstetricians were also worried about moral issues but they had a more prosaic objection, namely that a law making abortions easier would lead to an excessive demand.

The grounds on which a legal abortion could be given under the Abortion Act 1968 were:

(*a*) where there was a serious risk of physical or mental injury to the mother;
(*b*) where it was likely that the child would be abnormal;
(*c*) where the mother was either mentally defective or was under sixteen and had become pregnant as a result of rape.

A Bill proposing further extension of the grounds for abortion

was "talked out" in 1977 but will presumably be reintroduced
later.

11. Family planning. Closely allied to the subject of abortion and
involving similar moral issues is the question of family planning.
This had been possible, on medical grounds only, under the
National Health Service Act 1946. A new Act, the National
Health Service (Family Planning) Act 1967 extended the arrangements for giving contraceptive advice and appliances to women
who objected on social grounds to having children. The Catholic
Church, together with the Society for the Protection of the Unborn Child, were again prominent in opposing the measure while
a number of organisations representing women's liberation move-
ments advocated it, mainly on the grounds that a woman's body
was hers to do with as she wished.

12. Who should control the health service? One of the fears expressed by the medical profession at the inception of the National
Health Service was that they would find themselves as civil servants with little professional autonomy. The fear was unjustified,
not least because the medical profession is inclined to be autocratic and, as professionals, they can and do have an influential
voice in major decisions. The last three decades have, however,
seen the rise of a new class of medical auxiliary, the hospital
administrator. His expertise is in management and, as hospitals
grow more complex, so the need for managerial skills increases.

Some doctors are concerned at what they see as an increasingly
bureaucratic trend. Control of professionals by laymen is always
fraught with problems, particularly when the professionals are as
traditional and conservative as the medical profession. The new
regional and area health authorities set up under the National
Health Service Reorganisation Act 1973 (*see* **8**) still ensured that
the professional view was well represented but these bodies were
approved rather than elected and critics were not slow to point
out that, even though certain representative bodies were required
to be consulted, there was still little chance of a strong voice being
heard to represent the views of the patient who was, after all, the
person for whom the system was ostensibly intended.

13. Costs. It is true, of course, that a nation will afford those
things which it considers important. It is also true that there is
unlikely ever to be agreement on the order of priorities. The

health service does not, and cannot, pay its way in the sense that a monetary profit can be shown. The actual expenditure in 1975/6 was £6,429 million and the estimated cost in 1977/8 is £5,461 million (figures published in *Public Expenditure Decisions*, Cmnd. 6393, 1975 and Cmnd. 6721, 1976). The benefits of the health service cannot be measured in financial terms, but are seen in improved standards of general health or in a growing expertise in the treatment of disease.

Aneurin Bevan's original estimate of the cost of the health service in 1946 was £150 million but the expenditure in the first year was considerably more than this and has risen consistently since then. It will be remembered that the Guillebaud Committee had examined the costs in 1956 and had found no evidence of maladministration (*see* 5). The proposals made at that time did not materially reduce the cost and, although both major parties and a number of opinion polls have indicated that the maintenance of the health service is consistently seen as a major political issue, the obvious solution, increased taxation, is unacceptable. A number of alternatives have been suggested from time to time, most of them aimed at reducing the burden of taxation which, at present, accounts for over 80 per cent of all health service income. The following are two of the main suggestions.

(*a*) *Increase the national insurance contribution*. National insurance accounts for about 10 per cent of the health service income and an increase in the flat-rate contribution would be administratively simple and could produce a much higher proportion of the total cost. Such an increase would, however, mean that lower-paid workers were contributing a larger proportion of their income than those who earned more, and an addition to the earnings-related portion of the contribution would be much more difficult administratively.

(*b*) *Patients to pay more*. There are about one million people who contribute to private medical insurance schemes and, perhaps, a similar number who are able to pay for hospital treatment without the aid of such schemes. It would be in line with the Conservative emphasis on private enterprise to encourage such payments as a method of reducing the health service bill. The Labour Party is, however, firmly opposed to such policies and in the February 1974 election pledged itself to phase out the private sector in National Health Service hospitals.

(*i*) The Conservative view is that those who can afford treatment and wish to pay for it should be allowed to do so.

(*ii*) The Labour view is that the provision of health services should depend upon need, not ability to pay.

(*iii*) Doctors are divided. Consultants generally favour the private sector, partly because it benefits them personally and partly because it is said to be of benefit to the health service to have an income from this source which can subsidise the service as a whole.

14. The brain drain. In 1960 it was estimated that some 300 doctors per year emigrated, mainly to America. Such doctors were, for the most part, newly qualified and concern was expressed that the cost of training them, which was considerable, was lost. The following suggestions were made to remedy this situation.

(*a*) Newly qualified doctors should be required to work in this country for a specified period, perhaps equivalent to the number of years they had spent training, before being allowed to emigrate. This suggestion was seen as an unfair restriction on their freedom of movement and, if adopted in principle, it could equally apply to specialists in other fields.

(*b*) Graduates, and particularly those qualified in medicine, should be required to refund the cost of their training before emigrating. Such a proposal would, however, negate the established principle in the provision of education, that education should be provided for those who wanted and could benefit from it without regard to their ability to pay for it.

However, it could be argued that the loss of qualified personnel was more apparent than real since, although English doctors may have emigrated, the loss by emigration was more than compensated for by the numbers of immigrants from the Third World who received their training in Britain and stayed on to staff the hospitals in the country where they had received their training.

PRESENT SITUATION AND FUTURE DIRECTIONS

15. The official view. In 1976 the Department of Health and Social Security issued a consultative document, *Priorities for the Health and Personal Social Services in England* (H.M.S.O., 1976). It was a new departure in that, for the first time, an attempt had been made to establish a system of priorities in both health and personal social services. The document recognised that cuts in public expenditure affected all public spending, including that on health and social services; but the cuts in this particular area were less severe than in some others and took the form mainly of a restriction in the amount of growth, rather than a halt to growth or cutting back. The White Paper on public expenditure 1979/80 envisaged a growth rate of 2 per cent per year for the personal social services and 1.8 per cent for the health services and it was within this context that the proposals for expenditure were made.

The document represents the Labour government's attempt to implement its election promises to improve the health service. Whilst it says nothing about the sensitive, political, issues like phasing out pay-beds and prescription charges, both of which were in the October 1974 manifesto, it does refer to the Secretary of State's intention to redistribute health services so that hitherto deprived areas should enjoy a greater share of the improved services. It also aims at joint planning between local authorities and health authorities in those fields, such as the care of the mentally handicapped, where responsibilities overlap.

16. Priorities. The first priority would be, in the words of the consultative document, "to put people before buildings". This statement has the advantage that it is not only an acceptable goal it is also a useful recognition that the building of new hospitals involves heavy capital expenditure which cannot be undertaken in a time of economic difficulty. Cynics might add that it enabled the government to break its election pledges.

The following are the main proposals in the consultative document.

(a) More personal social services are to be provided for groups like the elderly, the younger disabled and the mentally handicapped.

(b) Family practitioner services are to be expanded at a rate of 3.7 per cent per year and the provision of health centres and other supporting services will continue to be given priority.

(c) Preventive medicine, including health education and family planning services are to be maintained and, where necessary, increased.

(d) There is to be a deliberate policy of giving priority in the provision of services to the mentally handicapped and the elderly. These services include geriatric and mental hospital provision and the provision of day care, residential homes and home helps.

(e) The expenditure needed for the elderly and the mentally handicapped would be met by a reduction in the rate of growth of expenditure in services for general and acute hospitals and for maternity services.

(f) Economies will clearly be necessary. The document sets out a number of areas in which they might be made.

(i) Doctors and other medical personnel could make more economical use of the facilities provided.

(ii) The N.H.S. bill for drugs is growing at a rate of about 5 per cent per year and over-prescription is to be avoided.

(iii) Procurement procedures need to be re-examined so that supplies for the health service may be obtained more economically.

(iv) Administrative costs continue to rise and arrangements have already been made to examine this aspect of health service expenditure. An official report will doubtless be published.

17. A further consultative document. *The Way Forward* (H.M.S.O., 1977) continued the discussion of health service strategy in the light of the Public Expenditure Survey Committee report for 1975 (*see* XIX, **12**(*a*)) and taking account of comments on the earlier document. These, together with revised projections of population and resources, resulted in a change of emphasis. The first priority was an increased stress on the need for preventive medicine, followed by an attack on what the document called "past neglect of services". The services to be improved were those for the mentally ill, the elderly and children. A large part of the improvement would be achieved by better use of existing resources and more careful budgeting. The use of Planned Programme Budgeting (P.P.B.) is an example of the way in which the Civil Service is borrowing management techniques from the private sector, a development recommended in the Fulton Report (*see* XVII, **6**).

18. Criticisms of the health service. An article in *New Society* called "Are we any healthier?" (8th September 1977) by Alwyn Smith looks at the progress made in the health service since its inception. The writer points out that whether or not the health service has made progress depends upon how "health" is defined. The National Health Service has pursued two complementary aims. One has been to reduce the amount of sickness in the society and the other is to devise roles suitable for those whose health does not permit them to take a full part in the life of the society.

On both these issues the writer is less than whole-hearted in his praise of the health service. In spite of the continually rising cost of the health service, Britain still spends far less than many other countries on the health of its citizens and, although there have been some improvements, the net result is, he believes, disappointing.

PROGRESS TEST 16

1. What was the main difference between the pre-war health service and that envisaged by the National Health Service Act 1946? **(1, 2)**

2. Give details of the principles and structure of the National Health Service Act 1946. **(3, 4)**

3. Trace the development of the health service in the 1950s and 1960s. **(5, 6)**

4. What events took place in 1968 in relation to the health service? **(7)**

5. List the main features of the National Health Service Reorganisation Act 1973. **(8)**

6. What problems arise for the legislator when dealing with (a) euthanasia, (b) abortion and (c) family planning? **(9–11)**

7. What alternative proposals have been made for the financing of the health service? **(13)**

8. What is the official view of the direction in which the health service is going? **(15–17)**

PART FOUR

PUBLIC ADMINISTRATION

CHAPTER XVII

The Civil Service

DEVELOPMENT

1. The permanent Civil Service. The basis of the modern Civil Service can be found in the Northcote-Trevelyan Report of 1853. Its full title was *The Organisation of the Permanent Civil Service* and its recommendations, although stoutly opposed in some quarters at the time, gradually won general support and continue, with modifications, to the present day. Trevelyan (and to a lesser extent Northcote) looked at the Civil Service of his day and found it unsatisfactory. Entry and promotion depended largely upon patronage and those clerks who had no patron were promoted by seniority. They could wait years for dead men's shoes and, when eventually promoted, they were frequently incapable of performing any duties higher than those to which they were accustomed. The Report considered that the system of patronage should be abolished, not so much because it was wrong (Northcote himself owed his nomination for the job of producing the Report to the patronage of Gladstone) but because it was inefficient.

The Report recommended that all government departments, previously largely autonomous, should be unified and that the rules which they advocated be applied to all.

(*a*) Entry should be by competitive examination.

(*b*) There should be two major classes, the higher class being recruited from university graduates between the ages of 21 and 25, and the lower class, the secondary clerks, being recruited from men (mainly) aged between 17 and 21 and "of good general education".

(*c*) Promotion should be by merit, although seniority was to be taken into account.

(*d*) The work in the various departments should be graded.

2. The Civil Service Commission. The proposals for the reform of the Civil Service were far-reaching and demanded not only a break with tradition but also, perhaps more importantly, the surrender by powerful political figures of the privilege of patronage. It was therefore decided that the proposals should be submitted to a number of persons and organisations. These included academics, officials, divines and prominent public figures. Their observations were published in 1855, following which, more as a sop to public opinion than because he considered it necessary, Palmerston's government issued an Order in Council establishing a Civil Service Commission. Its three members were required to satisfy themselves as to the suitability of candidates for the Civil Service.

(*a*) Candidates were to be examined and successful applicants were to be given a certificate of qualification.

(*b*) Age limits were prescribed for various posts in different departments.

(*c*) There was to be an examination of physical fitness and moral character.

(*d*) The commissioners had to satisfy themselves that the applicant had the requisite knowledge and ability for the post.

3. The next hundred years. The next hundred years were a period of consolidation with open examinations introduced in 1870 for all departments, except the Home and Foreign Offices, and Royal Commissions sitting at intervals of about twenty years.

(*a*) The Playfair Commission (1874) made recommendations about the tests to be applied to higher grade Civil Servants and advocated uniform pay scales for the first time.

(*b*) The Ridley Commission (1890) advocated changes in the pay scales and urged the recruitment of typists to replace copyists and boy clerks.

(*c*) The Macdonnell Commission (1914) produced a Majority and a Minority Report but the outbreak of war meant that little was done about either.

(*d*) The Gladstone Commission (1918) was formed to consider the problems of recruitment after the war and, with the help of a subcommittee of the Whitley Council for the Civil Service, produced the recommendation that there should be four major grades in the Civil Service:

(*i*) administrative,

(*ii*) executive,

(*iii*) clerical, and

(*iv*) writing assistants (later called clerical assistants).

(*e*) The Tomlin Commission (1931) is chiefly remembered for its definition of a Civil Servant: "Civil Servants are servants of the Crown, not being holders of a political or judicial office, who are employed in a civil capacity and whose remuneration is found wholly and directly out of monies voted by Parliament".

(*f*) The Priestly Commission (1953) was concerned with conditions of service and the remuneration of Civil Servants. It set up a Civil Service Pay Research Unit, charged with collecting information on the rates of pay paid by "outside" employers. The unit was to be staffed by Civil Servants but was to be independent (*see* **20**(*d*)). It did not decide pay scales but provided the information on which negotiations about Civil Service pay could be based. It continued in operation until 1975 when its work was suspended because of the economic situation.

BUREAUCRACY

4. The power of the Civil Service. The spate of post-war legislation and the increasing government involvement in all aspects of the life of the nation led to more power being exercised by the Civil Service. It was not suggested that the power was used corruptly, simply that it was concentrated in too few hands and that those who wielded it were not answerable to the electorate. These considerations, widely voiced in the 1960s, led to the appointment of the Fulton Commission (*see*, **6**).

Before considering Fulton's proposals it would be as well to consider the characteristics of bureaucracies in general. All large organisations tend to have bureaucratic control; and the larger the organisation the more inevitable the bureaucratic process becomes. It has five major characteristics.

(*a*) *Written rules.* Laws, regulations, statutes, codes and instructions ensure that the purposes and functions of the organisation are known. Decisions given by the organisation are based on the rules and justified by reference to them.

(*b*) *Specialisation by function.* The Civil Service has different departments dealing with different subjects. Specific individuals have precise responsibilities.

(*c*) *Hierarchical structure*. In the Civil Service a job becomes a career and the Civil Servant moves from one rung of the ladder to the next.

(*d*) *Impartiality*. It is the office which is important, not the holder of it.

(*e*) *Separation of ownership and control*. The Civil Servant, however important, does not own the "firm" for which he works.

5. Advantages and disadvantages. A bureaucratic system has strengths and weaknesses which can be related to the characteristics listed in **4** above.

(*a*) Written rules ensure predictability. The same situation dealt with by different bureaucrats should, in theory at least, be dealt with in the same way. Written rules, however, tend to become complex and inflexible.

(*b*) Specialisation by function means that it should be possible to pin-point the organisation and individual responsible for a particular subject. But the specialist, by definition, has a narrow outlook.

(*c*) Hierarchical structure gives the Civil Servant security of tenure. This makes for continuity but it also means that he has little incentive to show initiative.

(*d*) Impartiality is fair, it is also impersonal. The charge that Civil Servants are "faceless men" is not without foundation.

(*e*) The separation of ownership and control allows the legislature to have the last word in its dealings with the executive, but it means that the Civil Servant does not have ultimate responsibility for his actions.

THE FULTON REPORT

6. The Fulton Report. The Report of the Fulton Commission, *The Civil Service* (Cmnd. 3638, 1968), was a bulky document which took three years to produce and included comparisons with the Civil Services of France and America. It saw the Civil Service of the 1960s as still basically a Northcote-Trevelyan concept and made six major criticisms.

(*a*) It was too generalist. By this it meant that the higher Civil Servants did not specialise and, in particular, they lacked the specialised techniques necessary to run their departments.

(*b*) The structure of the Civil Service, with its classes and grades within the classes, was out-moded.

(*c*) Any specialists employed in the Civil Service were not adequately represented at the top management level.

(*d*) Management skills were lacking at all levels.

(*e*) The Civil Service was too exclusive and needed more contact with industry and commerce.

(*f*) Establishment work, i.e. that dealing with recruitment, promotion and training, was inadequate.

7. Recommendations. Having made its criticisms the Fulton Report emphasised that it regarded the Civil Service as basically sound. It recommended changes to enable the Civil Service to improve.

(*a*) There should be a continuous review of the work and staffing of the Civil Service.

(*b*) Treasury control of the Civil Service was restricting. A new department, the Civil Service Department, should be formed to be responsible for some of the functions undertaken by the Civil Service Commission and to take over control of management and pay from the Treasury.

(*c*) The permanent secretary of the new department should also be head of the home Civil Service, subject to the oversight of the Prime Minister.

(*d*) The class structure of the Civil Service should be abolished.

(*e*) More professionalism was needed. Training should be given in such subjects as economics, finance and social administration.

(*f*) Departments should have more say in the choice of staff allocated to them.

(*g*) A Civil Service college should be set up and some places in the college should be allocated to students from outside the Civil Service.

(*h*) Career management and promotion procedures should be reviewed.

(*i*) Management service units should be set up in all departments and management accountability should be encouraged.

(*j*) There should be more movement in and out of the Civil Service so that Civil Servants could learn about outside practices and the Civil Service in general could benefit from the expertise of outsiders. It was also possible that the Civil Service had something to offer to those outside.

(*k*) All departments should have a policy adviser who would be an important official and would have charge of a planning unit.

(*l*) Technical departments could have a technical head, i.e. a scientific department could be headed by a scientist, not an administrator.

(*m*) Policy advisors, chief specialists and the permanent secretary of each department should confer regularly. The permanent secretary would continue to be head of the department but it would, of course, be possible for him to be a specialist in his own right.

(*n*) Ministers should be able to employ their own experts.

(*o*) The proposals should be implemented as soon as possible and their implementation should be monitored, perhaps by a parliamentary committee.

There were a number of other matters which Fulton considered should be examined but he considered that further enquiries should be made before firm proposals were put forward. These matters included:

(*p*) hiving off, i.e. delegating official work to other bodies;

(*q*) ways of reducing unnecessary secrecy;

(*r*) new methods of staff consultation with trade unions and others;

(*s*) new and better methods of recruitment.

POST-FULTON DEVELOPMENTS

8. The Civil Service Department. The government accepted the main recommendation of the Fulton Report and announced the formation of a new department, the Civil Service Department (C.S.D.), on the day that the report was issued. Sir William Armstrong (now Lord Armstrong) was its first permanent secretary and also head of the home Civil Service. It took over most of the functions of the Civil Service Commission and the pay and management divisions of the Treasury and was responsible, throughout the Civil Service, for five areas of work. These were:

(*a*) personnel management, including the selection and recruitment of candidates and the management of their subsequent careers;

(*b*) training; individual departments continued to be responsible for some training but the C.S.D. had general oversight, with particular responsibility for training in administration and management techniques; training responsibilities also included responsibilities for operational research and for computers;

(*c*) supervision of expenditure and manpower; this included the responsibility for pay and pay negotiations;

(*d*) grading, classes and occupational groupings;

(*e*) superannuation and allied matters.

9. Personnel management. Fulton had recommended that graduate recruits should be allocated on the basis of the relevance of their degrees to the work of the department to which they were sent. The government rejected this proposal, largely on the basis that a youngster's potential was more important than the subjects studied for a first degree. Once appointed, the new Civil Servant's career would be developed logically. This would be done in a number of ways.

(*a*) First postings would be suited to the individual as far as possible and would take account of education, aspirations and abilities.

(*b*) A system of annual reports would ensure that the suitability and progress of all staff was kept constantly under review.

(*c*) Appropriate training would be given as and when required.

(*d*) Movement to different jobs and different departments would be facilitated in order to enhance the career prospects, particularly of youngsters.

(*e*) Promotion was to be by merit.

10. Training. Training in the Civil Service prior to the Fulton Report had been largely based on the recommendations of the Assheton Report (1943). The bulk of it was carried out within departments although some central training was carried out by the Centre for Administrative Studies for higher grades only. The Fulton concept, which owed a great deal to the French *Ecôle Nationale d'Administration*, was that there should be a Civil Service college (*see* 11 below) which would offer a range of courses for all grades throughout the service. After Fulton, departmental training was retained but considerably strengthened. All departments, except the smallest, now have their own training organisation which works in conjunction with the Civil Service Department. External training, i.e. training carried out outside the Civil Service, was continued and supplemented where necessary by day-release schemes for younger staff.

11. The Civil Service College. The college was opened in 1969 in three centres, London, Sunningdale and Edinburgh, but the Edinburgh centre was later closed as an economy measure.

The subjects covered by the college include economics, statistics, personnel management, social administration and public administration. The emphasis of all courses was to be on management and allied areas.

The staff of the college were to have been a mixture of Civil Servants on secondment and academics on short-term contract, usually five years. The original intention was that the proportions should be roughly 75 per cent Civil Servants and 25 per cent academics, but by 1974 there were about half of each.

Training by and for the civil service conducted in this way could easily become introspective and sterile. Links are therefore maintained with outside courses run by polytechnics and business colleges as well as with European organisations concerned with business studies and public administration. Exchange visits are sometimes arranged and sabbatical leave is available to staff of the college so that the research function can be strengthened.

Although the college was not intended to be as élitist as its French counterpart, there were criticisms in its first few years that it devoted too much of its resources to small élitist groups, the administration trainees and higher executive officers (A) (*see* **15**). This point was made in an appraisal of the first years of its existence and published by the Civil Service Department under the title *Civil Service Training*.

12. Specialists and generalists. One frequently-voiced criticism of the pre-Fulton Civil Service was that the "mandarins", i.e. the higher Civil Servants, were out of touch. They had been appointed in an earlier age, when a classical education was thought to fit a man for the job of running the country, and their attitudes and approach were an anachronism in the second half of the twentieth century.

One group who felt very strongly about this particular issue was the Institute of Professional Civil Servants whose evidence to the Fulton Committee ranged over the Civil Services of six different countries. The gist of their evidence was that there were two type of higher Civil Servant, the specialist and the generalist and in the main the specialist was subordinate to the generalist. If the generalist was to justify and maintain his position, he too should acquire a special skill, namely management. The direct entrants to the higher Civil Service at that time (assistant secretaries and assistant principals) received only three weeks' training on appointment and, although there was clearly some merit in learning the job by doing it, there was a good case for much more theoretical training in administration and management subjects. Fulton agreed with the criticism and the Civil Service College (*see* 11 above) now runs courses at all levels of management from executive officer to under secretary.

13. Supervision of expenditure and manpower. The Civil Service has changed considerably since the discussions which led to the Fulton Report. It grows each year (*see* Tables VII and VIII) partly because of the increasing volume of legislation, no matter which party is in power, and partly perhaps because of an in-built tendency to grow (Parkinson's Law) which is aggravated by union demands for more staff to cope with the complexities of new legislation. The growth was restricted in 1976–7 because of cuts in public expenditure.

TABLE VII.   NUMBER OF CIVIL SERVANTS IN APRIL
OF EACH YEAR (THOUSANDS)

1969	1971	1973	1975	1976	1977
699.0	700.1	700.2	701.4	747.6	745.6

Source: Civil Service Department Statistics.

TABLE VIII.   CIVIL SERVICE EXPENDITURE AND MANPOWER

	1961	1971	1975
Total public expenditure (£ millions)	10.319	24.327	54.465
Total number employed by central government* thousands	1,773	1,929	1,246
as a percentage of all employment	7.3	7.9	9.0

* These are not all Civil Servants (*see* 17).

Source: Social Trends, 1976.

14. Composition. The composition of the Civil Service is also changing. The old stereotype of the bowler-hatted Whitehall warrior has been unrealistic for decades. Only about 20 per cent of Civil Servants actually work in inner London and the work done by the majority in the provinces is unlike that which the traditional picture suggests. Men still outnumber women by about 3:2 but among the clerical staff, who tend to be more numerous outside London, the proportions are reversed. The rise in status of "blue-collar workers" since the war has meant that the "white-collar" Civil Service job is no longer regarded as prestigious and the increasing militance of trade unionism has meant that today's breed of young Civil Servant will not tolerate conditions which his predecessors would have accepted quite happily. For these and similar reasons the job of staffing the Civil Service has changed and manning levels which once were adequate have to be increased whenever new legislation requires implementation.

Fulton recommended that the distinction between administrative, executive and clerical staff should be abolished and that the many and various occupational groups which made up the Civil Service should be integrated into a unified structure. This integration is proceeding and the administrative, executive and clerical grades have been amalgamated, since 1971, in an administration group.

15. Administration Trainees. One innovation proposed by Fulton was the introduction of a "fast stream" composed of the brighter graduates who would enter the Civil Service in a special new grade (administration trainee) and would be intensively groomed for stardom. Those who survived the concentrated initial training would move quickly to the higher ranks of the Civil Service. Those who were unable to do so would be eligible for ordinary promotion in the normal way. The grade of administration trainee (A.T.) is open to graduates or those with equivalent qualifications, aged under 28, and from both within and outside the Civil Service. The original intention was that there should be about 250–300 such posts, half of which would be filled by internal candidates. In fact the proportion from outside has proved greater than was originally envisaged and the Society of Civil and Public Servants (the trade union representing the executive grades) is currently having second thoughts about the whole scheme because of the effect on the promotion prospects of its members. The successful A.T. (about one-third of the total) can expect to be promoted to higher executive officer (A) within four years and to be further promoted to the rank of principal within about three years. Both A.T.s and H.E.O.(A)s receive extensive and specialised training, particularly in management subjects, and their postings are designed to give them a broader view of the work of the Civil Service than that which is available to normal entrants.

16. Civil Servants and trade unionism. The British Civil Service prides itself on its political neutrality. It serves whichever party is in power with the same degree of enthusiasm and co-operation. That, at least, is the theory. Critics claim that it is unreasonable to expect that Civil Servants should be neutral and that, in the higher Civil Service at least, there is a strong Conservative bias (*see* A. Sampson, *The New Anatomy of Britain*, Hodder and Stoughton, 1971).

The question of Civil Servants' participation in the Trades Union Congress is therefore important since the T.U.C. is frequently seen as a strong supporter of the Labour Party, if not of Labour governments. Post-war developments and, in particular, the legislation in the mid-1970s (*see* XII, **9**) have highlighted the problems of Civil Service trade unionists. Whilst the official line is to encourage all Civil Servants to join their appropriate union they are still expected to remain politically neutral. For many years therefore Civil Service unions refused to affiliate to the T.U.C. since this might be seen as compromising their political neutrality. However, a survey by the Institute of Professional Civil Servants in 1963 showed that none of the major political parties saw membership of the T.U.C. as of political significance.

In 1946 the Civil Service Clerical Association (now the Civil and Public Services Association) became affiliated to the T.U.C. Several other Civil Service unions followed later. Political bias has not been seen to any large extent and, although some of the clerical unions are more militant than they once were, this may be due as much to the changing times as to the support given by T.U.C. membership.

The situation becomes difficult when the T.U.C. opposes government policy, as it did over *In Place of Strife* (*see* XII, **6**), or when the government as legislators take action which conflicts with their role as employers, e.g. the imposition of public expenditure cuts and the suspension of the activities of the Pay Research

Unit (*see* 3(*f*)). In such cases the Civil Servant trade unionist may have divided loyalties between the government and the T.U.C., and may feel that his interests are best served by the T.U.C. in its opposition to the government.

17. Unified structure. There are about two million people employed by the government (*see* Table VIII) but not all are Civil Servants as defined by the Tomlin Commission (*see* 3(*e*)). The total number of Civil Servants on 1st July 1977 was 739,700 (*Hansard*, December 1977) of whom about 180,000 were industrial Civil Servants, mainly manual workers in government industrial establishments. The non-industrial Civil Servants are currently being integrated into nine separate categories with common patterns of pay and grading (*see* Table IX). About 70 per cent of such Civil Servants have been so far integrated.

18. Recruitment and promotion. Recruitment is controlled by the Civil Service Commission and by individual departments. Entry into the administration group is by open competition based upon academic ability. Broadly, the brightest graduates enter at administration trainee level (*see* **15**), other graduates and those with "A" Level passes enter at executive officer level and others enter the clerical grades. Junion staff, i.e. clerical and manual grades, are selected by departments but the Civil Service Commission issues a certificate of qualification for all permanent appointees. Professional and technical staff are appointed on the basis of their qualifications, usually by means of an interview. Promotions at the highest level, Deputy Secretary and above, have to be approved by the Prime Minister but other promotions are either by means of centrally conducted examinations or from grade to grade. Both new entrants and promotees have to serve a period of probation in the post to which they are appointed. The length of the period depends upon the grade of the post.

19. Specialised Civil Servants. Most government departments, whatever their size, function or structure, have certain features in common. Their head is usually a permanent secretary and they will have their own finance, establishments and information divisions working to rules agreed by the Civil Service Department. Some comparatively small departments have a specialised role and their arrangements are somewhat different.

(*a*) *The Cabinet Office* works directly to the Prime Minister and comprises the Cabinet Secretariat (*see* XVIII, **12**), the

TABLE IX.   CATEGORIES OF NON-INDUSTRIAL STAFF IN THE CIVIL
SERVICE

Category	Number of staff
General	
Administration group	230,000
Economists	300
Statisticians	450
Information officers	1,350
Librarians	350
Science	
Scientists engaged in research and planning	18,000
Professional and technical	
Professional and technical group, including architects, engineers and support staff	40,000
Illustrators (graphics officers)	500
Training	
Instructional officers in crafts and trades	4,000
Legal	
Two groups of lawyers, one for England and Wales and one for Scotland	850
Police	
Policing of Ministry of Defence establishments	4,000
Secretarial	
Typists	23,000
Personal secretaries for higher Civil Servants	4,600
Data processing	
Computer operators etc.	8,000
Social security	
Staff of local social security offices	43,000
Total	378,400*

Source: Britain 1977 (H.M.S.O.). * The table shows only those staff currently integrated into the new grading structure.

Central Policy Review Staff (*see* XIX, 13), the Central Statistical Office and an historical section, responsible for the preparation of official histories.

(*b*) *The Civil Service Department* is also under the control of the Prime Minister. Its permanent head (Sir Ian Bancroft) is in addition head of the home Civil Service, and it is responsible for both the Civil Service Commission and the Parliamentary Counsel Office which is responsible for the drafting of government Bills and subordinate legislation. Its functions are described in 8 above.

(*c*) *The diplomatic service* provides staff for the Foreign and Commonwealth Office and for U.K. diplomatic missions. It has its own grade structure and entry is usually at honours degree level. Its work is carried out in embassies, consulates and delegations throughout the world and involves matters of trade, finance, aid, defence, energy and technology. It has a staff of about 6,500.

(*d*) *Scottish Civil Servants* are part of the U.K. Civil Service but are the responsibility of the Scottish Office, presided over by the Secretary of State for Scotland. Certain administrative functions are carried out by five specifically Scottish departments:

    (*i*) Department of Agriculture and Fisheries for Scotland;
    (*ii*) the Scottish Development Department;
    (*iii*) the Scottish Economic Planning Department;
    (*iv*) the Scottish Education Department;
    (*v*) the Scottish Home and Health Department.

(*e*) *Northern Ireland* has its own legislature and executive. Although the legislature was dissolved in 1975 the executive, i.e the Civil Service, continues to function as a separate body. It is modelled on its British counterpart and exchanges between British and Northern Ireland Civil Servants can, in theory, take place subject to agreement between the two employing departments.

CRITICISMS OF THE CIVIL SERVICE

20. The Expenditure Committee Report. The Eleventh Report of the Expenditure Committee, *The Civil Service* (H.M.S.O., 1977), made a detailed examination of the post-Fulton Civil Service and was critical of some aspects. Its most damaging criticism was that the higher Civil Service had too much power and obstructed the work of government (*see* XVIII, **19**). The other major points made in the report are considered below.

(*a*) *Expenditure.* The control of both the expenditure of the Civil Service and its efficiency was, prior to the Fulton Report, the responsibility of the Treasury. Fulton suggested the creation

of a Civil Service Department to deal with manpower and expenditure but left overall responsibility for efficiency with the
Treasury. The Expenditure Committee felt that the arrangement
had not worked particularly well and that there were grounds for
either giving both responsibilities back to the Treasury (since in
their view they could not be divorced) or creating a new Department of Expenditure and Manpower Control, in which case there
would not be much for the truncated Civil Service Department
to do.

(b) *Training*. The Committee was critical of the Civil Service
training programme and pointed out that only 9 per cent of it
was undertaken by the Civil Service College. The rest was done
by departmental training organisations. It recommended that the
Civil Service Department should monitor departmental training
schemes with a view to diverting even more work to either the
departments or to non-Civil Service educational establishments.

(c) *Oxbridge bias*. It is frequently alleged that the higher Civil
Service is staffed by graduates of Oxford and Cambridge, and
that a high proportion of those who did not go to Oxbridge are
the products of independent schools. The evidence is conflicting.
On the one hand, only six of the twenty permanent under secretaries went to public schools, but on the other hand, from 1971
to 1975 nearly a quarter of all applicants for administration
trainee posts and half of those who were successful in their application came from Oxbridge. It could be argued, of course, that
this is hardly surprising since Oxbridge produces the best graduates or, alternatively, that youngsters who intend to make a
career of the Civil Service go to these universities because it has
been shown that doing so will enhance their prospects.

(d) *Pay and superannuation*. In 1976–7, during a period of pay
restraint, the question of Civil Service pay and, more particularly, their inflation-proof superannuation scheme came in for
some criticism. The Committee in considering these matters decided that the Civil Service was not overpaid; but it did call
attention to the fact that the Pay Research Unit (*see* 3(*f*)) was
staffed by Civil Servants.

PROGRESS TEST 17

1. What did the Northcote-Trevelyan Report recommend? (1)

2. How was the Civil Service Commission to satisfy itself as to the suitability of candidates for the Civil Service? (2)

3. What are the characteristics of a bureaucracy? (4, 5)

4. What did the Fulton Report recommend? (6, 7)

5. Outline the developments in the Civil Service following the Fulton Report. (8–15)

6. What are the problems associated with the affiliation of Civil Service trade unions to the T.U.C.? (16)

7. List the more important of the specialised government departments. (19)

8. What did the Expenditure Committee say was wrong with the present-day Civil Service? (20)

CHAPTER XVIII

Policy Making

POLITICAL PARTIES

1. Who governs? This book is about government and, in particular, the British system in which Parliament is sovereign. There is a sense however in which Parliament is not master of her fate. The decisions which she makes and the laws which she enacts are the result of a complex process in which the formal proceedings of the legislature are but the final step. The seeds of legislation may lie in party conferences, in the activities of pressure groups, in Cabinet decisions or in the personality of the Prime Minister, to mention but a few of the possibilities.

The policy which is adopted by the governing party is a reflection of the views of the party as expressed at party conferences and in party caucuses (*see* VI). These views are published, at the time of an election, in the form of a manifesto and it is sometimes claimed that the programme outlined in the party manifesto gives the successful party a mandate to proceed in a certain way (*see* 18).

2. Labour Party. The Labour Party has an annual party conference consisting of delegates from affiliated organisations, M.P.s, parliamentary candidates, local agents and members of the National Executive Committee (N.E.C.). The N.E.C. which is elected by the conference, meets regularly between conferences and is responsible for the interpretation and implementation of conference decisions and for liaison with the Parliamentary Labour Party, i.e. those party members who are M.P.s. The N.E.C. also draws up the conference programme and is thus in an extremely strong position to influence Parliament. Its treasurer is invariably a leading member of the parliamentary party and it includes among its members the leader and deputy leader of the party who will, of course, be the Prime Minister and the deputy if the party is in power. The leader is chosen by ballot and stays as leader until he resigns. The system of balloting was devised in

1976 when Mr. Wilson, as he then was, resigned as Prime Minister.

(a) Labour M.P.s (but not Labour peers) may vote.

(b) The winner must poll over 50 per cent of the votes (which means that there may have to be a number of eliminating heats).

(c) Candidates may not enter the contest after the first round.

3. Conservative Party. The Conservative Party also has its conference, its head office and its special procedures for electing a leader; but they differ from those of the Labour Party in a number of important respects. The conference consists of representatives of the National Union (the full name of the Conservative Party, not often used these days, is the National Unionist Association of Conservative and Liberal Unionist Associations), constituency organisations, and election agents. Its function is different from that of the Labour Party conference in that it is the leader, rather than the conference, who decides policy. The leader must of course consult closely with colleagues and must be aware of the views of party members generally. For the Conservatives, however, the annual conference is more of a sounding-board than a policy-making body.

The Conservative Party has no one central body equivalent to Labour's N.E.C., instead it has a number of bodies responsible for different aspects of party organisation.

(a) Central Office is the administrative headquarters and looks after party finances. It is headed by the chairman of the party (not the leader) and studies political issues which will form the party manifesto. In this it is aided by a research department.

(b) The Central Council is, theoretically, the national governing body of the party and consists of all Conservative M.P.s together with adopted candidates and constituency representatives and its main function is to act as a link between members and constituents.

(c) The Executive Committee of the National Union is responsible for the day-to-day affairs of the Central Council and does some of its most important work by means of specialised sub-committees.

4. The Conservative leader. Prior to the election of Mr. Heath in 1965 the election of the leader of the Conservative Party was a mysterious process which, said its critics, owed much to the "old boy network". In that year a new system was devised relying, like the Labour Party system, on a ballot.

(*a*) All Conservative M.P.s may vote.

(*b*) The winner must have a clear majority over all other candidates, which means that there will probably be a number of ballots.

(*c*) Unlike the Labour system, candidates may enter after the first ballot (as happened when Margaret Thatcher succeeded Edward Heath in the struggle for Tory leadership in 1975).

THE PRIME MINISTER

5. Origins. The title Prime Minister is of comparatively recent origin, dating back no further than the reign of George I (1714–22). Since the King could not speak English he did not attend Cabinet meetings and his place as chairman was taken by the First Lord of the Treasury (Horace Walpole) who chose his colleagues and was regarded by them as *primus inter pares*, first among equals. The first man to whom the title Prime Minister was applied was Pitt the Younger, who held office between 1783 and 1801 and between 1804 and 1806. However, it was not until 1905 that official recognition was given to the office, by a Royal Warrant nominating the Prime Minister fourth in order of precedence on state occasions. The Chequers Estate Act 1917 was the first time that the office was referred to in a statute and final recognition, in the form of a salary, had to wait until the Ministers of the Crown Act 1937.

It will be seen that the office owes more to convention than to statute, and convention also decrees that the holder shall be a member of the House of Commons.

(*a*) He is the leader of the government. He forms it and appoints the Cabinet. He is responsible, both to Parliament and to the electorate, for the success or failures of his party.

(*b*) He is the link between government and sovereign. He keeps the Queen informed on important state and political matters and advises her on the dissolution of Parliament. (However, his role should not be confused with that of the Speaker, who is the link between Parliament and the sovereign.)

(*c*) He directs and controls policy. As chairman of Cabinet meetings (and as the leader of his party) he translates party policy into government activity.

(*d*) He is the representative of the nation. In international affairs, particularly since the Second World War, the "summit conference" has assumed greater importance and although the Foreign Secretary can, and does, conduct negotiations on behalf of the nation the Prime Minister plays an increasingly important part in these affairs.

(*e*) He makes recommendations for important appointments (*see* 7). Although the appointments are nominally made by the Queen they are, in fact, from nominations supplied by the Prime Minister.

6. The power of the Prime Minister. The Prime Minister's functions appear to give him a great deal of power. In one sense this power is real; he can exercise it so long as he holds the office. But his tenure of office depends upon a number of factors over which he may have very little control (the size of his majority, the strength of his support within his party, the popularity of his government to name but a few). Within these constraints, however, his position has been strengthened in this century by a number of developments.

(*a*) Increasing complexity in political matters, and the growing involvement of the government in the life of the nation, have resulted in the subjection of a large part of the national life to governmental control and influence.

(*b*) The growth of party politics means that M.P.s are now more dependent upon the party machine for election than previously. Once elected they are subject to the whip system and the Prime Minister is therefore assured of at least nominal support on most issues.

(*c*) The creation of the Cabinet Secretariat (*see* 11) and various co-ordinating committees has increased Cabinet efficiency and thus the power of the Prime Minister. He can now make decisions without consulting the Cabinet. He does not normally do so of course, since he relies on their support in a number of ways. The plans for the Suez crisis, in 1956, however, and the abdication of Edward VIII, in 1936, were both matters about which the Cabinet later complained that they had not been consulted.

7. The power of patronage. Among the appointments made by the sovereign on the advice of the Prime Minister are the following:

(*a*) Church of England archbishops, bishops and deans;

(*b*) judicial offices, including Lord Chief Justice, Lords of Appeal in Ordinary and Lord Justices of Appeal;

(*c*) Privy Counsellors;

(*d*) Poet Laureate;

(*e*) Constable of the Tower of London;

(*f*) chancellorships and vice-chancellorships of some universities;

(*g*) appointments to public boards, royal commissions and similar bodies.

The Prime Minister also makes recommendations for the award of honours and pensions paid from the Civil List.

8. Elected monarchy. The functions and responsibilities exercised by the Prime Minister are functions and responsibilities formerly exercised by the monarch. It is therefore sometimes said that the Prime Minister is an elected monarch, a president, and that his regime is nearer to that of a presidency, e.g. the U.S.A., than a constitutional monarchy.

In support of this view one could cite the following arguments.

(*a*) He can appoint and dismiss members of the Cabinet as he chooses. At meetings he controls the agenda and takes the chair.

(*b*) The timing of the dissolution of Parliament is his personal decision. In this respect he is in a stronger position than the President of the U.S.A. whose government is elected for a fixed term.

(*c*) As political head of the government he controls the appointment of senior Civil Servants to some extent.

(*d*) He personifies the government, e.g. it is usual to refer to the Heath government, the Wilson government or the Callaghan government.

The following arguments can be used to show that prime ministerial government is not like, for example, the U.S. presidency.

(*a*) The president of the U.S.A. is elected for a fixed term, the Prime Minister is not.

(*b*) The Prime Minister can ensure the passing of his party's political programme. The majority in Congress may be of a rival party.

(*c*) The tenure of the Prime Minister is dependent upon his support within his own party, that of the President is not.

Neither a prime minister not a president can be successful without:

(*a*) good health;
(*b*) a good public image;
(*c*) the co-operation of the Civil Service.

THE CABINET

9. Evolution. Prior to the reign of George I the Privy Council was the chief executive body but, during his reign, the Cabinet became more important and its importance has grown over the years. Traditionally the work of government is carried out by ministers and in one sense the Cabinet can be seen as a co-ordinating body. Its powers are, however, more extensive than co-ordination; it actually makes policy decisions and it is, above all, a political organ dependent upon the confidence placed in it by the House of Commons. Until 1867 it rarely contained more than sixteen members but the tendency since then has been for the numbers to grow. The rising numbers reflect the change in the nature and scope of the decisions with which the Cabinet is concerned. Before the First World War these were mainly questions of foreign policy and internal regulation. Since then, however, the emphasis has altered. Increasing social and economic involvement on the part of the government, and Britain's declining position in world affairs, has altered and increased the areas of government concern. The Cabinet has become more complex and less autonomous.

10. Size of the Cabinet. A large Cabinet, containing all the ministers, will be representative of all aspects of government but will be unwieldy. A small Cabinet is likely to be more efficient but less representative. The Prime Minister, in forming his Cabinet, must weigh up the balance of advantages and must also consider whether he needs the services of a particular individual or the views of a particular department. Some outstanding individuals will be given important posts which ensure a seat in the Cabinet. The Lord Chancellor, the Lord President and the Chancellor of the Exchequer, for example, have always been included in the Cabinet, as have the Secretaries of State for Scotland and Wales ever since the posts were created.

The history of the post of Minister of Health is an interesting example of the way in which the importance of the person who fills a post determines whether or not it is represented in the Cabinet. From 1945 to 1951 it was held by Aneurin Bevan, an important member of the Labour Party who was responsible for introducing a great new concept, the National Health Service. He was a member of the Cabinet during this period but his successor was not. The Conservative administration which followed also included the Minister of Health in its Cabinet for a while but later excluded him. Enoch Powell's promotion to the Cabinet in 1962 probably owed more to his ability than to his post as Minister of Health and the Labour administration of 1964 did not include the Health Minister in its Cabinet. It was not until the creation of the Department of Health and Social Security in 1968, when the Secretary of State for that department gained wider responsibilities, that health was again represented.

11. The Haldane Report. The *Report of the Machinery of Government* (Cmnd. 9230, 1918) set out the functions of the Cabinet and the conditions necessary to ensure that they were carried out. The functions included the control of the executive, the formulation of policy and the co-ordination and delimitation of the activities of government departments. The following conditions were necessary for the Cabinet to achieve these aims.

(a) It should be small in number. Haldane recommended not more than twelve, but the smallest Cabinet within the past fifty years was Churchill's Cabinet of 1951 which contained sixteen members. The normal number is now around twenty-three. Callaghan had twenty-two at the beginning of 1977 and both Sir Alec Douglas-Home and Harold Wilson had twenty-three. In Wilson's case however he created an inner cabinet of senior ministers in 1968 which had only six members.

(b) It should meet frequently. In fact it meets once or twice a week but can be convened at any time if necessary.

(c) It should be well informed.

(d) It should consult all ministers likely to be affected by its decisions.

(e) It should be able to ensure that its decisions are carried out.

12. Cabinet Secretariat. The Cabinet Secretariat was set up in 1916 as a temporary war-time measure but was retained following the Haldane Report and is now an integral part of the machinery of government. It is part of the Cabinet Office (*see* XVII, **19**(*a*)) and the Secretary of the Cabinet has access to a wide range of information which enables policy to be co-ordinated at the highest level. His responsibilities include:

(a) the circulation of documents required by the Cabinet;

(b) preparing agendas for Cabinet meetings in conjunction with the Prime Minister;

(c) recording and circulating minutes of meetings;

(d) follow-up action as necessary.

POLICY-MAKING CONSIDERATIONS

13. Factors to be considered. In shaping government policy, the party in power will have to take account of the views and representations of many groups. Some of them, like the party conference, are purely political. Some, like the Civil Service, are ostensibly non-political (but *see* XVII, **16**) and some, although they have political aspects, are basically pressure groups who happen to be interested in the political aspects of proposed legislation. Links with such groups may be formal or informal. Broadly speaking, the more links the government has with a group the more formal will be the arrangements for consultation with them. Some of the larger groups are considered below.

14. Trades Union Congress. (*See* also XII, **4**.) The T.U.C. is the largest and best known of the trade union organisations in Britain. One of its major functions is to present the views of the trade unions to the government, particularly on social and economic matters, and it is widely consulted by the government on those subjects. Its representatives, together with those of the Confederation of British Industry (*see* **15**), sit regularly on government committees and the expertise and resources which it can command are influential in the formulation of government policy.

15. Confederation of British Industry (C.B.I.). The C.B.I. is of more recent origin than the T.U.C. It was founded in 1965 as an amalgamation of employers' organisations, the chief of which was the Federation of British Industries. Like the T.U.C. it is a federation and it represents about 10,000 companies and 200 employers' organisations. It functions as an advisory and consultative body and is recognised by governments of both main parties as the official spokesman for employers. It frequently works in conjunction with the Association of British Chambers of Commerce, the Scottish Chamber of Commerce and the

Northern Ireland Chamber of Commerce and Industry. It is also represented on government committees, usually together with the T.U.C., and, like the T.U.C., it has a recognised role to play in the day-to-day administration of legislation which affects its members. Thus it has representatives on the National Economic Development Council (*see* XII, **16**(*c*)), the Manpower Services Commission and the Health and Safety Commission.

The involvement of the T.U.C. and C.B.I. in the decision-making process ensures that:

(*a*) legislation is assured of widespread acceptance;

(*b*) the process of dissemination of information is more efficient;

(*c*) resources and expertise are available to the government;

(*d*) the influence of pressure groups (for that is what they are in addition to their other functions) is exerted on both the legislature and the executive.

16. The Commonwealth. Most Commonwealth countries are now independent and their relationship with Britain is that of equal partners. It might appear, therefore, that their influence on British policy is now insignificant. However, there are still two important factors to be considered: firstly, the continuing aid given to some of the poorer countries in the form of both grants and technical co-operation (the provision of skilled personnel, advice and training), and secondly the continuing importance of the Prime Ministers' Conference.

The Prime Ministers of all the Commonwealth countries meet for an annual conference in London to discuss Commonwealth, international and economic affairs. Although the conference has no power to make decisions which are binding on its members it is a useful sounding-board on matters of mutual interest and a manifestation that, in some senses at least, the concept of a Commonwealth of Nations still has meaning and validity. The social problem of the Ugandan Asians and the economic problems created by Britain's membership of the European Community are examples of the types of concern which have been on the agenda. The implications of Britain's membership of the Common Market were discussed with Commonwealth representatives before Britain made a formal application to join.

Another important sphere of mutual interest is in the field of higher education. About 46 per cent of all overseas students in Britain are from Commonwealth countries and regular Common-

wealth education conferences are arranged by the Commonwealth Education Liaison Committee.

17. The national interest. In deciding its policy on world affairs
the government must act in what it considers is the national
interest. This is defined in two ways.

(*a*) Internally, the national interest is defined by a consensus of
the views of political parties, public opinion, interest groups, the
media and the Civil Service.

(*b*) Externally, the interests of Britain as a nation may be seen
as less important than, say, the interests of the European Community (*see* X) and pressures exerted by other countries, multi-
national corporations or world politics may modify the rather
narrow concept of "national interest" into something approach-
ing a world view which nevertheless, in the long run, may be seen
to be more beneficial to Britain.

18. Manifesto and mandate. Political parties seeking election publish manifestos setting out their party programme. If returned
to power they frequently claim that they have a mandate from
the electorate to carry out the promises made in the manifesto.
The claim has a superficial validity only. Whilst it makes sense
for a party to proclaim its programme so that the voters can
judge for themselves who they consider would be most fitted to
govern, the position may well have altered by the time they
achieve power. Promises are frequently based on assumptions
and if the assumptions prove incorrect there is a good case for not
implementing the promises.

A more important consideration however is that, in one sense,
governments are hardly ever truly representative. Since 1918,
for example, the government only once represented more than
half of the electorate, and that was the coalition government of
1931. M.P.s are, or should be, representatives, not delegates. As
a party member the M.P. has a mandate from his party to carry
out their programme and he must calculate the balance between
obedience to the party and responsibility to the electorate. The
party whip is important, and not lightly to be ignored, but this is
not to say that it never can be ignored. There may be times when
it can and should be.

CIVIL SERVANTS

19. The Civil Service. The charge is made from time to time that it is the Civil Service, rather than Parliament, which really governs the country. The Eleventh Report of the Expenditure Committee (H.M.S.O., 1977) (*see* XVII, **20**) contained an appendix contributed by one of its members, Brian Sedgemore M.P., which alleged that senior Civil Servants frequently delayed and obstructed policies with which they disagreed. He singled out the Department of Industry and the Home Office for particular condemnation. His fellow committee members rejected the allegations and they may therefore be seen as a minority report. It may be, however, that his conclusions were correct but that the reasons for them were wrong. Following are some of the factors which may affect the extent of Civil Service power.

(*a*) Ministers are transients and part of the Civil Service responsibility is to preserve continuity. The late R. H. Crossman M.P. calculated that it took a new minister two years to learn the work of his department, and most do not stay in one ministry for that length of time.

(*b*) Civil Servants have expertise and ability and may well see valid reasons why a course of action proposed by a minister is impracticable.

(*c*) The way in which a political issue is resolved between a minister and his Civil Servants depends upon a number of factors:

(*i*) the political sensitivity of the issue;

(*ii*) the minister's view of the importance of the subject;

(*iii*) the manner in which the issue is raised, e.g. whether a pressure group approaches either the minister or his ministry in the first instance;

(*iv*) the pressure of work within the department;

(*v*) timing, e.g. whether a general election is imminent may affect the way in which an issue is dealt with; in general, the nearer the election the more likely it is that the issue will be left to the department to resolve;

(*vi*) the ability of the minister to delegate. It could be argued that if a minister lets his Civil Servants make the decisions he cannot blame them for doing so.

20. Ministerial control. If ministers feel that they do not have adequate control over their departments there are a number of courses open to them.

(*a*) They could insist on their right to be kept fully informed.

(*b*) They could insist on changes within their departments.

(*c*) They could make more use of advisers from outside the Civil Service.

(*d*) In the case of a conflict of personalities between the minister and his senior Civil Servants the minister could insist on the removal of the Civil Servant (it being understood that such a removal would not jeopardise the Civil Servant's career).

21. Secrecy. Civil Servants tend to be secretive. This is a tradition and is often justified on the grounds that their work is confidential and that anonymity makes for efficiency. All Civil Servants are, in any case, subject to the provisions of the Official Secrets Act 1911 and there are good grounds for reform of its provisions (*see* III, 3(*b*)). Sir William Armstrong, ex-head of the home Civil Service, defended Civil Servants from this charge on the grounds that secrecy frequently stemmed from ministers who wanted secrecy in the first instance for political reasons. If secrecy starts in this way it filters down to the departments and becomes difficult to prevent even when unjustified.

PROGRESS TEST 18

1. How do political parties affect the policy of governments? (1–4)

2. What are the functions of the Prime Minister? (5–7)

3. In what sense is the Prime Minister an elected monarch? (8)

4. What are the arguments for and against a large Cabinet? (10)

5. List the recommendations of the Haldane Report. (11)

6. What does the Cabinet Secretariat do? (12)

7. Discuss the importance of (*a*) the T.U.C., (*b*) the C.B.I., (*c*) the Commonwealth and (*d*) the national interest in the formation of public policy. (14–17)

8. What is meant by the mandate? (18)

9. Why do Civil Servants appear to have too much power? (19–21)

CHAPTER XIX

Legislative and Administrative Control

ADMINISTRATIVE AGENCIES

1. Who implements the laws? When parliamentary decisions have received the Royal Assent, they become the laws of the land and are then the responsibility of the executive to carry out (*see* I, **16**). The main agencies for the implementation of laws are:

- (*a*) government departments;
- (*b*) administrative tribunals;
- (*c*) public corporations;
- (*d*) nationalised industries;
- (*e*) *ad hoc* public bodies.

2. Government departments. Government departments are the main instruments for giving effect to legislation. They are staffed by Civil Servants (*see* XVII) and either headed by a minister or, in the case of some smaller departments, represented in Parliament by the minister of another department. They range in size from the Ministry of Defence, with some 258,700 staff, to the Treasury Solicitor's Department with a few hundred. Most major departments are headed by a permanent secretary with one or more deputies and a number of under-secretaries. They will also have their own finance, personnel and organisation officers. Smaller departments tend to reflect this pattern of management but the grades of the more senior officers will be lower and there will be fewer of them. The pattern of organisation within the department will reflect the job which the department was set up to perform. Thus the Department of Health and Social Security is responsible for paying pensions and benefits throughout the country and has a large network of offices in most towns supported by regional and headquarters offices. The Ministry of Agriculture, Fisheries and Food, which has national and international responsibilities, carries out most of its advisory functions from a centralised headquarters and does not need a local office network.

It is impossible, in a book of this size, to do more than indicate the size and scope of a few of the larger departments. An excellent short account of some of the others is to be found in *Britain 1977* (H.M.S.O., 1977).

(*a*) *The Ministry of Defence* is the largest government department with some 258,700 staff. It is responsible for defence policy and for the administration and control of the armed services.

(*b*) *The Chancellor of the Exchequer's Departments*, for which the Treasury ministers are responsible, employ about 129,300 staff and include the Treasury, the Customs and Excise Board, the Inland Revenue, the Department for National Savings, the Treasury Solicitor's Department, the Royal Mint and the National Debt Office. These departments are responsible for the control of public money.

(*c*) *The Department of Health and Social Security* employs 98,300 people and is responsible for the administration of the National Health Service, the national insurance and supplementary benefit schemes and for local authority social services.

(*d*) *The Department of the Environment* is an amalgamation of the ministries of Housing and Local Government and Public Buildings and Works, and employs about 75,000 staff. It is responsible for a wide range of functions covering all aspects of the physical environment. Its duties include the planning, conservation and development of both town and country and the provision and maintenance of most government buildings, the latter being undertaken by a separate Property Services Agency.

(*e*) *The Department of Employment* Group is responsible for manpower policy and includes a number of specialised agencies dealing with particular aspects. They are the Advisory, Conciliation and Arbitration Service which deals with industrial relations, the Manpower Services Commission which deals with problems of employment, unemployment and training, and the Health and Safety Commission which deals with health and safety at work. The combined staff of the Group numbers about 52,500.

(*f*) *The Cabinet Office, Civil Service Department and Treasury* have special functions in relation to the Civil Service as a whole (*see* XVII, **8, 19** and **20**).

DELEGATED LEGISLATION

3. The advantages of delegated legislation. It should be noted that Parliament can not only make laws but also empower other people to do so. Such laws, called delegated legislation must, however, be ratified by Parliament. The advantages of delegated legislation are as follows.

(*a*) The range and complexity of modern legislation would prove impossible to handle if Parliament dealt with it alone and did not delegate.

(*b*) Delegation reduces pressure on parliamentary time. Parliament can agree the general scope of legislation by means of a Bill and can then delegate responsibility for details to another body.

(*c*) Expert knowledge can be used effectively. Some legislation is highly technical and there is a case for leaving the detailed work on such law-making to experts in the particular field covered by the legislation.

(*d*) If a body has delegated authority it can experiment on occasions and can amend the rules in the light of changing circumstances.

(*e*) Delegation can be used in emergencies. Thus the Prevention of Terrorism (Temporary Provisions) Act 1976 enables a system of travel controls to be imposed between Britain and Northern Ireland as a means of combatting terrorism.

4. The disadvantages of delegated legislation. The Donoughmore Committee was set up in 1929 to consider both delegated legislation and administrative tribunals (*see* **6**). Its findings were reported in the *Report of the Committee on Minister's Powers* (H.M.S.O., 1932) but were not implemented at the time. Donoughmore saw four major dangers in the practice of delegating legislation.

(*a*) Increasing delegation of legislation tends to decrease the liberty of the subject.

(*b*) Unless delegated power is rigorously controlled the citizen could lose the protection of the courts, e.g. if a Statutory Instrument contains a phrase such as "Such actions shall be at the discretion of the minister" then the courts cannot protect an individual who thinks that the minister has used his discretionary powers in a harsh or excessive manner.

(*c*) If delegated authority is not closely defined there will be uncertainty as to its use.

(*d*) The giving of due notice and where possible, consultation of interested parties are an integral part of parliamentary procedure and could be overlooked or ignored when legislation is delegated.

5. The control of delegated legislation. The disadvantages which the Donoughmore Committee outlined can be overcome if delegation is adequately controlled. There are a number of procedures for ensuring such control but critics have doubted their effectiveness. They include the following.

(*a*) *Parliamentary scrutiny.* The House of Commons has a number of select committees one of which, the Statutory Instruments Committee (sometimes called the Scrutiny Committee), examines Statutory Instruments and calls the attention of Parliament to those which appear to infringe the rights or liberties of the subject.

(*b*) *Parliamentary questions.* On four days each week during the Parliamentary session an hour or so is set aside for question time when any member can question any minister about the work of his department. Questions can also be asked about matters which arise as a result of delegated legislation but, unless an important issue of policy arises, it is unlikely that question time is among the more effective ways of controlling delegated legislation.

(*c*) *Motions of censure.* Any minister can be censured on the work of his department, and a minister who has delegated some of his responsibility can be censured on the delegated legislation. In practice this method of control, like question time, is not altogether satisfactory since a censure motion may divide the House along party lines and the outcome could be more a reflection of party loyalty than of a search for justice for the individual.

(*d*) *Supply motions.* Estimates of the cost of providing the services needed to run the country are submitted to the House of Commons every February. They include some costs of delegated legislation and the debate on such estimates provides an opportunity to criticise the way in which delegated legislation is administered.

ADMINISTRATIVE TRIBUNALS

6. Administrative law. The British legal system does not officially recognise a separate body of law called "administrative law" which regulates the rights and duties of the individual in his dealings with the state. Increasingly, however, with new legislation in fields as diverse as national insurance, transport, race relations, rent and industrial matters, the individual has recourse, not to a special body of law as in France (*droit d'administratif*), but to a lay tribunal entrusted with certain powers under delegated legislation. This has certain advantages (*see* 3) but it also has disadvantages, particularly if the decisions of the tribunal are of a quasi-judicial nature. In such cases the individual is, in effect, subject to the law without adequate opportunity for legal redress. Although in theory he can appeal to the High Court (in Scotland the Court of Session) on a point of law this is, in practice, difficult to do. The phenomenon is not new. Constitutional lawyers have been alarmed for years at the growing number of such tribunals and at the range of their powers. The title of a book published in 1929 by Lord Hewart, *The New Despotism*, reflects the fears of the lawyers at that time, and the fears have increased since then.

Since tribunals frequently sit in private, are not bound by the rules of evidence and may deprive a citizen of his legal rights there needs to be strong evidence as to their advantages to explain their increasing use. Such evidence can be summed up briefly.

(*a*) *Cost*. They are much cheaper than courts, members of some tribunals being unpaid or only receiving a nominal fee.

(*b*) *Speed*. The courts move slowly and matters dealt with by tribunals tend to be those in which a quick decision is required.

(*c*) *Informality*. The majesty of the law has its place, but it may well prevent recourse to law over a comparatively trivial matter. If a citizen can get justice in the courts but is not prepared to use them then he does not in fact get justice.

(*d*) *Expertise*. In subjects as widely diverse as supplementary benefit, planning legislation and rent questions there is a great body of expert opinion which may need to be consulted. It makes sense for such opinion to be available to specialised tribunals.

(*e*) *Equity*. Justice must not only be done, it must manifestly be seen to be done. Advocates of tribunals claim that the informal atmosphere, the "non-legal" approach and the specialised subject matter are more likely to produce a result which the appellant will see as "fair" (prior to the introduction of national insurance it was frequently said that claims for workmen's compensation were unfairly dealt with because wealthy employers could hire better lawyers than could injured workmen).

7. The Franks Committee. In 1954 the owner-occupier of some land was threatened with dispossession by a tribunal set up under

the Agricultural Act 1947. The case focused attention on tribunals in general and agricultural tribunals in particular. Sir
Oliver Franks was asked to investigate the powers and procedures of tribunals. Whilst accepting the need for, and the value of,
independent tribunals he proposed a number of safeguards which
were incorporated in the Tribunals and Inquiries Acts 1958, 1966
and 1971.

(a) A Council on Tribunals was to be set up by the Lord
Chancellor in order to supervise the working of those tribunals
with the power to make decisions affecting citizens.

(b) Recognised tribunals were to be listed, and subsequent
additions to the list were to be authorised by the Lord Chancellor.

(c) Rules of procedure governing the conduct of tribunals were
to be agreed by the Council.

(d) Decisions of certain specified tribunals could be contested
on a point of law in the High Court (Court of Session in Scotland).

(e) The appointment of members of some tribunals would be
on the recommendation of the Council.

PUBLIC CORPORATIONS

8. What is a public corporation? A public corporation is a semi-
independent body, neither a government department nor a
private company, but combining elements of both. The term
"quango" is sometimes used to refer to such bodies; the word
stands for quasi autonomous national organisation. The concept
is not new. The Elizabethan Commission on Sewers and the
eighteenth-century turnpike trusts were both examples of govern-
ment-sponsored private enterprise. Public corporations come in
many forms and are created for different purposes. They share,
however, certain common characteristics.

(a) They are created by Parliament or by Royal Charter.

(b) Control is by a board of management, usually appointed
by a minister.

(c) Powers of re-appointment and dismissal of members are
usually vested in a minister.

(d) The government can exercise control of the organisation
by means of its power to nominate and dismiss its management.

(e) Boards of management tend to be made up of "outsiders"
rather than those within the organisation.

(*f*) The broad aims of the organisation are defined by Parliament but day-to-day control is left to the organisation. When such an organisation is set up a' statement of the respective spheres of responsibility is frequently published.

(*g*) An annual report is normally published.

(*h*) A public corporation is a legal entity. It can sue and be sued.

(*i*) Employees are not Civil Servants although they frequently enjoy comparable conditions of service.

(*j*) Financially they enjoy a certain amount of independence. They are not required to submit estimates to Parliament but they are normally expected to break even taking one year with another. They may borrow money from the government for capital development.

9. Examples of public corporations. Given the wide variety and increasing number of public corporations it would not be possible to describe them all. The list which follows is, therefore, selected as representative of the whole range.

(*a*) Nationalised industries are public corporations (*see* XII, 1–3).

(*b*) The United Kingdom Atomic Energy Authority was established in 1954. It is subject to stricter governmental control than most public corporations but is able to be more flexible in its approach than would be the case if it were a government department. It is unrealistic to suggest that such an organisation should be in the hands of private enterprise even if a private entrepreneur could be found wealthy enough to underwrite it.

(*c*) The Bank of England was nationalised in 1946 and the Post Office changed from a government department to a public corporation in 1969. In both cases the links with government were, and remain, very close. The Bank of England was nationalised because it was considered that the links should be tightened, while the change in the Post Office's status was made because there was a case for making the links looser.

(*d*) Post-war development of new towns created a series of development corporations. In the course of time they had fulfilled their primary purpose, that of getting new towns developed, and they were replaced by a Commission for New Towns set up under the New Towns Act 1959.

(*e*) The supply of electricity throughout the country is a commercial concern; but it is too important to leave entirely to private enterprise. There are, therefore, three public boards charged with responsibility for administering it. They are, the Central Electricity Generating Board, the Electricity Council and the South of Scotland Electricity Board.

(*f*) Both the British Broadcasting Corporation (B.B.C.) and the Independent Broadcasting Authority (I.B.A.) are public corporations with a considerable degree of freedom in the day-to-day running of their affairs. Both are answerable to Parliament through the Home Secretary.

(*g*) The Mersey Docks and Harbour Board is one of the earlier public corporations having been set up in 1857 as a joint board to deal with overlapping areas and services in the docks of Liverpool and Birkenhead.

10. Why have public corporations? The political arguments for and against nationalisation are discussed in XII, 1–3. Below are considered some of the other factors which may influence a decision to create a public corporation.

(*a*) A monopoly organisation may be able to avoid taking into account the interests of consumers. However, when a monopoly organisation is also a public corporation, e.g. the Post Office, it can be required to have regard to this constraint.

(*b*) Some industries are important to the country as a whole but only the government has enough money to finance them properly, e.g. British Airways.

(*c*) Some industries need considerable technological development which the owners cannot or will not undertake. This was one of the considerations which led to the nationalisation of the mines.

(*d*) Some services can be provided more cheaply if they are provided on a national scale, e.g. gas and electricity.

(*e*) Government control is necessary in some circumstances to ensure that government policy is carried out. This was one of the reasons for the nationalisation of the Bank of England.

(*f*) With some activities there may be an element of risk to the public which the government needs to control, e.g. the U.K. Atomic Energy Authority.

CENTRAL CONTROL

11. The Cabinet and the Civil Service. The relations between the legislature and the executive are complex and there are critics who suggest that it is the Civil Service rather than the government which really runs the country (*see* XVIII, 19). Whether this is true or not is for the reader to decide in the light of such information as is available to him. No consideration of this aspect of government would be complete, however, without a look at the ways in which the activities of the Civil Service are controlled.

12. The Treasury. The Treasury is the most important of the financial departments. It controls the spending of the Civil Service as a whole and it accounts to the government for both actual and proposed expenditure by the Civil Service. To do this it uses two specialised committees.

(*a*) *Public Expenditure Survey Committee* (*P.E.S.C.*). This committee is concerned with inter-departmental co-ordination and advises the Chancellor of the Exchequer on the financial implications of departmental programmes. It started as a Treasury committee in the 1960s and is responsible for producing an annual report for ministers on the decisions to be taken in relation to public spending. Its other major function is to provide a medium of exchange of views on technical and theoretical problems.

(*b*) *Programme Analysis and Review Committee* (*P.A.R.C.*). This committee is, as its name suggests, responsible for the analysis and review of departmental programmes. Its work is concerned with programme planning and, as is to be expected, there is a considerable overlap in membership of this committee and P.E.S.C. Reports submitted to P.A.R.C. are serviced by the Treasury's public expenditure divisions and particular attention is paid to alternative ways of achieving departmental aims and the measurement of the likely costs and outcomes of the alternatives suggested.

13. Central Policy Review Staff (C.P.R.S.). The Central Policy Review Staff (sometimes referred to as the "think tank") is part of the Cabinet Office and advises ministers collectively on policy matters. It was set up by Edward Heath in 1970 and its first head was a Labour peer, Lord Rothschild. The original intention was to rationalise, some said legitimise, the system by which individual Prime Ministers gathered around them a number of advisers with undefined status and responsibilities. Lloyd George had a body of advisers who were known as the "garden suburb" and Harold Wilson had what was sometimes called a "kitchen cabinet" whose members advised him from time to time on political matters. The White Paper, *The Reorganisation of Central Government* (Cmnd. 4506, 1970), which contained proposals for the setting up of the C.P.R.S., stipulated that "This staff will form an integral element of the Cabinet Office and . . . will be at the disposal of the government as a whole".

14. The Parliamentary Commissioner for Administration (P.C.A.). The Commissioner, sometimes called the Ombudsman, is a public official whose responsibility is to ensure that the laws enacted by Parliament are administered fairly and he investigates complaints of maladministration. The proposal to appoint an Ombudsman, an office known in Sweden since 1809, was the outcome of the Whyatt Report, *The Citizen and the Administration: The Redress of Grievances*, published in 1961.

This report drew attention to the concept of "ministerial responsibility" (*see* V, **15**) and pointed out that a minister's responsibility was something of a myth since he could be held responsible for minor decisions of which he could not possibly be expected to have personal knowledge. In any case his responsibility was to the letter of the law, not to the way in which perfectly correct decisions might work to the detriment of the citizen. The Critchel Down case (*see* V, **15**) was an excellent example of a situation in which a minister had acted within his lawful powers but where the results had been grossly unfair to an individual. The French legal system, with its recognition of administrative law, enabled a citizen to obtain redress from specialised courts in those cases where correct decisions had resulted in an abuse of power.

The recommendations of the Whyatt Report were taken up by the Labour administration of 1964, and the Parliamentary Commissioner Act was passed in 1967. The first occupant of the new post of Ombudsman was Sir Edmund Compton, a senior Civil Servant who had served in the Treasury and as Auditor General.

15. The Ombudsman's duties. At the outset it was clear that the duties of the Parliamentary Commissioner were to be restricted in scope. He could only investigate a complaint if it was submitted to him by a Member of Parliament. His field was to be that of central government. Whilst this might appear to be reasonably wide it covered only forty-seven bodies and excluded local authorities, nationalised industries and a range of government activities such as action by the police and the armed services and internal Civil Service matters. There was to be a time limit of one year after which, unless there were special circumstances, cases would be outside his scope. His powers and procedure were as follows:

(a) The procedure was intended to be informal. Legal representation would be allowed but legal aid was not available since representation was to be the exception rather than the rule.

(b) He had the power to decide whether or not a particular complaint came within the scope of his powers.

(c) He was concerned with administrative faults, not matters of government policy.

(d) He was required to submit annual reports to Parliament and special reports if circumstances appeared to warrant it. It would be for Parliament to decide what action (if any) to take on the reports.

The scale of operations was, from the beginning, modest. The Commissioner's staff numbered fifty-nine and the first full year showed that, although 1,340 cases had been referred to the P.C.A.'s office by M.P.s, over half had been rejected as being outside his terms of reference. In all a total of thirty-eight cases of maladministration were found.

16. The benefits and disadvantages of the Ombudsman. The institution of the Parliamentary Commissioner filled a gap. It provided a "watch-dog" for the ordinary citizen. The watch-dog had few teeth however. It was even suggested that the appointment of a Civil Servant to this particular post was in itself unfortunate since he might well find himself called upon to criticise ex-colleagues. This view was not widely held and was in any case seen to be unjustified when the Commissioner came to make his first report.

The Commissioner himself, in his second report, set out what he saw as the benefits and drawbacks of his work. On the credit side he listed those cases in which he had either caused matters to be put right or had confirmed that there was no maladministration and expressed his belief that the existence of the Parliamentary Commissioner had improved the quality of administration.

On the debit side was what the first Commissioner, Sir Edmund Compton, described as "the extent to which this new office adds to the coefficient of friction in government". His officers occupied a considerable amount of the time of the Civil Servants whose job it was to answer the queries which he raised and in an article in *Public Administration* (Spring 1970, vol. 48) he speculated whether the net result might be that departments which were normally helpful to the public might play for safety and refuse to advise members of the public. Finally he argued that the principle of ministerial responsibility might mean that, since ministers would be answerable to the Parliamentary Commissioner, they might be less prepared to delegate. Such a trend would, in the long run, work against the public interest.

PROGRESS TEST 19

1. List some of the more important government departments. (2)

2. What are the advantages and disadvantages of delegated legislation? (3, 4)

3. How can delegated legislation be controlled? (5)

4. What is the "new despotism"? (6)

5. What characteristics are shared by public corporations? (8)

6. What reasons, other than political considerations, can be given for the creation of public corporations? (10)

7. What agencies are available to the Treasury to enable it to control public expenditure? (12)

8. What is the Parliamentary Commissioner and how does he function? (14–16)

Bibliography

GENERAL PUBLICATIONS

There are a vast number of books about government and politics and it would be impossible to list them all. The list which follows is a selection only and must be supplemented by wide reading of contemporary reports in newspapers, journals and government publications, some of which are listed below. There are a number of "classics" of which the student should be aware. These books, e.g. Erskine May, *Parliamentary Practice* (Butterworths, 19th edition, 1976) are cited as works of reference rather than as books which are to be read from cover to cover. Others in this category include:

Bagehot, Walter, *The English Constitution* (Fontana, 1973). (Note particularly the introduction by R. H. Crossman.)

Blondel, J., *Voters, Parties and Leaders* (Penguin, 1976)

Crick, B., *In Defence of Politics* (Penguin, 1969)

Dicey, A. V., *Introduction to the Law of the Constitution* (Macmillan, 10th edition, 1959)

Jennings, Sir Ivor, *Parliament* (Cambridge University Press, 2nd edition, 1957)

Minogue, M. (ed.), *Documents on Contemporary British Government*, Vol. I. *British Government and Political Change*, Vol. II. *Local Government in Britain* (Cambridge University Press, 1977)

POLITICAL IDEAS

The following relate primarily to Part One of this book although most have sections relevant to other parts.

Birch, A. H., *Representative and Responsible Government* (Allen and Unwin, 1964)

Mackenzie, R., *British Political Parties* (Heinemann, 1963)

Mackintosh, J. P., *The Government and Politics of Great Britain* (Hutchinson, 1970)

Open Government: The British Interpretation (Royal Institute of Public Affairs booklet, no. 5, 1977)

Punnett, *R. M., British Government and Politics* (Heinemann, 1970)

Zander, M., *A Bill of Rights?* (Barry Rose, 1975)

INSTITUTIONS

This section covers the legal system, local government, decentralisation and supra-national government.

Banks, J. C., *Federal Britain?* (Harrap, 1971)

Calvert, H. (ed.), *Devolution* (Professional Books, 1975). (This has a useful chapter on the attitude survey mounted for the Kilbrandon Report.)

Griffiths, A., *Local Government Administration* (Shaw, 1976). (This was written for the Institute of Chartered Secretaries and Surveyors.)

Jackson, E. W., *Local Government in England and Wales* (Penguin, 1977)

Jackson, R. M., *The Machinery of Justice in Great Britain* (Cambridge University Press, 1967)

Kitzinger, U., *Diplomacy and Persuasion: How Britain joined the Common Market* (Thames & Hudson, 1973)

Redcliffe-Maud, Lord and Wood, B., *English Local Government Reformed* (Oxford University Press, 1974)

PROBLEMS AND ISSUES

Most of the issues discussed in this HANDBOOK are dealt with in L. J. Macfarlane's book, *Issues in British Politics Since 1945* (Longman, 1975) which has useful bibliographies at the end of each chapter. The issues are also dealt with, but in a different way, in *Penelope Hall's Social Services of England and Wales*, edited by J. Mays (Routledge and Kegan Paul, 9th edition, 1975) which, again, has comprehensive bibliographies. F. W. S. Craig has collected political manifestos up to 1966. They are published under the title, *British General Election Manifestos, 1918–1966* (Political Reference Publications, 1969). Public opinion on these and other topics is examined by D. Butler and D. Stokes in *Political Change in Britain: Forces shaping electoral choice* (Pelican, 1971). Other recommended publications on specific topics include the following.

(a) *Education*. Cox, C. B. and Dyson, A. E., *The Black Papers on Education* (Davies Poynter, 1971)

(b) *Employment and industry*. *Report of the Royal Commission on Trade Unions and Employers' Associations* (Donovan Report) (H.M.S.O., 1968)

(c) *Housing*. Donnison, D. V., *The Government of Housing* (Penguin, 1967)

(d) *Immigration and racism*. *Racial Discrimination, a guide to the Race Relations Act 1976* (Home Office, 1977)

(e) *Poverty and health*. The annual reports of the *Department of Health and Social Security* (H.M.S.O.)

PUBLIC ADMINISTRATION

Britain, an Official Handbook is published annually by H.M.S.O. and is a useful work of reference. It contains a great deal of material which is also published separately in the form of Central Office of Information Reference Pamphlets. Other recommended works include the following.

Birch, A. H., *The British System of Government* (Allen and Unwin, 3rd edition, 1973)

Cross, J. A., *British Public Administration* (University Tutorial Press, 1970)

Hanson, A. H. and Walles, M., *Governing Britain* (Fontana, 1970)

Harvey, J. and Bather, L., *The British Constitution* (Macmillan, 1972)

Kimber, R. H. and Richardson, J. J. (eds.), *Pressure Groups in Britain: a Reader* (Dent, 1973)

Mackintosh, J. B., *The British Cabinet* (Methuen, 2nd edition, 1968)

Smith, de, S. A., *Constitutional and Administrative Law* (Penguin, 1971)

Stacey, F., *The British Ombudsman* (Oxford University Press, 1971)

OTHER READING

There are a number of important annual publications produced by Her Majesty's Stationery Office (H.M.S.O.). They include reports of various departments and of the Council on Tribunals and the Parliamentary Commissioner for Administration. Select committees mentioned in the text of this HANDBOOK also publish reports. Such reports should be read preferably in conjunction with contemporary newspaper comments on them. Three other publications are particularly commended for general coverage.

Mosley, R. K., *British Government and Politics*. (This is a small, privately produced book, issued annually and obtainable from the author at 8 Cedar Avenue, Shirley, Southampton SO1 5GW)

Parliamentary Affairs (Hansard Society, quarterly)

Who does what in Parliament? (Mitchell and Burt, Westminster Bookstall). (New editions of this work of reference are published from time to time as the composition of Parliament changes. The latest edition is no. 6, 1975.)

PERIODICALS

The student should cultivate the habit of wide reading. *The Times*, the *Daily Telegraph* and the *Guardian* all give adequate and regular coverage of matters relating to government and politics but readers of such accounts should appreciate that there are other points of view. A paper such as the *Morning Star* might well provide an alternative view. Professional journals, such as the *Local Government Chronicle* and *Local Government Review* provide yet another approach, as does the quarterly, *Public Administration*. Periodicals of more general interest frequently contain matters of interest to the student of government. Such periodicals include the *Listener*, *New Society*, *New Statesman* and *The Economist*.

Examination Technique

1. Before the examination. It is useful to practise answering questions set in previous examinations. This has a number of advantages but the student should beware of the danger of trying to guess what topics will be covered on the basis of their frequency, or infrequency, on previous occasions. The fact that a topic has appeared for the past three years does not guarantee that it will appear on the fourth, neither does its absence in previous years indicate that it must come up this time. Some examining bodies, e.g. the Local Government Training Board, issue reports on previous examinations and the student, having answered an earlier question-paper, can read how past questions were answered and, more importantly, how the examiners thought that they should be answered. At this stage he should re-read his own answers and satisfy himself that he knows how they should have been presented.

2. Learn to recognise different types of questions. Most questions demand a mixture of facts and commentary and the tendency in this subject is for credit to be given for analytical answers, i.e. those which consider the various aspects of a problem and their relationship to each other. It is necessary to know about the various Reports, White Papers, legislation etc., which are relevant to the question; but it is even more important to know the thinking which lies behind the official pronouncements.

3. Assess your weaknesses. Answering previous examination questions and reading the comments upon them should show both your strengths and your weaknesses. Concentrate on improving those areas where your performance seems most frequently to be unsatisfactory. The following questions may help.

(a) Do you always answer the question which the examiner has set? It is easy, if you know something about a topic, to display your knowledge, but it may not answer the question.

(b) Are you good at essay-type questions? This means more

than just writing a lot. The writing must be relevant, it must be as concise as the question will allow and it must be couched in good English. Good English does not mean high-flown or classical language, it means appropriate language. Slang, and a personal approach, should be avoided, as should "padding" (it shows).

(c) Do you have difficulty in memorising facts? If so, when revising, work out some mnemonics. The *Report on the Machinery of Government* is also known as the Haldane Report. If you have a mechanical turn of mind it may stick in the memory because of its association with machinery. If you know someone called Haldane his name might provide the "trigger". Those with a literary turn of mind might find an association with Hamlet, who was a Dane, more helpful. There are endless possibilities, the main point is that an elusive fact can often be dredged up from the memory if it is associated with other facts which are well-known to you.

(d) Do you make best use of your time? Some people spend too long looking at the questions, considering alternative answers and pondering on the exact form of words to use. Others, probably the majority, go to the other extreme and rush at the question paper, dashing off ill-considered answers and becoming aware of it only when it is too late to correct it. Decide which of the two extremes is nearest to your approach and then make a conscious effort to compensate.

4. At the examination. Read the paper carefully. Make sure that you understand what the questions ask. Check your understanding. Could the question be asking something other than what you first thought it to mean? When you are satisfied that you know what all the questions mean, decide which ones you intend to answer and the order in which they are to be answered. There is something to be said for starting with one which appears easy. This will give you confidence but should not be allowed to cause over-confidence.

5. Draw up an outline of the answers. The outline should be headings and sub-headings only and should be consulted from time to time as the examination proceeds. If it is written in an appropriate part of the examination paper itself, it may possibly gain one or two extra marks since, if you are unable to finish in time, the examiner will at least know the ground which you intended to cover.

6. Time. Consider the time at your disposal and allocate equal proportions of it to each question. You should also allow time at the end for checking all your answers. If, in answering a question, you come to the time limit which you have imposed upon yourself you should stop and go on to the next question. If time permits you can go back to the question which you have left and if time does not permit you will at least have attempted more questions.

7. Some rules.

(*a*) Define your terms.

(*b*) Avoid personal views, particularly political ones. There is a place for the personal view but it should be related to other views and should be justified, if used, by reference to recognised authorities. Matters on which you hold strong political views are probably best left alone, since it will be more difficult to be objective.

(*c*) Check for relevance. However interesting you may consider a fact or opinion to be it has no place in your answer unless it is relevant.

(*d*) Watch spelling, grammar and presentation. Examiners are human and will find a well-presented essay easier to mark.

Test Papers

G.C.E. "A" LEVEL

The following questions are reproduced by kind permission of The Associated Examining Board.

Paper 1. Political Behaviour—Britain
Time allowed—three hours. Five questions to be answered. All questions carry equal marks.

1. Who rules Britain?
2. Suggest ways in which pressure groups may (*a*) help, and (*b*) hinder democratic government.
3. "Despite the shortcomings of the party system, a democracy must have political parties." Discuss.
4. It is often claimed that ours is a homogeneous society. How, then, do you explain the recent success of nationalist groups?
5. What is the role of the annual conference of each of the major political parties?
6. "Proportional representation has been far too easily belittled by political commentators who are tied to an out-dated two-party system." Discuss.
7. How far can, and should, a government give a lead that is not widely popular?
8. What is meant by "the British political culture"?
9. If you were introducing a foreigner to British politics how much attention would you devote to history and how much to modern social conditions?
10. How do people try to influence their M.P.? Do they affect the M.P.s behaviour in any way?
11. What purpose is served in the political process by public opinion polls?
12. With what degree of accuracy can one refer to Britain as having a two-party system?
13. Consider some of the symbols and rituals that strengthen loyalty to British institutions.

Paper 2. Political Institutions—Britain

Time allowed—three hours. Four questions to be answered. All questions carry equal marks.

1. "We need a new Bill of Rights." Do we? What might it contain?

2. Why do we still have a monarchy?

3. How far, and by what means, does the central government control local government?

4. Why has there been serious discussion in recent years about establishing a written constitution for Britain?

5. "Whatever the text-books say, Parliament is not sovereign now." Discuss.

6. "With a two-tier system of local government in England there is no need for, or room for, any regional authority." Discuss.

7. Consider the possibly conflicting claims that may be made on an M.P. by: (*a*) his party, (*b*) his constituents, and (*c*) his own self-respect.

8. "Even if the powers of the Prime Minister have not increased in recent years, television has made it appear that they have increased." Discuss.

9. "It is easy to criticise our top Civil Servants; what we need to do is to realise their considerable worth." Discuss.

10. Consider the relationship between (*a*) councillors and officials, and (*b*) ministers and Civil Servants. Point out any similarities and differences between the two relationships.

CERTIFICATE IN MUNICIPAL ADMINISTRATION

The Certificate in Municipal Administration is set and marked at the standard of a university pass degree and the syllabus states that "Candidates will also be expected to be acquainted with the most important British official reports of recent years on various aspects of government". The following test papers are compiled from questions set in 1976 and 1977 and are reproduced by kind permission of the Local Government Training Board.

Paper 1. Government and Public Administration I

Time allowed—three hours. Four questions to be answered.

1. How effective has the British Parliamentary Commissioner for Administration been in protecting the citizen from maladministration? In the light of experience would you recommend any change in his powers? (1976)

2. What services should be based on, and administered by, a regional authority in Britain today? Should the regional authority be elected and be politically responsible for its actions? (1976)

3. To what extent have the principles of the British Constitution been affected by membership of the E.E.C.? (1976)

4. Consider the view that British government would be more effective if the House of Commons, through an electoral process based on proportional representation, reflected more accurately the wishes of the voter. (1976)

5. "The problem with pressure groups is that the bigger and more influential they become, the less they represent the views of their rank and file members." Discuss. (1976)

6. "Politics is the means used to reconcile conflict between competing interests; in one-party states there can be no politics." Discuss. (1977)

7. Of whom and of what is "representative government" supposed to be representative? (1977)

8. Consider the assertion that in a democracy political parties should be subject to "democratic" control by their members. (1977)

9. "The search for new forms of government in the U.K.—devolution, regionalism, new local authorities—is nothing more than a manifestation of the country's poor economic performance." Discuss. (1977)

10. Discuss the assertion that what Britain needs is not a written constitution containing a Bill of Rights but Members of Parliament prepared to resist governmental encroachments on the citizen's rights. (1977)

Paper 2. Government and Public Administration II
Time allowed—three hours. Four questions to be answered.

1. "The role of the expert has increased, is increasing and ought to be diminished." Discuss this view of the British Civil Service. (1976)

2. How far would you agree that patronage is not a problem in the British system of government? (1976)

3. In 1968 the Select Committee on Nationalised Industries recommended that a single ministry be responsible for the supervision of nationalised industries. Examine the merits and demerits of this suggestion. (1976)

4. What administrative problems are likely to arise from the proposals to devolve powers to Scotland and Wales? (1976)

5. "The independence of local authorities makes it more difficult for the national government to exercise effective control over economic policy." Discuss. (1976)

6. "Ministerial responsibility has come to mean ministerial irresponsibility." Consider this view. (1977)

7. Give an assessment of the advantages and disadvantages of administrative decentralisation. (1977)

8. How have the procedure and the influence of the British Parliament been affected by our membership of the European Economic Community? (1977)

9. Should political parties be subsidised by the state? (1977)

10. Consider whether the dissatisfaction with the results of the Local Government Act 1972 provides a strong case for further reorganisation. (1977)

G.C.E. "A" LEVEL, UNIVERSITY OF LONDON

The new syllabus in Government and Political Studies was examined for the first time in June 1978. The syllabus is designed to highlight the relationship of ideas and concepts to institutions and structures. There is one compulsory paper (Paper 1, *Political Institutions and Concepts*) and a choice of four other papers, one of which must be taken. The optional papers allow a wider choice of subject matter. The following questions are taken from specimen papers provided by the University of London's University Entrance and School Examinations Council whose permission to reproduce them is hereby acknowledged.

It should be noted that the questions are taken from various papers to show the range of subjects. They do not, however, include questions from Paper 5, *Comparative government*.

Paper 1 Political Institutions and Concepts

1. (Short answer questions carrying one-third of the total marks. There are twelve of these questions, of which ten must be answered.)

(*i*) Distinguish between the idea of representative and that of responsible government.

(*ii*) Distinguish between anti-constitutional and unconstitutional.

(*iii*) Distinguish between devolution and federalism.

(*iv*) Distinguish between "the state" and "the government".

(*v*) Define the concept of "parliamentary sovereignty".

(*vi*) Define the concept of "consensus".

(*vii*) What are the powers of the Prime Minister?

(*viii*) Who may not vote in British parliamentary elections?

(*ix*) Why do constituencies have unequal numbers of voters?

(*x*) When may the Upper House legally reject legislation from the Commons?

(*xi*) Define the concept of "ministerial responsibility".

(*xii*) Define "equality" differently as a Conservative would and as a Socialist would.

2. How can it be said that there is constitutional law in Great Britain when there are no sanctions if the government ignores the constitution?

3. State a case for and a case against having a more political, that is less politically neutral, Civil Service.

4. "The powers of the Prime Minister do not explain his authority." Discuss.

Paper 2. *Modern British Politics*

(This paper too has a compulsory question carrying one-third of the marks and consisting of a selection of short-answer questions. The subject matter of these questions is dealt with in Part Three of this HANDBOOK. Samples of other questions include the following.)

1. Account for the differences between what the politicians and what ordinary people perceive to be the most important political issues.

2. How are the parties financed? Should they be financed by the state?

3. Name one successful pressure group. How did it obtain what it wanted?

Paper 3. *Modern Political Ideas and Doctrines*

(These subjects are dealt with in Part One of this HANDBOOK. This paper also has a series of short-answer questions carrying one-third of the total marks. Samples of other questions include the following.)

1. Discuss the view that all political doctrines are simply the self-interest of some élite.

2. Why do some people think that ideology is a distinctively modern phenomenon?

3. What kinds of political doctrines have been and can be built

upon a belief that ultimately, in the modern world, all problems are technical problems?

Paper 4. Public Administration

(This paper is reflected in Part Four of this HANDBOOK. The series of short-answer compulsory questions again account for one-third of the marks. Other specimen questions include the following.)

1. With the aid of examples drawn from cases you have studied, evaluate the role of pressure groups in making government policy.

2. Assess the effectiveness of the Parliamentary Commissioner for Administration. What extensions in his terms of reference appear desirable?

3. In what ways have relations between central and local government changed over the last twenty years?

4. After the Bains Report, corporate planning was adopted by most local authorities. What is likely to be its effect on the power and influence of the lay councillor?

Index

Abdication, 230

Abel-Smith, B, 184

Acts of Parliament

Abortion Act 1968, 202, 204

Act for the Union of Great Britain and Northern Ireland 1800, 109

Act of Settlement 1701, 12, 29

Act of Union 1707, 109

Agriculture Act 1947, 244

British Nationality Act 1964, 179

Catholic Emancipation Act 1829, 29

Chequers Estate Act 1917, 229

Cinematograph Acts 1909–52, 29

Coal Industry Act 1967, 150

Coal Industry Nationalisation Act 1946, 150

Commonwealth Immigrants Act 1962, 175, 177, 178

Commonwealth Immigrants Act 1968, 180

Companies Act 1948, 43

Crown Proceedings Act 1947, 42

Defamation Act 1952, 28

Defence of the Realm Act 1939, 18

Disabled Persons (Employment) Act 1944, 155

Education Act 1944, 70, 142, 143, 145

Education and Libraries (Northern Ireland) Order 1972, 145

Education (Scotland) Act 1962, 145

Employment Protection Act 1975, 154

Equal Pay Act 1970, 33, 156

European Communities Act 1972, 128, 129

Factory Act 1802, 30

Family Allowances Act 1945, 194

Furnished Houses (Rent Control) Act 1946, 166

Government of Ireland Act 1920, 109

Health and Safety at Work etc. Act 1974, 57

Health Services and Public Health Act 1968, 199

House of Commons (Disqualification) Act 1957, 14

Housing Acts 1957–69, 164

Housing (Financial Provisions) Act 1958, 164

Housing Rents and Subsidies Act 1975, 168

Housing Rents and Subsidies (Scotland) Act 1975, 168

Housing Repairs and Rent Act 1954, 165

Incitement to Disaffection Act 1936, 28

Industrial Relations Act 1971, 20, 57, 153

Industrial Training Act 1964, 138

Iron and Steel Act 1967, 151

Land Commission Act 1967, 170

Life Peerages Act 1958, 42

Local Government Act 1888, 93

265

Acts of Parliament—*cont.*
  Local Government Acts
    1933–58, 106
  Local Government Act 1972,
    94, 96, 100, 106
  Local Government Act 1974,
    168
  Local Government (Financial
    Provisions) Act 1963, 100
  Mauritius Independence Act
    1968, 133
  Ministers of the Crown Act
    1937, 229
  Ministry of Social Security
    Act 1966, 113, 169, 179, 187,
    189, 191, 194
  Municipal Corporations Act
    1835, 93
  National Assistance Act 1948,
    168, 189, 193
  National Health Service Act
    1946, 70, 100, 198, 205
  National Health (Abortion)
    Act 1967, 204
  National Health Service
    (Family Planning) Act 1967,
    201, 205
  National Health Service
    (Reorganisation) Act 1973,
    58, 100, 202, 205
  National Insurance Act 1946,
    196
  New Towns Act 1946, 170
  New Towns Act 1959, 245
  Official Secrets Act 1911, 19,
    28, 238
  Parliament Act 1911, 7, 72
  Parliament Act 1949, 7
  Peerages Act 1963, 42
  Prevention of Terrorism Act
    1976, 241
  Public Order Act 1936, 28, 60
  Race Relations Act 1965, 180
  Race Relations Act 1968, 156
  Race Relations Act 1976, 28,
    181
  Rating Act 1966, 106

Reform Act 1832, 31, 71, 92
Reform Act 1867, 30, 71
Rent Act 1954, 163
Rent Act 1957, 163, 165, 166
Rent Act 1965, 166
Rent Act 1974, 167
Representation of the People
  Act 1969, 63, 102
Sex Discrimination Act 1975,
  33, 157
Social Security Act 1973, 197
Social Security Pensions Act
  1975, 67, 197
Supplementary Benefits Act
  1976, 194
Test Act 1673, 29
Theatres Act 1968, 28
Town and Country Planning
  Act 1947, 170
Trade Disputes Act 1927, 151
Trade Disputes and Trades
  Unions Act 1945, 151
Trade Unions and Labour
  Relations Act 1974, 154
Water Act 1973, 96
Wireless and Telegraphy Acts
  1949 & 1967, 18
Additional member system, 122
Administrative devolution, 113
Administrative law, 242–3
*Administrative structure of
  medical and related services in
  England and Wales, The*, 202
Adversary politics, 120
Advisory, Conciliation and
  Arbitration Service, 154
Aims of Industry, 150
Anarchists, 73–4
Anti-constitutional, 39–40
Area Health Authorities, 113, 202
Aristocracy, 2
Aristotle, 2
Assheton Report, 217
Authority, charismatic, 32

Bains Report, 98
Bank of England, 245

Barlow Committee, 169
Benefits,
  lack of take-up of, 187
  universality of, 185
Bentham, Jeremy, 31
Bevan, Aneurin, 198, 201, 233
Beveridge Report, 31, 189
Bill of Rights 1689, 33
Board of Trade, 110
Bow Group, 23
Boyson, Dr. Rhodes, 141, 193
British Airways, 246
British Board of Film Censors, 29
British Broadcasting
  Corporation, 18, 246
British Communist Party, 74
British Iron and Steel Federation,
  150
British Medical Association, 24,
  204
British Psychological Society, 139
British Steel Corporation, 151
British Union of Fascists, 60
Brussels Treaty, 125
Buchanan-Smith, Alec, 118
Bureaucracy, 213–14
Burke, Edmund, 60, 65

Cabinet, 62, 232
Cabinet Office, 222, 233, 240, 248
Campaign for Labour Democracy,
  23
Capital gains, 170
Censorship, 28
Central Council, the, 228
Central Electricity Generating
  Board, 246
Centralisation, 114
Central Land Board, 170
Central Policy Review Staff, 247
Central Statistical Office, 223
Centre for Policy Studies, 23
Certiorari, 99
Chairman of Ways and Means, 46
Chamber of Commerce, 234
Chancellor of the Exchequer, 232

Chancellor of the Exchequer's
  Departments, 240
Charity Organisation Society, 31
Chief Whip, 47
Child Benefits, 195
Child Poverty Action Group, 187,
  188, 192
Chiltern Hundreds, 14
Churchill, Sir Winston, 61
Circumstances of Families, 194,
  196
Civil Servant, definition of, 213
Civil Service
  administration group, 220
  administration trainee, 220, 225
  career management, 215
  College, 215, 218, 225
  Commission, 212, 216, 222, 224
  Department, 213
  Expenditure Committee's
    comments on, 224
  "generalists", 218
  grading, 220
  head of, 215, 224
  higher executive officer (A), 221
  management service units, 215
  manpower, 219
  Oxbridge bias, 225
  Pay Research Unit, 213, 225
  personnel management, 216,
    217
  policy adviser, 216
  promotion, 222
  recruitment, 222
  Scottish, 224
  secrecy in, 238
  specialised, 218, 222
Claimants Union, 189, 192
Clerk to the House of Commons,
  47
Coalition government, 48
Code of practice, 154
Coke, Lord Chief Justice, 132
Collective bargaining, 152
Colquhoun, Maureen, 50
Commissioner for Local
  Administration, 104

Commission for New Towns, 245
Commission for Racial Equality, 181
Commission on Industrial Relations, 152
Commonwealth, 235
Commonwealth Education Liaison Committee, 236
Communism, 17, 59, 74
Community care, 201
Community Relations Commission, 181
Computers and Privacy, 35
Confederation of British Industry, 234
Congress (U.S.), 13
Consensus, 20
Conservative Central Office, 71, 228
Constitution,
    American, 40–1
    federal, 41
    flexible, 41
    rigid, 41
Constitutional government, 39
Constitutional monarchy, 4
Constitution, Royal Commission on, see Kilbrandon Report
Convention, 5, 34, 42, 133
"Cooling-off period", 152, 153
Council of Ministers (E.E.C.), 127
Council on Tribunals, 244
Court of Justice (E.E.C.), 125, 127, 136
Court of Session, 244
Crime, Police and Race Relations, 1970, 183
Critchel Down case, 64, 248
Crossman, R. H., 55, 56, 237
Crown Dependencies, 40
Crowther Report, 142

Day nurseries, 156
Declaration of Independence, 13, 29
Defence, 68
    Ministry of, 240

Delegated legislation, 129, 240
Democracy, 2
Department
    of Agriculture and Fisheries for Scotland, 224
    of Economic Affairs, 111
    of Education and Science, 140
    of Employment group, 240
    of the Environment, 170, 240
    of Expenditure and Manpower Control, 225
    of Health and Social Security, 10, 233, 240
Deprivation, cycle of, 188
Deputy Speaker, 46
Development corporations, 245
Devolution, 68, 111, 115
Devolution Bill, 117
Devolution: the English dimension, 118
Diplomatic Service, 224
Disablement Resettlement Officer, 155
Discrimination, 181
Divine right, 16
D notices, 18
Donovan Report, 152
Donoughmore Committee, 241
Droit d'administratif, 243

East African Asians, 179
Ecole National d'Administration, 217
Economic planning boards, 111
Education,
    adult, 138
    alternative, 143
    Black Papers, 140
    Committee for the Advancement of State, 145
    comprehensive, 139
    curriculum, 146
    de-schooling, 143
    direct grant schools, 140
    eleven plus, 139
    H.M. Inspector of Schools, 100

leaving age, 143
liberal studies, 138
"positive discrimination", 142
priority areas, 143
private schools, 140
school governors, 144
selection, 139
teachers, 141
teachers' aides, 143
Education: a framework for Expansion, 141, 143
Education in Schools: A Consultative Document, 137, 145
Elected monarchy, 231
Election (*see also* Vote, Voting), 44
Electioneering, 22
Elective dictatorship, 26
Electoral reform *see* Reform
Electricity Council, 246
Elites, 17
Employment,
  disadvantages, 154
  problems of the disabled, 155
  Rehabilitation Centre, 155
  sheltered, 155
Environment, 169
Equal Opportunities Commission, 157
Ethnic minorities, 156
Euratom, 126
European Assembly, 127
  direct elections to, 134
European Coal and Steel Community, 125, 126
  High Authority, 125
European Defence Committee, 126
European Economic Community, 21, 126, 158
  membership of, 129
European Free Trade Area (EFTA), 126
European Social Fund, 158
Euthanasia Society, 203
Expenditure Committee Report, 237

Expression, freedom of, 67
Executive Committee of the National Union, 228
Eysenck, Professor, 176

Fabian Society, 23, 112
Family Allowance, 190
Family Expenditure Survey, 188
Family Income Supplement, 195
Family planning, 205
Family Welfare Association, 31
Fascism, 60
Federalism, 115
Federation of British Industries, 234
Federations, 40
Feudal system, 1
Finer Committee, 192
First Lord of the Treasury, 229
Foot, Michael, 119
Franks Committee, 243
Freedom, 33
  of association, 29
  of expression, 67
  of person, 27
  of religion, 29
  of speech, 27
  under the law, 27
Fulton Report, 37, 214
Future shape of local government finance, 105

Gallup Poll, 19
"general will", 32
Gingerbread, 192
Gladstone Club, 23
Gladstone Commission, 212
Government
  departments (*see also* Departments), 239
  machinery of, 9
  representative, 62
  responsible, 64
Grotius, 124
Grunwick Film Processing Laboratory, 29
Guillebaud Committee, 200

Habeas Corpus, 27
Hague Conventions, 124–5
Hailsham, Lord, 26
Haldane Report, 233
Hansard, 3
Hansard Committee on Electoral
  Reform, 50, 120
Hansard Society Commission,
  120
Health and Safety Commission,
  235
Heath, Edward, 118, 247
High Court, 84, 244
Hitler, Adolf, 60
Hobbes, 124
Hospital administration, 205
Housing,
  Barlow Committee, 169
  community involvement, 170
  controlled tenancies, 166
  environmental legislation, *see*
    Environment
  "fair rents", 167
  furnished tenancies, 166
  Government Social Survey, 162
  homelessness, 168
  home ownership, 163
  housing subsidies, 164
  in Greater London, 167
  Old Houses into New Houses,
    164
  option mortgage scheme, 164
  "Part III accommodation", 168
  rate rebate, 167
  regulated tenancies, 166
  rent officer, 166
  rent rebate, 167
  rent restriction, 165
  Scott Committee, 169
  slum clearance, 163
  squatting, 169
  Uthwatt Committee, 170
House of Commons, 44
  procedure, 47
  Select Committee on
    Procedure, 129
House of Lords, 7, 42

Howard League for Penal Reform,
  22

Ideological parties, 73
Ideology, 58
Immigration, 57
Industrial action, 22
Industrial Arbitration Board, 156
Industrial Board, 152
Industrial Rehabilitation Units,
  155
Industrial Revolution, 30
Industry, training for, 137
Independent Broadcasting
  Authority, 18, 246
Independent Television
  Authority, 246
In Place of Strife, 57, 152
Institute of Professional Civil
  Servants, 218
International
  Court of Justice, 125
  law, 124
  Monetary Fund, 133
Irish Home Rule, 70
Iron and Steel Corporation, 150

James Committee, 141
Jensen, Arthur, 176
Job Creation Programme, 159
Joseph, Sir Keith, 188
Judicial committee of the Privy
  Council, 117, 119
Judicial power, 11
Jus Gentium, 124
Justinian, 124

Kilbrandon Report on the
  Constitution,
  Majority Report, 37, 41, 56,
    114
  Minority Report, 116, 128

Labour Party conference, 227
Law Lords, 44
Layfield Report, 107

Leader of the House, 46
Leader of the Opposition, 44, 47
League of Nations, 125
Legal-rational authority, 31
Legislation, *see* Acts of Parliament
Liberty, *see* Freedom
"Lib–Lab pact" (1977), 69
Lobbying, 22
Local government (*see also* Redcliffe-Maud Committee Report)
  block grants, 106
  Boundary Commission, 93
  chief education officer, 99
  community councils, 96
  corporate management, 99
  county councillors, 102
  district authorities, 96
  district councillors, 96
  finance, 105
  functions, 99, 101
  local authorities, 102
  local income tax, 108
  local Ombudsman, 104
  metropolitan authorities, 96
  non-metropolitan authorities, 96
  parish councils, 96, 102
  party politics in, 103
  percentage grants, 106
  rate support grant, 106
  regional water authorities, 96
  town clerk, 99
  town manager, 99
  two-tier system, 95
Local Government in England: proposals for re-organisation, 96
Locke, 72, 124
London Passenger Transport Board, 149
Lord Chancellor, 6
Lord President, 232
Lords
  of Appeal in Ordinary, 44
  spiritual, 43
  temporal, 43

Macdonnell Commission, 212
Machiavelli, 36
Magna Carta, 27
Mandamus, 99, 102
Mandate, 40, 227, 236
Manifesto, election, 227, 236
Manpower Services Commission, 235
Maoists, 73
Mass media, 18
May, Erskine, 47
Mein Kampf, 60
Meritocracy, 62
Member of Parliament,
  full-time, 52
  qualifications for, 44, 46
Mill, John Stuart, 92
Minister of Health, 232
Ministerial
  control, 237
  responsibility, 64, 128, 248
Ministry
  of Agriculture, Fisheries and Food, 113, 239
  of Defence, 240
  of Housing and Local Government, 110
  of Transport, 110
Monarchy, 1, 4
Monday Club, 23
Money Bill, 43
Montesquieu, Baron de, 13
Morning Star, 74
Moseley, Sir Oswald, 60
Motions of censure, 242

National Chamber of Trade, 24
National Coal Board, 150
National Coalition Government, 48
National Council for the Unmarried Mother and her Child, 192
National Economic Development Council, 160
National Enterprise Board, 68, 160

National Executive Committee, 70
National Farmers Union, 24
National Foundation for Educational Research, 139
National Front, 74
National Industrial Relations Court, 153
National Insurance, 190, 196
Nationalisation, 68, 149, 245
National Opinion Polls, 19
National Party, 75
National Union of Conservative and Unionist Associations, 70, 228
National Union of Mineworkers, 150
National Water Authority, 96
Natural law, 124
Natural rights, 29
Nazism, 59
New Left, the, 73
Newsome Report, 142
Nietzche, 60
1922 Committee, 23
North Atlantic Treaty Organisation (N.A.T.O.), 125
Northcote-Trevelyan Report, 211
Northern Ireland Chambers of Commerce, 235
Northern Ireland Civil Service, 224
Northstead, Bailiff of the Manor of, 14

Oligarchy, 2, 18
Ombudsman, *see* Parliamentary Commissioner for Administration
Open government, 36
Orders in council, 5
Organisation for Economic Co-operation and Development, 125

Our Changing Democracy: Devolution to Scotland and Wales, 117
Overlords, 10

Parliamentary
  government, 42
  questions, 242
  scrutiny, 242
  sovereignty, 26, 48, 128, 132
Parliamentary Commissioner for Administration, 48, 104, 248
Parliamentary Counsel Office, 224
Parliamentary Labour Party, 227
Participation, 55, 102
Party government, 42
Patronage Secretary, 46
Permanent Court of Arbitration, 125
Picketing, 152, 154
Pitt the Younger, 229
Plaid Cymru, 73, 118
Playfair Commission, 212
Plowden Report, 56, 142
Pluralism, 3
Plutocracy, 3
Political
  culture, 16
  issue, 66
  parties, 227
  pressure groups, 22–4
Political and Economic Planning, 177
Polity, 2
Porritt Report, 201
Post Office, the, 245
Powell, Enoch, 174, 179, 233
Power and authority, 31
Prentice, Reginald, 50
Prerogative, 5
Prescription charges, 200
Pressure groups, 20–2
Priestly Commission, 213
Prime Minister, 229
Prime Ministers' Conference, 235
Privacy, Report of the Committee on, 35

Privy Council, 232
Privy Council, Judicial
    Committee of, 117, 119
Proclamations, 5
Programme Analysis and Review
    Committee, 247
Prohibition, 99
Proportional representation,
    119-22
Protest, 22
Public corporation, 244–6
Public Expenditure Survey
    Committee, 248
Public opinion, 18, 134

"Quango", 244
Queen in Parliament, 7, 11
Question Time, 47, 52, 242

Race Relations Board, 181
"Rachmanism", 167
Racialism, 66, 173
Redcliffe-Maud Committee
    Report, 94, 104
Redress of grievances, 47
Referendum, 30, 40, 118, 126,
    130
Reform,
    electoral, 52, 69, 119–22
    of the legislature, 119–51
Regional health authorities, 202
Registrar of trade unions and
    employers' associations, 152
Registration officer, 102
Remploy, 155
Re-organisation of Central
    Government, 9, 37
Representatives, types of, 63
Residual freedoms, see Freedom
Revolutionary Socialist League,
    23
Ridley Commission, 212
Robbins Report, 137
Rothschild, Lord, 247
Rousseau, Jean-Jacques, 30
Royal
    Assent, 6

Pardon, 6
Prerogative, 5
Royal College of Obstetricians,
    204
Rule of law, 67
Runnymede Trust, 182
Russell Report, 56

Sainsbury Committee, 201
Sanctions, 24
Scott Committee, 169
Scottish
    Chamber of Commerce, 234
    Development Department,
        224
    Economic Planning
        Department, 224
    Education Department, 224
    Grand Committee, 113
    Home and Health Department,
        113, 224
    nationalists, 72, 118
Scrutiny Committee, 129, 242
Secretary of State
    for Scotland, 232
    for Wales, 232
Secretary of the Cabinet, 233
Sedgemore, Brian, 237
Selectivity, 185
Selsden Group, 23
Senior, D., 95
Separation of the Powers, 10–15
Separatism, 115
Serjeant-at-Arms, 47
Shadow cabinet, 17
Shaftesbury, Lord, 31
Short, Edward, 141
Skeffington Report, 56, 57, 171
Social
    class, 75
    dividend, 192
    wage, 30
Social and Democratic Alliance,
    23
Social Contract, 30, 124
Socialist Workers Party, 74
Social Services, paying for, 193

Social Survey (1947), 163
Society for the Protection of the Unborn Child, 204
South of Scotland Electricity Board, 246
Sovereign, 5
Sovereignty of Parliament, 26, 48, 128, 132
Soviet Marxism, 17
Speaker, 46
Speech from the throne, 6
Standard of living, 67
Standing Committee, 47
Standing orders, 47
Stansgate, second Viscount, 42
Stanstead airport, 171
Statutory Instruments, 242
Steel, David, 202
Stormont, 40
Supplementary Benefit, 194
Supplementary Benefit Commission, 169
Supply motions, 242
Supreme Court (U.S.A.), 41
Switzerland, 41

Tameside, 101
Technocracy, 61
Thatcher, Margaret, 118
Theocracy, 4
"Think-tank", 247
"Three-line whip", 47
Tolpuddle Martyrs, 35
Tomlin Commission, 213
Totalitarian regimes, 50
Trades Union Congress (T.U.C.), 30, 151, 234
"Programme for Action", 153
Trade unions, 151
Traditional authority, 32, 60
Traditionalism, 60
Transport and General Workers Union, 151
Treasury, 215, 216, 224, 247
Treaty of Accession, 128
Treaty of Rome, 126, 132, 134

Tribunals, 242
Trotskyists, 73

Ultra vires, 11, 100, 117
Unconstitutional, 39
Unemployment, 157
Unfair industrial practices, 153
Unitary constitutions, 40
United Kingdom Atomic Energy Authority, 245
United Nations Organisation, 125
Universal Declaration of Human Rights, 34, 125

Vote,
alternative, 121
block, 121
cumulative, 121
limited, 121
single transferable, 122
Voting,
additional member system, 122
double ballot, 121
list system, 121
West German system, 121

Walpole, Horace, 229
Webb, Beatrice, 31
Webb, Sidney, 31, 112
Wedgewood Benn, Anthony, 42
Welfare Rights Project, 187
Welsh National Water Development Authority, 96
Welsh Office, 114
Western European Union, 126
West Germany, 41
Whyatt Report, 248
William Tyndale school, 137
Wilson, Sir Harold, 247
"Women Against Rape", 12
Women's liberation, 205

Younger Committee, 35
Youth Opportunities Programme, 159

For full details of other Macdonald & Evans
Handbooks send for the FREE M & E
Handbook list, available from: Department E6
Macdonald & Evans Ltd., Estover Road,
Plymouth PL6 7PZ